CLIO'S CORNER

CLIO'S CORNER

The History of Nursing in Massachusetts - Articles from the Massachusetts Report on Nursing

2004-2016

Mary Ellen Doona, RN, EdD

Published by American Nurses Association Massachusetts

ISBN: 1530335191
ISBN 13: 9781530335190
Library of Congress Control Number: 2016903599
CreateSpace Independent Publishing Platform
North Charleston, South Carolina

Clio, the Muse of History, is one of four statues (Peace, Soldier and Sailor are the others) on the Soldier and Sailor's Monument erected in 1877 on Boston Common's Flagstaff Hill to commemorate America's Civil War (1861-1865). Clio wears the laurel wreath of victory and holds a book in one hand with a pen poised in the other to write in the Book of History.

TABLE OF CONTENTS

FOREWORD

Clio, the Muse of History, is one of four statues - Peace, a Sailor and a Soldier are the other three - that adorns the Civil War (1861-1865) monument erected on Boston Common's Flagstaff Hill in 1877. Noted sculptor, Martin Milmore (1844-1883), depicts Clio in the dress of the Golden Age of Athens and crowns her head with the laurel wreath of victory. With her eyes fixed on the horizon, Clio grasps a pen in one hand ready to record significant deeds in the Book of History she holds in the other. Fittingly as the daughter of Mnemosyne (Memory) Clio treasures the present as it becomes the past and privileges its remembrance as the inspiration for creating the future.

The articles collected here were published in each issue of the *Massachusetts Report on Nursing* from 2004 to 2016. The Massachusetts Association of Registered Nurses, which in the Spring of 2014 was renamed the American Nurses Association Massachusetts, (ANA Massachusetts), distributes this newsletter to every registered nurse in the Commonwealth. Nurses have been fulsome in their praise for Clio's Comer. Some remember the nurses and events that are subjects of the articles, while others are learning about these subjects for the first time. Their enthusiastic acceptance suggests that nurses have a sense that without their history they are disinherited and even paupers. For history is to nursing what memory is to the individual nurse.

This collection is in a sense a continuation, after an interim of a few years, of articles that were written for *The Massachusetts Nurse,* the publication of the Massachusetts Nurses Association. Those articles were compiled into *Eyes on the Future* in time for the American Nurses Association's convention in Boston in 1990. Copies of the monograph are deposited in the History of Nursing Archives at the Howard Gotlieb Archival Research Center at Boston University; at the Mary L. Pekarski Nursing Archives at the Bums Library at Boston College; and, in the open shelves of the nursing collection at the Thomas P. O'Neill, Jr. Library at Boston College.

As solitary as the research process is, no one works alone. The restoration of nursing history as a central part of the profession's life in Massachusetts rests with the late Richard Tierney RN. As MNA's executive director, he sensed the membership's response to articles in *The Massachusetts Nurse,* starting with "The Cause is Just," that recounted Mary E. P. Davis's stalwart efforts in the movement to professionalize nursing. She and her classmate, Sophia Palmer, had been students of Linda Richards at what became the Massachusetts General Hospital Training School for Nurses. At the turn of the twentieth century, these three nurses were at the forefront of creating professional organizations, which became the American Society of Superintendents of Training Schools for Nurses in 1893 (later the National League for Nursing), and in 1896 the National Alumnae Association (later the American Nurses Association). By October 1900 nurses also had their own journal, the *American Journal of Nursing,* with Palmer as its editor, Davis as its business manager and Linda Richards as a columnist each month on training schools and hospitals.

Tierney reported the membership's interest to MNA's Board of Directors which after due deliberation created the *Lucy Lincoln Drown Nursing History Society,* at the one time responding to the membership and honoring MNA's first historian of years before. Drown's first report was on the founding of the Association at Faneuil Hall February 26 1903. Also present at this momentous occasion was Mary E. P. Davis. Palmer sent her greetings from up-state New York and Richards sent hers from Taunton, Massachusetts. In 1983, eighty years later, MNA's Board appointed me as MNA Historian and chair of the *Society's* Executive Committee. Tierney, Ann-Marie Giannetta and Denise Sullivan, the Editor of *The Massachusetts Nurse,* staffed the *Society's* Executive Committee, which at first included: Alice Friedman, Maryann Matzo, Claire Scigliano, Joanne Garvey with Ann Donovan, Janet Wilson James, the notable women's historian, and Susan Reverby, a labor historian serving as consultants. Committee membership changed over the years adding Ursula Van Ryzin, Jeanine Young Mason, Patricia Tyra, Joellen Hawkins and Loretta Higgins as earlier members resigned. Patricia Brigham RN and later, ethicist Sarah Moroney RN staffed the executive committee as did nursing's north star, Shirley A. Duggan RN. My article "A Spotlight on Nursing," published in the September 2009 issue of the *Massachusetts Report on Nursing* details some of the *Society's* activities.

After almost two decades, the *Society* effectively ended once the Massachusetts Nurses Association disaffiliated from the American Nurses Association to become a labor organization. The Massachusetts Association of Registered Nurses, incorporated on March 23, 2001, became the organization for nurses who were committed to continuing their membership with ANA. By 2004, MARN was firmly on its feet and had established the *Massachusetts Report on Nursing,* its newsletter with Myra Furman Cacace as its deft editor.

Cacace immediately got in touch with me and asked me to contribute articles on the history of Massachusetts nurses and nursing. Clio's Comer was born June 2004 and for twelve years has appeared in each issue of the *Massachusetts Report on Nursing*. On the eleventh of April 2014 during its annual meeting, the Massachusetts Association of Registered Nurses changed its name to the American Nurses Association Massachusetts. ANA Massachusetts better conveys the Association's local and national import, while at the same time uniting its members and strengthening its public image.

INTRODUCTION

During my tenure as editor of the *Massachusetts Report on Nursing*, I have had the privilege to work with so many amazing and dedicated nurses. On nurse in particular, Mary Ellen Doona, has dedicated herself to preserving the rich history of nursing in Massachusetts. Throughout the last 10 years, Mary Ellen has provided us with glimpses of nursing greatness in the days when our profession was making great strides to become the powerful profession that we are today.

Mary Ellen taught me that the past informs our present and points to our future. Through her wonderful articles in Clio's Corner, nurses in Massachusetts understand that they have so much to be proud of. I hope that you will enjoy this book, and appreciate the great fortune that we all have to be nurses in Massachusetts.

Myra Cacace MS, GNP/ADM-BC
President (2015-2016)
ANA Massachusetts

PRESERVING OUR HISTORY -
THE HISTORY OF NURSING ARCHIVES

A TRIBUTE TO HOWARD GOTLIEB:
PRESERVER OF NURSING'S MEMORY

(originally published March 2006)

Nurses must stop for a minute in their important work to honor the memory of Dr. Howard Gotlieb (October 24, 1926-December 1, 2005), the director of Special Collections at Boston University's Mugar Memorial Library, who died December 1, 2005 at the age of seventy nine. It is only fitting and proper that nurses remember Dr. Gotlieb. Since February 18, 1966 he preserved nursing's memory in the History of Nursing Archives situated on the fifth floor of Mugar. Dr. Gotlieb's death is a significant loss for nurses.

A pioneer in collecting the popular culture, Gotlieb aimed to create "an archive that was not only useful today but that in one hundred years would allow researchers to write definitively about the twentieth century." As his long-time associate, Vita Paladino, who manages Special Collections remarked, Gotlieb was a visionary in collecting "contemporary archives when no other institution was doing it." So successfully did he achieve that objective, on September 30, 2003 the University honored Gotlieb with a gala banquet and an exhibit: Capturing the Century: Forty Years of Collecting excerpted from what he had collected over forty years. Sprinkled among the correspondence, diaries and photographs on display were television's Emmys, the theatre's Tonys, the cinema's Oscars and other awards. A pair of Fred Astaire's dancing shoes was there as well. Grateful to Gotlieb for amassing the papers of two thousand individuals, sixty million documents, 150,000 rare books and artifacts, the Board of Trustees capped its tribute by renaming the Department of Special Collections the Howard Gotlieb Archival Research Center.

Gotlieb collected information on individuals who had stamped their signature on the twentieth century in the performing arts, literature, public policy, academia, theology and journalism. Among these individuals were: opera personalities such as Rïse Stevens and

Sir Rudolph Bing; journalists Alstair Cooke, Dan Rather, Frances Fitz Gerald and Stewart Alsop; public policy makers Speaker of the House of Representatives, the Honorable John McCormack and the Honorable Edward Brooke the former Senator from Massachusetts; Sue Grafton and Margaret Drabble from popular literature and Somerset Maugham and Robert Frost from the world of letters. Among those representing stage and screen were: Bette Davis, Fred Astaire, Gene Kelly, Roddy McDowell, Joan Fontaine, Sam Wanamaker, Claire Bloom, Rex Harrison and Angela Lansbury.

Some were already stars when Gotlieb sought their papers but others such as Martin Luther King Jr. and David Halberstam were at the beginning of their careers. Martin Luther King Jr. had not made his march on Selma that kicked off the Civil Rights Movement when he agreed in 1964 to give his papers to Boston University. David Halberstam was just back from Vietnam and had not begun to write his books which by 2006 number nineteen. Perceptive man that he was, Gotlieb anticipated their success and persuaded them to give their papers to Boston University before the world also recognized their preeminence.

Nestled safely among the documents and artifacts of these public figures are the precious personal and professional papers of the nursing profession thanks to the foresight of Mary Ann L. Garrigan (1926-2000). Two years after Gotlieb arrived at Boston University from Yale and just before the new Mugar Memorial Library was completed, Garrigan approached him with a proposal to establish the History of Nursing Archives. As Gotlieb considered Garrigan's proposal, he pondered important questions: Why should Special Collections embark on this untried field? Were there any primary sources—papers, manuscripts, memorabilia and the like? Why should the Mugar Memorial Library collect nursing's primary sources when no other institution was doing so? And a most important question, would scholars use the History of Nursing Archives?

No student was ever more prepared for an exam! Garrigan had long been one of Clio's servants. She had been teaching the history of nursing to Boston University School of Nursing students for fifteen years. She was first a member and then chaired the Massachusetts League for Nursing's Committee on Historical Source Materials in Nursing. She had the facts ready at hand and using her considerable charm and persuasive powers, urged Gotlieb to include nursing in his quest to document the twentieth-century.

In answer to the question about primary sources Garrigan said there were sources galore and many of them were in danger of being lost forever by "benign neglect." More urgently, she reported that significant resources were misplaced, cast away and frequently destroyed." She also argued that Special Collections should collect nursing because it was undergoing an enormous change as more and more of its education was taking place in institutions of higher learning. Their success in caring for sick and wounded men during World War II had made nurses the nation's heroes. A grateful country poured money into nursing education with the Boston University School of Nursing founded in 1947 only one of many examples of this educational reform. Nursing would shuck off hospital domination to become an independent profession. In 1947 change was still to come. There would be still more change when the Women's Movement emerged several decades later. Before long feminists in search of a use-able past would find nursing's long and troubled journey to full professional status a subject for research. Gotlieb and Garrison did not know that future when they were discussing the possibility of a History of Nursing Archives in 1966 but they spotted the signs that academics were becoming more interested in the profession's past. What is more, they were developing skills to research that past.

Gotlieb's prescience in selecting individuals prior to their emergence as stars in their fields was operative here in his prediction that nursing would become a more important subject for researchers as the years went by. He made his decision. After gaining the neces-sary approval of the library system, on February 18, 1966 Gotlieb welcomed the History of Nursing Archives to Mugar's fifth floor. The Nursing Division of the United States Public Health Service seconded Gotlieb's judgment by granting five years of funding for the fledging History of Nursing Archives. These funds made it possible to collect and classify nursing's documents. In addition, the funding supported: improving the quality of how nursing history was taught; preserving historical source material; and, fostering historical research.

Gotlieb guided Garrigan as she assumed her new position as Curator of the History of Nursing Archives. He in turn was willing to be educated about nursing's rich past. In Garrigan he had a master teacher. Gotlieb and Garrigan became partners in amassing a nursing collec-tion that gathered the papers of nurses who were making history during the twentieth-century. They also collected the papers of nursing organizations that reached back to the last quarter of the nineteenth-century when nursing education began in the United States and to mid-nine-teenth century when Florence Nightingale emerged as the hero of the Crimean War (1854-56).

The Boston University School of Nursing gifted the History of Nursing Archives with the Rawlinson Collection of fifty Florence Nightingale letters. Most of them were written after the Crimean War but the relationship between Nightingale and Sir Robert Rawlinson was forged in Constantinople. By 1974, when Professor Lois Monteiro edited the Letters of Florence Nightingale there were 151 Florence Nightingale letters. Irene S. Palmer, the dean of the Boston University School of Nursing, wrote several papers based on her research of these letters. By 2006 there are more than 300 letters. The Florence Nightingale letters gave added luster to an enterprise that was already gleaming with glory.

But all this and more were still to come on February 18, 1966 when Garrigan moved the small history of nursing collection from the School of Nursing to climate-controlled Mugar. The History of Nursing Archives would grow over the years to two hundred collections, 1400 rare nursing books and hundreds of Florence Nightingale letters. At its beginning there were the fifty rare nursing books of Boston University School of Nursing's founding dean, Martha Ruth Smith. Marie Farrell, the dean in 1966 gave her papers and the papers of the Boston University School of Nursing to the new History of Nursing Archives. It was a small but auspicious beginning.

The Archive did not stay a local enterprise for long. Within five years the History of Nursing Archives had collected the papers of the *American Journal of Nursing* and its Sophia Palmer Historical Collection. In 1972 the American Nurses Association recognized the History of Nursing Archives as the national depository for materials important to nursing history, and then, sent its papers dating back to 1896 to Boston University. Other organizations followed. The American Nurses Foundation, the American Public Health Association, the US Public Health Service: Department of Nursing, the National League of Nursing Education and the National Student Nurses Association also gifted their papers to the History of Nursing Archives. Local Massachusetts nursing organizations did the same. Among them were: the Massachusetts Nurses Association, the New England Organizations of Nurses, and the Massachusetts League for Nursing.

Within seven years the History of Nursing Archives had amassed 1500 rare nursing books and eighty manuscript collections. During this time, nursing's educational revolution dominated nursing's scene. The American Nurses Association issued its Position Paper in December 1965 stating that nursing education should take place in colleges. This preempted the National League for Nursing's Resolution 5 that called for an orderly transition of nursing education from hospital-based schools to collegiate programs. This set off an explosion. Viewed from the distance of four decades later the energy unleashed in the ANA/ NLN debate served to move nursing education onto college campuses.

The History of Nursing Archives was perfectly positioned at this critical turning point to gather in the documents of schools that closed. That reassured nurses who were dedicated to the hospital schools of nursing that their work did not evaporate into the ether. Instead it had a treasured place in the History of Nursing Archives. Researchers who have since used these papers to tell the story of the beginning of nursing education in the United States were the beneficiaries as was nursing history itself.

Among these collections are the papers of the alumnae associations of the Beth Israel Hospital and Massachusetts Memorial Hospital Schools of Nursing and the Vassar Training School of World War I vintage. Among the hospital schools of nursing that gave their papers to the History of Nursing Archives are: the Peter Bent Brigham Hospital, New England Baptist Hospital, Children's Hospital, Boston City Hospital, Mount Auburn Hospital, Newton Wellesley Hospital, Rhode Island Hospital and the New England Hospital for Women and Children where the first diploma in nursing was awarded to Linda Richards in the summer of 1873, and where six years later Mary Eliza Mahoney, America's First African-American Nurse, received her nursing diploma. The Waltham Hospital School of Nursing Collection contains the story of Dr. Alfred Worcester's attempt in 1885 to scuttle the autonomy of the young profession. He saw nursing becoming medicine's art once medicine began to concentrate on its science. Nursing declined the "honor."

The Boston Visiting Nurses Association (the successor to the Boston Instructive District Nurses Association) gave its papers to the History of Nursing Archives thus providing scholars with documents that dated to February 1886 when Amelia Hodgkiss, a graduate of the New England Hospital for Women and Children, made the first home visit. That historic venture preceded the public health movement that burst on the scene with the new century.

Gotlieb often spoke figuratively of getting callouses on his knees from being on them so often begging people to give their papers to Boston University. Garrigan followed his example as she educated nurses why they should be interested in the profession's history. Then, as now, nurses were more comfortable immersed in nursing's urgent present than they are with reflecting on nursing's past. Such was the force of Garrigan's personality she was able to educate nurses and nursing's organizations on the value of documents that might have otherwise been scrapped. She could summon up nursing's past like an old friend and enchant nurses with stories of their predecessors.

She spoke at conventions and attended organizational board meetings. She found historically significant documents in nursing's literature for the nursing journals to reissue. She mentored practitioners, faculty, students and friends of nursing about nursing's history and won many devotees to her project. No venue and no nurse were beyond Garrigan's reach. She had been watching Gotlieb enticing, cajoling and persuading people as he pursued their papers. Garrigan added Gotlieb's skills to her own. Energizing the efforts was her commitment to save the documents of nursing's past and to collect contemporary papers of importance. And, as her mentor had done, Garrigan anticipated who would become a star and collected their papers before they knew they would shine in nursing's firmament.

Garrigan had no trouble persuading Virginia Henderson about the disposition of her papers. Henderson, long an admirer of her former student, eagerly gave the History of Nursing Archives her extensive collection of manuscripts, drafts of her books, lecture notes, presentations, books, awards and memorabilia. In her encomium Henderson states:

> [Garrigan] has a fine mind, a great capacity for sustained effort and a wonderful sense of humor. Even more conspicuous is her humanity—her ability to identify and sympathize with others—her gift for friendship. Her qualities are such as to define the term nurse but in addition, her work as archivist has been a beacon to nursing in this country where nurses have been singularly . . . [remiss] in developing and preserving all sorts of scholarly resources.

Henderson was a one-woman public relations department throughout the United States, Europe and Asia for the History of Nursing Archives and for its singular curator. Henderson practiced what she preached. The first chapter of her classic Principles and Practice of Nursing is a brilliant summary of nursing's past. Nurses should know the ideas and event that preceded them, the chapter infers, before they began to make their own mark on the profession.

Stella Goostray, (1886-1969) was still another nursing celebrity who was devoted to the History of Nursing Archives. The Director of the Childrens Hospital School of Nursing from 1927-1946 Goostray used her position of prominence as a national nursing figure—she was at various times president of the *American Journal of Nursing* (1930-37), president of the National League for Nurses (1940-44) and president of the National Nursing Council for War Services (1942-45)—to educate the profession about collecting nursing's primary sources. She wanted nurses to "hunt for and save" nursing's historical materials.

Goostray was similar to Gotlieb in urging nurses to save contemporary materials as well as to search out materials from the past. She assuaged her own guilt at having once discarded papers that she later discovered were the only copy. She advised other nurses not to do the same. In 1948 she joined Isabel Stewart and Helen Munson on the new Committee on Early Source Material which the next year became the Committee on Historical Source Materials in Nursing of the National League for Nursing. From 1948 until 1964 Goostray served this important work in various capacities as well as served as consultant for the North Atlantic region.

Goostray extended her efforts for nursing history beyond the profession. She served on the Advisory Committee for the Elizabeth and Arthur Schlesinger Library on the History of Women at Radcliffe and in the same capacity for its first three volumes of Notable American Women: 1607-1950, a biographical dictionary. She contributed to it a biographical sketch of Linda Richards and ensured that other nurses would be included. Earlier Goostray authored books on material medica and in 1941 wrote the history of the Children's Hospital School of Nursing. *Nursing Outlook* published her "Nation-wide Hunt for Nursing's Historical Treasures" in 1965.

After years of service to nursing history, the founding of the History of Nursing Archives must have filled Goostray with joy! Her collegiality with Garrigan and their admiration for nursing's storied past merged in Goostray's service as a consultant to the federal grant for the History of Nursing Archives. Goostray was eighty years old and a walking archive of nursing history when Garrigan supplied her with a tape recorder. Associates from the Children's Hospital gave her copies of National League for Nursing documents that jogged her memory as she journeyed back over her career. Goostray intended these informal reminiscences would be added to the Stella Goostray Collection. The History of Nursing Archives thought otherwise and in 1969 published *Memoirs: Half a Century of Nursing*. Goostray died that year in her eighty-third year.

Soon after the History of Nursing Archives sponsored research conferences taking advantage of the growing scholarship in nursing's history. The blend of nurses researching nursing's past and social historians researching the profession made these conferences lively affairs. The papers were excellent and as is so often the case at such conferences, the liveliest discussions happened in the corridors and over dinner. The proceedings were published for those unfortunate enough to have missed the sessions.

Such conferences publicized the History of Nursing Archives as did the many honors nursing groups sprinkled on its curator. Although Garrigan would eschew any attempt to monumentalize her, she readily accepted awards that would throw glory on the History of Nursing Archives. She was granted honorary degrees from Boston University and the University of San Diego. Sigma Theta Tau, nursing's honor society, awarded Garrigan its most prestigious award, the Edith Copeland Founders Award. Boston College gave her the Joseph Coolidge Shaw Award during its Year of the Library. The Academy of Nursing accepted Garrigan as one of its fellows, the Massachusetts Nurses Association made her an honorary member and Boston University School of Nursing's chapter of Sigma Theta Tau named its leadership award in Garrigan's honor.

Garrigan graciously accepted these awards and then got back to the work at hand. During this same time Garrigan chaired the committee that created the American Nurses Association's Hall of Fame. Established to celebrate the country's Bicentennial Year (1976), ANA's Hall of Fame continues to honor notable nurses at each convention.

The History of Nursing Archives Associates was established in 1970 with Dean Marie Farrell as its first president. In 2006 the Associates continue to support the development and goals of the History of Nursing Archives in its efforts to collect, preserve, research, study and publish the materials of nursing history. More important the Associates provide necessary professional and financial support to recruit new members, educate the profession about the value of the History of Nursing Archives and secure new materials that add breadth and depth to the Collection.

Each spring, the Nursing Archives Associates gather for their annual meeting and listen to a presentation on nursing's history after which they join the speaker and colleagues in a festive reception. Every year Dr. Gotlieb opened the proceedings with his gracious welcome to the attendees. He shared with them his pride in the achievements of the History of Nursing Archives and then brought them up to date with a brief report on its present state and future goals. This was especially welcomed in 1988 after President John Silber and the Board of Trustees closed the BUSON. The History of Nursing Archives was secure, said Gotlieb, indeed it was one of the Center's most used collections bringing scholars from across the nation and from abroad to Boston University. Former faculty and alumnae of the School remain active supporters of the History of Nursing Archives.

Thanks to Garrigan's determination and Gotlieb's support in 1966 nursing's precious documents are today preserved in the Mary Ann Garrigan Vault in the Howard Gotlieb Archival Research Center. Their belief in the value of nursing's history has been validated over and over again. Their service to history is honored in their names being on what they established.

The Center and the History of Nursing Archives are flourishing. Now connected to the world via the internet, the History of Nursing Archives' web site receives almost 13,000 hits per year. There are nearly one hundred researchers using the collections each year. The American Nurses Association Collection attracts lots of scholars as does the History of Military Nursing Collection. Nursing's past is seen through the various prisms of nursing history, labor history, feminist history, organizational history and biography. There is no end to the stories that scholars are extracting from the Collection. The stories of Linda Richards, Mary Eliza Mahoney, Frances Slanger, Mary Maher, the founding of the Massachusetts Nurses Association, the evolution of the Boston City Hospital School of Nursing and oral histories of nurses from World War II are among some of the stories that have been told.

As W. Perry Barton who mounted the Capturing the Century: Forty Years of Collecting exhibit has said about the four nurses (Ethel Brooks, Helen Parks, Alice Clarke and Frances Slanger) he excerpted from their collections: "Four women with four stories that reach out to you from time gone by . . . [and present] a tiny slice of what we may now call history that is as resonant to us today as it was to those women years ago."

Thus it is only fitting and proper that nurses pause in their important work to honor Howard Gotlieb. Mary Ann Garrigan answered his questions of why Special Collections should collect nursing. Howard Gotlieb's accomplishments and Mary Ann Garrigan's achievement will continue on, way beyond their passing. And in a hundred years from now, scholars will ask for the Massachusetts Association of Registered Nurses Collection so they can discover what Massachusetts Nurses were doing in 2006.

HISTORY OF NURSING ARCHIVES:
FORTY YEARS YOUNG

(originally published September 2006)

The occurrence this year of the fortieth anniversary of the establishment of the History of Nursing Archives at Boston University's Mugar Memorial Library in 1966 provides an opportunity to pause for a moment and reflect upon just how significant this achievement was. There is a particular reason why nurses should take note of this anniversary. The reason lies in nursing's recognition that its history is not dry antiquarianism but a vital element in the present life of the profession. Nursing understands how knowledge of the past is needed to guide and inspire forward movement. This knowledge, says Mildred Newton (1965, 20), allows charting the profession by events that show how one generation uses the ideas, theories, practices and research of past generations and passes this knowledge on to the nurses of the future.

What was the social environment in which the History of Nursing Archives was founded? In 1966 NASA was planning its trip to the moon, Medicare became a reality and the Vietnam War was at its beginning.

A birth control pill tested in 1954 and on the market in 1960 became available to any married couple in 1965 thanks to a Supreme Court ruling. The pill became available to everybody who wanted it in 1975 after a Bill Baird-led rally in Boston. Nurse Margaret Sanger (1883-1966) who went to jail in 1917 for providing women with birth control information died in 1966 as the pill became the center of women's reproductive rights.

A multimillion dollar library was opened at Boston University and Mary Ann L. Garrigan (1914-2000) seized the opportunity that the completion of the new library at Boston University presented. Negotiating with Howard Gotlieb (1926-2005) the Director of Special Collections, and then with his colleagues in the library system, Garrigan was able to convince these authorities that Boston University should establish the History of Nursing Archives. Supporting Garrigan in her efforts was Stella Goostray of Boston's Childrens Hospital. She had used her bully pulpit as past president of the National League for Nursing Education (subsequently the National League for Nursing) to educate the profession about preserving its documents (Goostray, 1965, 26-29). Only the year before the establishment of the History of Nursing Archives, Goostray voiced her hopes for a central depository where nursing's documents might be "catalogued, reported and made available for reference" (Goostray, 27). Until that hope might be realized, Goostray made sure that the Arthur and Elizabeth Schlesinger Library on the History of Women in America at Radcliffe College— now Harvard's Radcliffe Institute—received a run of the American Society of Superintendents of Schools of Nursing Reports (1912-1952).

Thanks to Goostray's relationship with Radcliffe, nurses were included among the biographies in *Notable American Women: A Biographical Dictionary.* Goostray wrote the biographies of Linda

Richards (1841-1930), America's first nurse to receive a nursing diploma and Sophia F. Palmer (1853-1920), Richards' student at the Massachusetts General Hospital School of Nursing and later the first editor of the *American Journal of Nursing.* Mary Eliza Mahoney (1845-1926), America's first African-American nurse and Maj. Julia Stimson (1881-1948) are other Massachusetts nurses featured in the biographical dictionary.

If the social environment in which the History of Nursing Archives was established is important, its professional context is crucial to understanding how significant an achievement it was. The lack of a central nursing archives prior to 1966 was only one of nursing's serious deficits. Disparate education, an inaccessible scholarly record and an uncatalogued research history were noteworthy others. Help to remedy these disparities came from beyond the profession. Post World War II gave a boost to nursing education. The GI Bill enabled nurses returning from the War to enroll in universities. The National Mental Health Act of 1946 addressed the dearth of psychiatric nursing preparation.

It was not until the 1950s that the National League for Nursing mandated that psychiatric nursing had to be part of the nursing curriculum. Ironically, prior to the full use of psychotropic medications, fifty percent of the nation's patients were hospitalized in psychiatric hospitals. Less than five percent of America's nurses cared for them. Kennedy's Community Mental Health Centers Act would revolutionize the treatment site. Federal funding for nursing education continued in the Eisenhower administration and President Lyndon B. Johnson signed into law the Professional Nurse Training Program.

Within a generation of this federal intervention, there were nurses prepared as educators and others with graduate degrees prepared to conduct research. Administration that had long been the destiny of nurses with advanced education receded in importance as clinical nursing rose in prestige and nursing research became important. The hospital diploma nursing schools continued to graduate nurses but slowly lessened in popularity as young women and men increasingly chose colleges and universities for their nursing education. This gradual movement away from the hospital and towards academia escalated in 1965 when the American Nurses Association published its position that all nursing education should take place in institutions of higher education.

This was not the first time nursing tried to establish its education at colleges and universities. Mary E.P. Davis and her MGH classmate Sophia Palmer promoted university education in the pages of the *American Journal of Nursing* and in their meetings with officials at Simmons College in 1903. The Rockefeller Foundation institutionalized the educational reforms recommended by the Goldmark Report (1923) at Yale University after Harvard declined the honor. Some years earlier Dr. Alfred Worcester of Waltham, Massachusetts had persuaded Harvard to establish a nursing school. All that was needed was funding, and that, a wealthy Bostonian promised to supply. Reversals of his Wall Street portfolio that year defeated the philanthropist's enthusiasm for the nursing school. The idea of a Harvard Nursing School never rose again.

Nursing programs at Minnesota, Columbia University and Simmons College in the Fenway were exceptions to the steady state of nursing education in hospitals. Necessary to the hospital economy when they were established in 1873, hospital nursing programs continued to benefit the operation of the hospital to the disadvantage of the profession's growth. The numbers were in: though there were more college educated nurses, they represented probably less than ten percent of the profession in 1964 (Simmons & Henderson, 1964, 29). Nurses educated at a graduate level were even fewer. Still, the university was nursing education's destination.

Unsurprisingly, the relocation of nursing education from hospitals to the university was not without turmoil. Tumultuous as this transition was, nursing was beginning to take its place among the learned professions. Unlike these professions which were skilled in researching their practice, nursing's scientific investigation focused mostly on education and administration and rarely on nursing practice. Nursing aspired to reverse this but was obstructed by the difficulty in accessing nursing's scholarly record. Accessing the literature was not impossible in 1966 but it was not comprehensive and decidedly labor intensive.

Almost from the beginning of nursing journals, nursing organizations addressed the need for an index to the nursing literature. For the most part nursing had to depend on the annual index to nursing journals. This may have been relatively easy in 1900 when nursing had only two journals: *The Trained Nurse* and the *American Journal of Nursing*. But even then, unless nurses had good memories or had personally indexed the journals as they arrived, accessing the current literature was a problem. The nursing literature needed to be indexed. Papers galore in the nursing journals from 1920 forward agreed. Major Julia Stimson, a Worcester, Massachusetts native, second dean of the U.S. Army School of Nursing and World War I veteran chaired a national committee for a number of years. Like much else in nursing's long and troubled journey to full professional status, the urgent need for an index fell to the bottom of the profession's agenda.

Lack of money was a major obstacle. Eleanor Cairns, the late nursing librarian from Connecticut, provided a telling image of the dire need for financial resources. If she had to cut any more corners, she said, she would be "going around in circles" (Pings, 160). There was also a dearth of opportunities for collaboration. What is more, most nursing libraries had been created without organizational theory or practical procedures. Then, few schools had qualified librarians. Some schools used retired nurses as voluntary librarians. Other schools had neither a nurse nor a librarian heading the library (Pings, 159). Such an ad hoc method of running nursing libraries spoke volumes on how little nursing education valued the library. Accreditation bodies may have exacerbated by not emphasizing nursing libraries. Later, when the National League for Nursing did ask about the adequacy of the library, no measures were given or sought (Pings, 166).

Nursing was confronting its lack of bibliographical control over its literature at the same time that nurses were having their research findings published in *Nursing Research*. This disparity was part and parcel of nursing's revamping its educational process to make it reflective of professional standards while at the same time it bent its best efforts towards discovering new knowledge. Often those committed to tradition's "we've always done it this way" as the evaluator of practice struggled against those who accepted independent thought and scientific investigation of nursing practice as essential. As long as nurses were separate from the scholarly record represented in nursing journals, nurses were incomplete scholars (Pings, 120).

At last, in 1964 the American Nurses Foundation commissioned Vern Pings PhD, RN, a medical librarian at Wayne State in Detroit, MI, to conduct a three month-long study. The aim of the study was to develop a plan for indexing nursing's periodical literature. Central to Ping's study was the belief that nursing could not continue to promote scholarship and produce literature and then not take responsibility for indexing its literature (Pings, 118). If nursing was to be a profession in word as well as in deed, it had to gain bibliographic control of its literature.

Pings asked how many of nursing's 91 journals schools subscribed to. One collegiate program stood out from all the others. The Boston College School of Nursing Library subscribed to 85 of the 91 titles and was the sole subscriber to 30 of these titles (Pings 190). In effect, states Pings, there are probably only three libraries in North America receiving the scholarly record of nursing: the National Library of Medicine, the Sophia F. Palmer Library of the *American Journal of Nursing Company* and Boston College [School of Nursing Library] . . . The only source of documents for a large share of the nursing scholarly record, five years after the establishment of a comprehensive index, would be Boston College and the National Library of Medicine, neither of which should be expected to service the entire community of nursing (190).

Only the Boston College School of Nursing Library had accepted the responsibility of preserving nursing's scholarly record (Pings 190). Ironically, when Mary Pekarski, newly graduated from Simmons College Library School, surveyed nursing libraries in 1947 she found that except for the Palmer-Davis Library at the Massachusetts General Hospital School of Nursing, nursing libraries were so deficient that she decided she could not be a nursing librarian. With the urging of a wiser head, she learned that her library did not have to be like those deficient nursing libraries. With her creativity unleashed, Pekarski created a world-renowned nursing library in 1947 that had no peer in 1966 nor has it a peer sixty years later.

A decade before Pings plan for bibliographic control of nursing's periodical literature, the National Committee for the Improvement of Nursing Service (1948-1953), the successor to the National Nurse Council (1940-1948) that Boston's Stella Goostray led during World War II, proposed that nursing studies be assessed. The need to keep up with published nursing research and to understand developing research trends drove the profession to seek the study. By the time that Leo Simmons and Virginia Henderson were appointed as co-investigators and the project funded in 1953, it had "widened and deepened" (Simmons & Henderson, 1964, 2). Rather than limit the project to 1942-1952 as originally planned, the project would reach back to 1870 when American nursing education began and go forward to the 1960s. It would study the beginnings of nursing research, the directions it took and the forces that had impeded or promoted its development (Simmons & Henderson, 4). In ten years time, the first of the four volume *Nursing Studies Index* (1963-1972) was published starting with the most recent studies. Earlier studies appeared in subsequent volumes. This made sense given students and researchers need for current research findings.

The co-investigators were stymied by the lack of library tools, a cumulative index to the nursing literature or a classification system. Simmons and Henderson (5) had to create their own categories as they developed a classification system that follows:

* Historical, philosophical and cultural studies
* Occupational orientation and career dynamics
* Specialties in nursing by occupational categories
* Nursing organizations and organizations including nursing
* Administration of nursing services in hospitals, clinics, public health and other agencies
* Nursing care
* Patients' reactions and adjustments to identifiable variables related to their illnesses
* Interaction patterns between nurse, patient, patients' families, other nurses, physicians, and other members of the health team
* Education for nursing
* Conducting research—facilities, personnel, support and method (71-72)

Among the foci for historical studies, Simmons and Henderson listed the following subject headings: aims, values and ideals; origins, epochs and events; movements, trends and patterns over stated periods; history of special agencies or institutions; general nursing services; specialized types of nursing; biographies and portrayal of the nurse in the arts, literature, drama and advertising (72).

The American Nurses Association had developed a *Master Plan for Research* in 1950 and then in 1962 published its *Blueprint for Research in Nursing* in the *American Journal of Nursing* (69-71). Barbara Schutt editorialized that with the publication of the *Blueprint*, "the most certain thing about it is that somebody's favorite subject has been missed" (45). Significantly, the *Blueprint* put nursing and its practice as the first among the six areas for research:

* Nursing and its Practice
* Nursing in the Social Milieu
* Communications and Decision Making in Nursing
* Organization and Operations of Nursing Services
* Education for Nursing
* Structure, Functions and program of the ANA

Schutt was correct. More than one nurse was disturbed that historical research was missing from the *Blueprint*. According to Mildred Newton the gap was not recognized until the Spring of 1965, but when it was, ANA's Committee on Research and Studies acted to remedy the error. It commissioned Newton to write "The Case for Historical Research" which *Nursing Research* published in its Winter 1965 issue. Not only had the Committee overlooked historical research in its 1962 *Blueprint for Research in Nursing*, it had also failed to mention historical research in its 1950 *Master Plan for Research*. Newton's argument that all researchers needed to develop historical mindedness could also be applied to the profession as a whole. Nursing had to habitually reflect the present against the background of the past if it was to develop perspective. What is more, Newton added, there was an urgency to increase historical research simply because there was too little of it (26).

Mary Kelly Mullane, the Chair of the Committee on Research and Studies, used the moment to appeal to nurses to identify and preserve nursing's primary documents, direct faculties and students towards opportunities for historical research and continue to broaden the search for places to house and preserve historical documents (1965, 25). The next year, 1966, one of Mullane's wishes came true. The History of Nursing Archives was established at Boston University. The profession finally had a place for its documents and artifacts.

Mary Ann Garrigan exclaimed "At Long Last! A Nursing Archive!" (1967, 11-12). Bowing in respect to the Committee on Historical Source Materials for its efforts over the years, Garrigan urged nurses, schools and agencies to preserve their historical papers. She included all of Massachusetts nurses when she asked, "Can you help us develop the Archives?" Nurses answered the question with another question. "Just what are you looking for?" nurses asked. Garrigan listed personal and organizational papers, records, reports, correspondence, memoranda, addresses to conferences, programs, clippings, photographs, runs of journals, biographical materials and old nursing books. Clearly, she was on a hunt for nursing's historical treasures and "anything that marked nursing's historical 'tracks'" became her quarry. She knew where valuable documents were apt to be. She urged, "Search your desks, closets, cellars and attics for memorabilia that will contribute to the factual development of the story of nursing as an integral part of the progress on civilization. Before you throw it away, [Garrigan advised], write or call" (12). She strengthened her pleas with recourse to authorities referring nurses to Simmons and Henderson's *Nursing Research: Survey and Assessment* and Newton's "The Case for Historical Research."

During this same time, many diploma nursing programs closed and made the History of Nursing Archives the repository of their decades-old records, photos and memorabilia. This new interest in preservation of the historical record of organizations coincided with Garrigan's collecting documents, teaching nursing's history and helping scholars access the collections. She used her positions on committees and review boards to promote the History of Nursing Archives. The receipt of a United States Public Health Service grant of $152,000 helped Garrigan get this work up to speed (Research Project, 1967, 289).

As Broadway was singing, "On a clear day you can see forever," Mary Ann Garrigan gained the advantage over a society and a profession in turmoil. She kept her eyes on nursing's future by esteeming its past. As curator of the History of Nursing Archives, Garrigan needed the skills of the nurse and the librarian. In this she was supported by Virginia Henderson who had been her teacher at Columbia and Mary L. Pekarski, nursing's librarian par excellence. The three professionals were members of the Interagency Council on Library Tools for Nursing founded March 4, 1960. They institutionalized their own collaboration when they founded the New England Council for Library Resources for Nurses. Henderson hosted the first meeting at Yale during the student unrest but thereafter nurses and librarians met each fall at the New England Center for Continuing Education at Durham, New Hampshire.

Then in 1971 the American Nurses Association named the History of Nursing Archives as the "national depository for nursing materials." ANA announced that it would deposit some of its historical paper at the History of Nursing Archives and encouraged other organizations and individuals to do the same (Boston University, 1971, 2090). With ANA's decision, the History of Nursing Archives changed from a local archives to a national one.

In the same issue, the *Journal* noted the 25th anniversary of the Boston University School of Nursing. Dean Irene Palmer presided over the symposia on the Social Significance of Education in Nursing that 300 guests attended. The uproar of previous years that had erupted with Palmer's changes to the curricula had dissipated, though certainly, it had not been forgotten. During her brief administration the School of Nursing in 1972 purchased 50 of Florence Nightingale's letters to Robert Rawlinson. Interestingly, they were written during the 1860s a hundred years before the History of Nursing Archives was established. If ANA's depositing its materials gave the History of Nursing Archives a national presence, these Nightingale letters made the History of Nursing Archives international in scope. What is more, the letters provided a link with the nineteenth-century nursing icon and the beginning of modern nursing. They also were primary sources of research. The History of Nursing Archives published the letters and Palmer authored two papers on Nightingale using these primary sources.

Other scholars were delving into the extensive records of early nursing schools housed in what Carnegie called an "academic research repository" (1974, 371). Biographical studies were done on Linda Richard, the first American to earn a nursing diploma and Mary Eliza

Mahoney, nursing's first African-American nurse both of whom graduated from the New England Hospital for Women and Children's School of Nursing. A study on Mary E.P. Davis focused on her helping nurses to form alumnae associations and the Associated Alumnae of the United States and Canada, the precursors to the American Nurses Association. The Association's collection attracted nurses and organizational analysts. Social historians writing history from the ground up focused on the many nursing students as opposed to the few founding mothers. Labor historians and military historians along with feminists from the 1970s Woman's Movement found the History of Nursing Archives a goldmine as they trolled the nineteenth- and early twentieth century's documents in search of a useable past.

Rare early nursing texts provided access to the profession's early ideas on ethics. Busy from the outset, the History of Nursing Archives has remained so over the forty years. Garrigan was the public face of the History of Nursing Archives. Accordingly she attended professional conventions, conferences and committees. In 1974 while at ANA's convention in San Francisco she addressed ANA's Council of Nursing Research. Collecting material for historical research, she told the attendees, is like collecting fine art. Not only do we search for the past, but we must identify directions of today and tomorrow and acquire meaningful material to continue the documentation of nursing's significant contribution to mankind's heritage (Carnegie, 1974, 371).

Garrigan had amassed significant primary sources that were inventoried and available to researchers. No one questioned nursing's proud history. Neither sources nor pride was enough to entice the profession to focus as much as it should on historical research if Lucille Notter's 1972 editorial in *Nursing Research* is credible (483). Two years later Carnegie's editorial echoed Notter's. The "historical approach to nursing research has been lagging conspicuously," wrote Carnegie who pointed her readers' attention to "the significant collection of historical materials in nursing" that were preserved in the History of Nursing Archives at Boston University's Mugar Memorial Library (1974, 371).

The profession's deliberate retrieval of its research studies in Henderson's *Nursing Studies Index*, the development of the cumulative index to nursing's scholarly record in the *International Nursing Index* and nursing's evolving reformation of its education were proceeding apace as Garrigan and her research colleagues tried to persuade the profession of the importance of the past in present choices and future directions.

The History of Nursing Archives was nearing its tenth birthday when the profession prepared to celebrate America's bicentennial. Garrigan and the History of Nursing

Archives were more than ready. *Nursing Research* noted that Garrigan was "an authority on the history of nursing in the United States" (Research Report, 1974, 75). Not surprisingly, ANA asked Garrigan to chair its Bicentennial Celebration Committee. An exhibit that accompanied the Hall of Fame in Heritage Hall was excerpted from artifacts and documents in the History of Nursing Archives. Nurses attending the convention could see lamps that Florence Nightingale might have used and first editions of her books, a replica of Linda Richards' uniform, the first issue (October 1900) of the *American Journal of Nursing,* a report of Henry Street Settlement, photos of nursing's early leaders, President Harry S. Truman's award to Stella Goostray for her service during World War II, photos, books and letters of America's African-American nursing leaders and early records of the national nursing organizations. When the *American Journal of Nursing* reported on Convention '76, Garrigan wrote its editorial and linked the spirit of nursing with the spirit of 1776 (Garrigan, 1976, 1101).

The Nation's bicentennial festivities began in Boston. ANA kicked off its Bicentennial celebration May 6, 1975 with a lecture in Boston's Faneuil Hall America's Cradle of Liberty. Hazelle Ferguson who chaired MNA's Bicentennial Committee welcomed ANA's Bicentennial Celebration Committee that Garrigan chaired. Senator Edward M. Kennedy sent his best wishes, gratitude and admiration for nursing's "fight for healthcare as a right for all Americans" (MNA, 1975, 4). Then ANA President Rosamund Gabrielson reminded nurses that their history reached back to the nurses who had cared for the sick and wounded in the Revolutionary War's Continental Army Hospital in 1777 and forward to the clinical nurse practitioners of the 1970s. In doing so Gabrielson unwittingly recorded nursing's renewal as a practice profession. The investment in nursing education following World War II had created a knowledge explosion in nursing which the *International Nursing Index* and the *Nursing Studies Index* facilitated. Professional prestige had shifted from administration to clinical practice. The Bicentennial gave added cachet to historical research. More and more nursing's storied past was being freed from old documents to inform current decision-making.

At MNA's convention later that year, Mary Ann Garrigan as chair of the ANA's Bicentennial Celebration Committee bestowed the ANA Bicentennial's Liberty Medal on Catherine Towers, the outgoing President of the Massachusetts Nurses Association. Garrigan cited Towers' for her leadership during the celebrations and for producing the *Landmarks in Nursing* booklet that recounted Massachusetts nursing history. Garrigan was especially complimentary about Towers' creating the lecture series which provided a "public platform from which to proclaim the contributions, goals, and directions of the nursing profession" (Garrigan, 1976/76, 6).

Garrigan might have been speaking of the History of Nursing Archives. In ten years time Garrigan had brought it to a place of prominence and prestige. At the fortieth anniversary of the History of Nursing Archives, nurses are educated in institutions of higher learning, nursing's research record is unbroken from 1870 to the present and nursing's literature is accessed with the click of a mouse. Thousands visit the History of Nursing Archive's website each year which leads to hundreds of reference requests to use the manuscript and book collections. Nursing's vision has become bi-directional. The profession looks back towards its past and forward to its future. To be sure there is never enough historical research but it continues to expand and to be reported in nursing's many journals.

The History of Nursing Archives is NOT an inanimate thing. It sprang from Garrigan's respect for nursing's past. To celebrate the fortieth anniversary of the History of Nursing Archives, then, is to celebrate its founding curator. Garrigan's distinction and achievement lay in her success in persuading Boston University to establish the History of Nursing Archives. She had the foresight to see beyond the professional and social turmoil of the 1960s and the imagination and scholarly insistence to proclaim that nursing needed its history as much as it needed educational reform, a cumulative index and an unbroken line of its research and studies.

Mary Ann Garrigan had the vision to conceive a central depository for nursing's documents and artifacts and the persistence to carry it through to its triumphant realization. Finally, her curatorship of the History of Nursing Archives was an amazing achievement in which she saw her dreams realized in a way given only to those who deserve success.

REFERENCES

Committee on Research and Studies. 1962. "ANA Blueprint Nursing Research," *American Journal of Nursing*, (62): 69-71.

"Boston University Named ANA Depository." 1971. *American Journal of Nursing* (71): 2090.

Carnegie, M. Elizabeth. 1974. "Towards More Clinical Research," *Nursing Research* (23): 371.

Garrigan, Mary Ann. 1976. "In the Spirit of '76," *American Journal of Nursing* (76): 1101.

---. 1976. *Heritage Hall/Hall of Fame: The Exhibition of American Nursing History.* Kansas City, MO: ANA.

---. 1975/1976. "68th MNA Convention," *Bulletin of the Massachusetts Nurses Association* (44): 6-7.

---. 1965. *Project Grant Application for Improvement of Instruction in the History of Nursing and Nursing Education.* Washington: D.C.: USPHS.

---. 1967. "At Long Last: A Nursing Archive!" *Bulletin of the Massachusetts Nurses Association* (36): 11-12.

Goostray, Stella. 1965. "Nationwide Hunt for Nursing's Historical Treasures," *Nursing Outlook*, 26-29.

MNA. 1975. "Bicentennial Lecture," *Bulletin of the Massachusetts Nurses Association* (44): 2-4.

Mullane, Mary Kelly. 1965. "ANA Blueprint for Research in Nursing," *Nursing Research* (14): 25.

Newton, Mildred. 1965. "The Case for Historical Research," *Nursing Research* (14): 20-26.

Notter, Lucille E. 1972. "The Case for Historical Research," *Nursing Research* (21): 483.

Pings, Vern M. 1966. *A Plan for Indexing the Periodical Literature of Nursing: Report of a Study of the Need for Bibliographic Control of the Scholarly Record of Nursing,* New York: ANF.

Research Reporter. 1967. "Boston University Establishes Nursing Archives." *Nursing Research* (16): 289.

Research Reporter. 1974. "Mary Ann Garrigan Named ANA Bicentennial Celebration Committee Chair," *Nursing Research* (23): 75.

Schutt, Barbara. 1962. "An Expanding Concern with Nursing Research," *American Journal of Nursing* (62): 45.

Simmons, Leo & Henderson, Virginia. 1964. *Nursing Research: A Survey and Assessment.* New York: Appleton- Century-Crofts.

MARY ANN GARRIGAN AND THE HISTORY OF NURSING ARCHIVES

(originally published June 2015)

As the fiftieth anniversary of the History of Nursing Archives approaches, it is a fitting time to honor the legacy of Mary Ann Garrigan, a former nursing professor at Boston University. The History of Nursing Archives, founded in 1966 with the aid of a U.S. Public Health Grant, preserves the collections of 152 individuals and 61 organizations and institutions. With the help of the Nursing Archives Associates, Garrigan collected the papers of hospital schools of nursing as they were closing due to the ANA's 1965 Position Paper on Nursing Education that stated education for the profession should take place in institutions of higher learning. Such was Garrigan's magnetism that she was able to entice many nursing's leaders to contribute their papers to the History of Nursing Archives.

Diane Gallagher, the Nursing Archivist who was recently honored as the first ANA Massachusetts Friend of Nursing, continues the legacy of Mary Ann Garrigan. Most recently Gallagher provided her special services to Ronna Krozy and Beryl Chapman, co-Presidents of the Beth Israel Hospital School of Nursing Alumni Association. They are currently gleaning historical data from the BIHSON Collection in preparation for the Centennial of the School in 2018. Preserved among the many institutional reports, documents, speeches and photographs, Chapman and Krozy found a video of the graduation of the class of 1935. Also in the Collection was a questionnaire asking nurses who had worked at Beth Israel prior to 1947 about their service during World War II. Still another precious document of the School's history is a small brochure: *Life at 330 Brookline Avenue, 1961.* Each item presents the life of the School as it was lived, as do artifacts such as a class pin dated 1921 and a student nurse uniform. The DVD that is being made for the Centennial will provide similar perspectives and perhaps the thrill of discovery to researchers of the future.

Another user of the History of Nursing Archives was Robert Welch, a journalist and resident of Eugene, Oregon. Using the Boston City Hospital School of Nursing Collection he researched Frances Slanger (1913-1944), a graduate who landed with the troops at Normandy during World War II. The young Army nurse was killed by enemy fire and is remembered in the USS Frances Y. Slanger hospital ship. As Welch was signing his book, *American Nightingale: The Story of Frances Slanger, Forgotten Heroine of Normandy* in Eugene, a young man asked him where he had done the research. When he heard 'Boston University', Terry Shugrue, the young man said, "I have a sister who works there. Her name is Diane Gallagher." Such a moment was put in the small world department once the author replied, "She was the nursing archivist who helped me with my book."

The History of Nursing Archives has more than 300 original letters written by Florence Nightingale. Through the efforts of Diane Gallagher and Vita Paladino, the Director of the Howard Gotlieb Archival Research Center at Boston University where the History of Nursing Archives is housed, a collaboration with the Nightingale Museum and other partners has resulted in the digitization and public availability of hundreds of these famous letters.

The Nursing Archives Associates provides support to the Archives and hosts an annual meeting every spring. Past speakers have included notable nurses such as Margaret McClure and Muriel Poulin, researchers who were instrumental in creating the foundation of the Magnet Program, Joyce Clifford, long time chief nurse at Beth Israel Hospital in Boston and Terri Arthur, author of *Fatal Decision: Edith Cavell, World War I Nurse*. Membership is open to anyone interested in preserving the history of nursing. (See http://www.bu.edu/dbin/archives/pdf/nursing.pdf for a membership form.) The History of Nursing Archives is open Monday through Friday from 9am to 3:45pm. An appointment must be made 48 hours prior to the intended visit by calling 617-353-3696 or by email at msdsg@bu.edu.

NURSING SCHOOLS IN MASSACHUSETTS

THE EMERGENCE OF ST. ELIZABETH'S
HOSPITAL TRAINING SCHOOL (PART 1)

(originally published in September 2007)

In 1868 Ann McElroy, Ann Dolan, Ann Doherty, Margaret McNarney and Elizabeth Carling opened their thirty-bed hospital for women at 28 Hanson Street in Boston's South End. Designed as an urban suburb for Boston's well-to-do, the South End had fallen into disfavor as new mansions rose along Commonwealth Avenue. South End estates were divided into boarding houses into which Irish immigrants escaping from the 1847 potato famine in Ireland flooded. The torrent of these new immigrants continued over the next decades changing the character of the city and inciting the wrath of native Bostonians against this "foreign population" (Handlin, 1974, 185; Vogel, 1989, 7).

The demand for domestic servants overrode the want ads that stated "no Irish need apply" and "Protestant girl" or "American girl" wanted. Protestant girls would not work as servants nor would Italian and Jewish immigrant women. Irish women ignored anti-Irish sentiments and domestic service's low status focusing instead on its advantages. Taking "their destiny into their own hands" these *Bridgets,* as the elite termed them, had emigrated from Ireland by themselves and for economic reasons. Their earnings helped other family members to emigrate out of Ireland's poverty and supported churches springing up in Boston. The same focus, as well as the independence and assertiveness it bred, shaped how Boston's more than 14,000 domestic servants in 1870 dealt with employers who detested them but were desperate for their labor (Diner, 1983, 1-29; Vogel, 1980, 7). Tradition has it that the five founders emerged from this group of domestic servants. Many daughters and granddaughters of these servants became nurses.

The South End's physical climate was more lethal than the prevailing anti-Irish prejudice. In 1870 consumption was the leading cause of death in Massachusetts and the Irish huddled together in unsanitary housing its primary victims. Boston's elite had little sympathy for the sufferers and claimed the Irish had imported the disease with them from Ireland. Understanding the cause and course of this and other infections and conquering sepsis in surgery would eventually change the original charitable thirty bed hospital into St. Elizabeth's Hospital, a scientific institution.

The constant in that change was St. Elizabeth's continued adherence to the founders' objectives. These lay members of the Third Order of St. Francis cared for women of all faiths, creeds, nationalities and colors taking their inspiration from Elizabeth (ca. 1207-1231), a princess who became a saint for her care of the poor in thirteenth century Hungary. With its thirty-bed capacity St. Elizabeth's was small compared to the one hundred and forty-bed Massachusetts General Hospital or the two hundred and ninety-two bed, Boston City Hospital. St. Elizabeth's, however, excelled as did other denominational and ethnic hospitals, such as St. Joseph's Home for Destitute Serving Girls with Consumption (1860), Carney Hospital (1863), the West End's Mt Sinai dispensary (1902), the South End's Plymouth Hospital (1908) and the Beth Israel Hospital (1917), in providing a milieu where patients' cultures and religious practices were respected and patients were treated as persons of worth and dignity.

Similar to other hospitals of that era, St. Elizabeth's distinguished between the virtuous and the vicious poor, that is, those who were sick through no fault of their own and those whose vices made them sick. The hospital discouraged mendacity and spent prudently the donations given or solicited to finance the work. An un-endowed institution St. Elizabeth's had what Brandeis' Abraham Sachar has termed a "living endowment" specifically, the unpaid labor of its sisters.

By the time the hospital was incorporated in 1872, it had moved a short distance away to 78 Waltham Street. A *Boston Evening Transcript* report shows how St. Elizabeth's was part almshouse and part hospital with little distinction drawn among acute, chronic and incurable cases. There were: twenty-eight sick persons, two or three of whom are bedridden, others are suffering from diseases that seem incurable, and one is in her second childhood. A great many of the cases are of the class that necessitate a great deal of lifting and there are some surgical cases that require a great deal of care, but all this arduous and disagreeable work is performed by the [seven] sisters (p. 1).

By 1883 when Archbishop John Williams invited the Franciscan Sisters of Allegany, New York to assume the domestic care of the hospital, it had extended its mission to include the care of men and renamed itself St. Elizabeth's Hospital of Boston. As from the beginning more patients sought admission than could be accommodated. Within a year of Mother M. Rose's O.S.F. (née Mary Ann Enright) arrival in 1884, the hospital moved to the former estate of historian and Harvard librarian, Justin Winsor (1831- 1897), at 61 West Brookline Street and added a four-story brick building at its rear. Fittingly, the hospital reopened on St. Elizabeth's feast day, November 19, 1885. Still the demand for care grew and within five years time, Mother Rose reported that the "capacity of the hospital was not sufficient" (*Corporation*, March 19, 1890). Before long, St. Elizabeth's expanded into the three adjoining estates, (numbers 59, 57 and 55). Fronting Blackstone Square, one of two parks that Charles Bulfinch had created in his grid plan of the South End, the "new" ninety-bed St. Elizabeth's Hospital was renovated from "attic to cellar" and its equipment updated. Many domestics and "respectable working-women" were receiving care in its medical department. The gynecology services continued as the largest and best in Boston and the surgical services were formalized into a department (*Ninth Triennial Report* 8-9).

At this point, August 28, 1895, the Corporation voted that the Board of Directors would establish a "training school in connection with the Hospital" (159). So began the school in 1895 that by 2000 would graduate more than four thousand nurses. Unknown is how Susan M. Foley (1869-1959), the first of ten children born to Thomas and Mary E. Thompson Foley and an 1894 graduate of the Boston City Hospital Training School for Nurses (BCHTSN) was chosen as superintendent. She was of Irish origins and Catholic in religious belief which would have recommended her. Her training under Lucy Lincoln Drown (1847-1934) whose own training at BCHTSN had been under Linda Richards (1841-1930), America's putative first trained nurse, was also in her favor.

More is known of Foley's choice of nursing. Following graduation from Willard High School in Quincy and before applying for nursing, she worked as a bookkeeper at Jordan Marsh. She believed that "every woman had a true vocation." After six years of much "thought, study and work" Foley concluded that her vocation was nursing. "For this reason and because of the greater chances of doing good than other works afford," she wrote Drown, "I desire to become a nurse" (*BCHTSN*, January 25, 1892). One reference cited her as a "wholesome girl who [would] work with conscience" and praised her as "an uncommonly bright pupil" who had "an intellect that was quite superior." Once accepted, Foley enthusiastically thanked Drown, writing, "I am truly grateful and will do all in my power to be a good nurse," (*BCHTSN*, March 14, 1892).

She was a woman of her word. During her two-month probationary period one head nurse found that Foley's only fault was that she talked too much but within the month she had improved. The other head nurse found her personal manners "pleasing but girlish." Both nurses remarked on Foley's good judgment, intelligence and quick perception. Her endurance for the labor intensive profession was rated "above average." As Foley moved through her program, she was found to be "a kind, helpful and reliable nurse." It would seem that Foley was careful about contagion and used the prescribed disinfectants in her work. Although she was sick thirty-five days because of a "very sensitive throat," she was far more fortunate than three of her classmates who died from scarlet fever, diphtheria and emphysema (Cheever, 1906, 212). Perhaps the clearest indication of Foley's maturation from talkative girlishness to nursing proficiency was her "executive ability" in managing a twenty-five bed typhoid fever ward (*BCHTSN*:Ledger).

BCH tried to persuade Foley to remain at the Hospital following graduation but like many other BCHTSN graduates, Foley chose instead to sign on with the Directory of Nurses at the Boston Medical Library. She accepted general medical and surgical cases for twenty-one dollars a week and contagious cases for three dollars more. Patients and doctors rated her nursing care as good, the top grade it could earn, with one patient exceeding the limits of the questionnaire to praise her as a "most satisfactory, faithful and skillful hospital attendant" (*Directory of Nurses*).

With the twenty-six year old Foley's appointment, St. Elizabeth's had an intelligent and competent nurse of sound judgment and executive skill. She had style, as well. St. Elizabeth's student uniform reflected 1890s fashion with its change from voluminous silhouettes with bustles to slimmer skirts with the fullness of fabric limited to Gibson Girl leg o mutton sleeves. A white apron with a six-inch hem over a blue chambray dress and a fluted cap atop the head turned fashion into a practical uniform. Foley's black silk superintendent's uniform announced her position while her BCHTSN cap declared her educational credentials. It also added four inches to her five foot three inch height. The prominence of Foley's right hand in the photograph symbolized her responsibility to shape students' intelligence and compassion into the practical care of the sick, a process that will be discussed in part two.

Susan Margaret Foley, First Superintendent of Nurses at St. Elizabeth's
Hospital Training School for Nurses 1895-1898
Courtesy John J. Burns Library, Boston College

REFERENCES

"A Triple Charity." *Boston Evening Transcript*, (October 13, 1879): 1.

Boston City Hospital School of Nursing Collection. History of Nursing Archives Howard Gotlieb Archival Research Center.

Cheever, David W. 1906. *A History of Boston City Hospital from its Foundations to 1904.* Boston, Municipal Office.

Diner, Hasia R. 1983. *Erin's Daughters in America: Irish Immigrant Women in the Nineteenth Century.* Baltimore: John Hopkins University.

Foley, Susan M. *Directory of Nurses.* Center for the History of Medicine, Countway Library of Medicine.

Handlin, Oscar. 1974. *Boston's Immigrants: 1790-1880,* (Rev.). New York: Athenaeum.

Ninth Triennial Report of the Directors of St. Elizabeth's Hospital: February 1, 1893-January 1, 1898.

St. Elizabeth's Hospital Corporation Records. Archdiocese Archives Boston.

Sachar, Abraham. 1995. *A Host at Last,* (Rev. ed.). Waltham: Brandeis.

"St. Elizabeth Hospital," *Boston Globe,* (November 11, 1885) 6.

Vogel, Morris, 1980. *The Invention of the Modern Hospital: Boston 1870-1930.*
Chicago: University of Chicago.

THE EMERGENCE OF ST. ELIZABETH'S HOSPITAL TRAINING SCHOOL (PART 2)

(originally published December 2007)

The trained nurse movement was twenty-two years old in the summer of 1895 when St. Elizabeth's Hospital's Corporation voted to establish a nurses training program associated with the hospital. The new school caught the attention of training school superintendents who in 1893 had organized into the American Society of Superintendents of Training Schools for Nurses (precursor to NLN). Until the nursing owned and operated *American Journal of Nursing* was created in 1900, the superintendents used the pages of Buffalo Hospital's *Trained Nurse and Hospital Review* to be in contact with nurses across the United States. The "In the Nursing World" column of the 1896 issue alerted these nurses that: "St. Elizabeth's Hospital, Boston, Massachusetts has just opened a training school for nurses and is now prepared to receive pupils" (NA, 1986, 91). The column provided more information the next year:

> To those wishing a course in training in a small hospital, St. Elizabeth's of Boston offers fine opportunities. [It was] recently enlarged, making it a general hospital of [90] beds, offering special work in gynecology and obstetrics, while general surgery and medical cases receive their full share. The hospital is under the charge of Sisters of St. Francis, but doctors, nurses and patients are nonsectarian, so this need make no difference to applicants. The course is three years, one year to be spent in private duty nursing. The hospital is probably not well known, being small, but the training school is in a flourishing condition (NA, 1897, 36).

Flourishing the new training school certainly was. The first enrollees, the Class of 1898, had already advanced to their senior year; the Class of 1899 to their second year; and, one student of the

Class of 1899 had just arrived at the time of this announcement. In 1898 when Susan M. Foley gave her first report as superintendent, the training school had 20 nurses in training and three probationers selected from a pool of 135 applicants from January 1, 1896 to January 1, 1898.

The Directors of St. Elizabeth's alluded to how the innovation was changing the nursing care within the hospital. "All the Sisters have put themselves under the instruction and training of the school," they reported, "and all nurses hold themselves in readiness, besides the regular work of the Hospital, to attend any outside cases in families that might desire professional service" (*Ninth Triennial Report*, 1898, 9). The medical staff noted that "In the Training School for Nurses ...there is a most efficient corps of nurses, and there is always a waiting list of applicants for admission to the school" (Ninth Triennial Report, 1898, 8). It was evident to the Trustees that their decision in 1895 to "give to women desirous of becoming professional nurses a systematic course of training and practice" was a success by 1898 (Ninth Triennial Report, 1898, 10).

Once accepted, a two-month probationary period provided students with the opportunity to show that they were able to use their good common school education, were physically fit for the labor and fatigue of the profession and were of good character. As important was their capacity for "self-denial, forbearance, gentleness, kindness and good temper," all necessary attributes of those who cared for the patients at St. Elizabeth's Hospital. The course of instruction had several components: the superintendent, Susan Foley, and the head Sisters taught students on the wards; 20 lessons of practical instruction on sick-room cookery were given by Miss Farmer of the Boston Cooking School, and 12 lessons on massage taught students a skill made necessary to prevent atrophy of muscles that resulted from bed-rest. Early ambulation following surgery was a World War II discovery.

Physicians lectured each week to students on nursing care. Dr. John G. Blake (1837-1918), an Irish born, Harvard Medical School educated physician who was an "unrivalled clinical teacher" according to his medical peers, gave the opening lecture. Blake was among the first physicians appointed in 1864 when the Boston City Hospital opened. He remained associated with the hospital until his death in 1914 while also serving at St. Elizabeth's and encouraging the founding of the Carney Hospital (Kelly & Burrage, 1920, 110-111). More than likely, Blake was the catalyst that brought the BCH-trained Susan Foley to St. Elizabeth's training school as its first superintendent.

He lectured on professional etiquette, specifically, the "duties and conduct of nurses." His son, Dr. John Bapst Blake, newly appointed as St. Elizabeth's opened its surgical department, lectured the students on surgical nursing, administration of anesthetics, emergencies, shock, collapse and hemorrhage. Other doctors lectured on medical nursing, obstetrical nursing, fever nursing, bandaging and fractures, administration of medication, as well as on anatomy and physiology. Special among the lecturers were members of the Nursing School Committee: Drs. Walter Burrage (gynecology), John Moran (physician) and George Thompson (children).

The required nursing texts provided still another aspect of the course of instruction. Danville's *Manual of Hospital Nursing*, Joseph Hutchinson's *Physiology, Anatomy and Hygiene* and Wilson's *Lectures on Fever* provided the first year students with basic principles. Still another text was *Materia Medica* that Lavinia Dock, nursing's premier nursing historian, had written in time snatched during night duty at Bellevue Hospital in New York City.

Anna Fullerton's *Obstetrical Nursing*, a compilation of lectures she had given to students in Women's Hospital in Philadelphia that went into multiple editions, stressed the importance of the nurse in obstetrical care. She called on nurses to recognize the value of cleanliness, antisepsis and eternal vigilance in adverting the dangers of childbirth. She directed other physicians to gain "a thorough understanding of the many details of scientific nursing" so that both the nurse and the doctor might work in harmony with the patient {Fullerton, 1895, ix).

Scientific nursing in the care of women was especially pertinent for students at St. Elizabeth's. Established as a women's hospital in 1868, it had been a general hospital since 1884 but in the 1895-1898 period its patients remained mostly women. Housewives and domestics predominated. Among others who sought treatment were dressmakers, working girls, school girls, nurses, professionals, clerks and women who listed no occupation. Fifty-three per cent of the 2627 patients who were admitted were treated for gynecological problems, the top ten of which were: endometritis, retroversion of the uterus, lacerated cervix, cystic ovaries, lacerated perineum, pyosalpinx, fibroid tumor, cancer, salpingitis and tubo-ovaritis.

As could be expected such a concentration of gynecological problems attracted doctors training for the specialty. The hospital took pride in maintaining the quality of the specialty that attracted such talent (Ninth Triennial Report, 1898, 9). Like the hospital itself, St. Elizabeth's did not discriminate on matters of race, color or creed in selecting doctors. This policy remained in effect until sometime around 1912 just before Cardinal William O'Connell broke ground for relocating St. Elizabeth's to Brighton. He "disbanded" the whole staff and reorganized the hospital with Catholic doctors in charge (O'Connell, 1934, 280).

Student nurses in these first three graduating classes came from Boston (5), Canada (4), Ireland (3) and New Hampshire (1). They were a small sample that shows the movement into Boston of immigrants from other countries and migrants from within the country. All these students met the age requirement. More than half the students were 20, 21 or 22 years old; the other students were equally divided between the mid twenties and early thirties.

Student nurses at St. Elizabeth's were referred to as nurses and not pupil nurses as at other training schools. Their days were twelve hours long and their experiences on the wards necessarily reflected the patient population. As Table 1 shows these students spent more weeks in gynecology than in other areas of the course of study.

TABLE 1
Weeks of clinical experiences of students in first three classes at St. Elizabeth's Hospital School of Nursing

Student	Gynecology	Op. Room	Medical	Surgical	Maternity
Ellen Coakley '98	44.5	35.5	22	14	12
Anne Hull '98	122	0	16	14	11.5
Mary Connolly '98	60.5	9	32	22.5	24
Mary Ryan '99	74.25	13	41	13.5	0
Catherine Casey '99	63.75	34	23.5	23	0
Margaret Murphy '99	45	5	37.33	38.33	15
Katherine Murphy '99	45	5	37.33	38.33	15
Frances O'Toole '00	56	12	16.25	55	7
Mary Donovan '00	50.5	12.5	28	39.25	19
Elizabeth Roche '00	40.5	39	40.5	17	10.5
Mary McDonald ' 00	48.75	25	7.5	26	114.5
Mary Shea "00	58.25	7	39	28	11
Laura Carney '00	49	12.5	33	25	11.5

Source:
Nurses Records from 1895-1905; Volume 1 St. Elizabeth's Training School Boston MA (Three Sisters of St. Francis-Magdalene, Raphael and Veronica graduated in 1898 but data on their clinical experiences were not in this ledger).

Students also did private duty nursing. Most often this was in the community but sometimes students took special care of one patient on the wards. It is not clear from the evidence how this decision was made. Often the patient was suffering from an infectious disease, but given the prevalence of infectious diseases at that time, this alone may not have been the specific criterion for placing a student with one patient. The one on one assignment may well have been to give the student the experience of private cases in preparation for careers following graduation.

With students as an ever-renewing labor force, hospitals required the services of only a few selected graduate nurses. Other graduate nurses left hospitals to care for patients in their homes, perhaps because it was more remunerative and provided more independence than did the hospital milieu. Susan Foley, for example, declined a position of the Boston City Hospital in favor of private nursing, and after her stint at St. Elizabeth's as its training school superintendent, she returned to private nursing. It is reasonable to assume that she was preparing her students for the realities of the profession.

With its training school, St. Elizabeth's joined those at the New England Hospital for Women and Children (1872), Massachusetts General Hospital (1873), Boston City Hospital (1881) and Childrens Hospital (1889) in educating nurses and providing better care to Boston's patients.

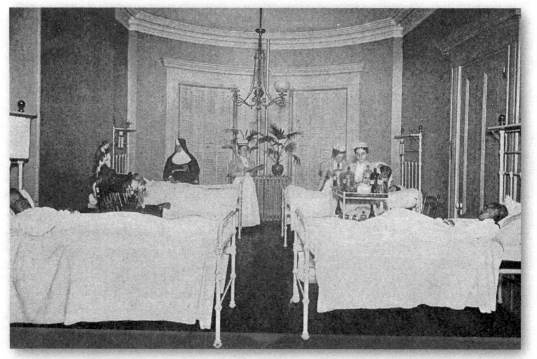

Students and Sisters caring for patients on the medical ward at St Elizabeth's Hospital
Source: *Triennial Report*

SOURCES CITED

Fullerton, Anna M. (1899). A Handbook of Obstetrics for Nurses, Students and Mothers, (Philadelphia: P. Blakiston's sons and Co).

Kelly, Howard A. and Burrage, Walter L. (1920). American Medical Biographies. (Baltimore: Norman Remington Co).

Ninth Triennial Report of the Directors of St. Elizabeth's Hospital; February 1, 1893-January 1, 1898.

[No author]. (Feb. 1896). "In the Nursing World," *The Trained Nurse and Hospital Review*, 15: 91.

[No author]. (Jan. 1897), "In the Nursing World," *The Trained Nurse and Hospital Review*, 28:36,

Nurses Records from 1895-1905; Volume 1 St. Elizabeth's Training School Boston MA.

O'Connell, William. (1934). Recollections of Seventy Years (Boston, Houghton Mifflin).

DR. ALFRED WORCESTER AND THE WALTHAM TRAINING SCHOOL FOR NURSES

(originally published September 2008)

The Trained Nurse Movement was a decade old in 1885 when Alfred Worcester, M.D. (1855-1951) an 1883 graduate of Harvard Medical School and his partner Dr. Edward Cutler opened a hospital in Cutler's house on Waltham's Main Street. The year before they had joined with medical peers to found the Waltham Fellows of the Massachusetts Medical Society. The following gives an idea of the state of medicine practiced at that point in Waltham. Appendectomies and caesarian sections were radical procedures, surgeries at home were a common practice, infectious diseases were the leading cause of death, antibiotics were a century away and refusal to believe that bacteria caused disease was ordinary.

It was in this climate that Worcester and his medical peers opened the Waltham Training School for Nurses. The doctors lectured pupil nurses on the basic sciences each week, first in a hired parlor, then in a former grocery store on the corner of Lyman and Main Streets and finally in rooms on the first and second floors of the new hospital. The doctors taught the pupil nurses how patients should be nursed and had volunteer women teach cooking, sewing and housekeeping. When Wilhemina Worth, Addie Kelton and Nettie Hathaway graduated, Mrs. Elizabeth Stone handed them their diplomas and her fellow lady business manager gave each a bouquet of "choice" flowers (Newsclipping, May 18, 1887). Several years later when Mary Hackett, a graduate of the Long Island College Hospital Training School came to Waltham to nurse her sister, Worcester persuaded her to join the School.

Worcester's concept of nursing was the neighbor nursing that he had witnessed and done as a child. When he was twelve years old he had nursed his friend during a bout of typhoid fever. Through the long night of watching the convalescent, Worcester changed his fever-ish friend's bedding, and then washed and dried the soiled linens. He had learned from the example of his mother and father that neighbors helped neighbors when they were sick. The tasks were various. Some provided nursing services as night watchers allowing the worn out family to get some rest, while others did housework, farm chores or read to a blind person. The occasional neighbor stood out for natural skill in caring for the sick, said Worcester, suggest-ing that in these "born nurses" rested the seeds of the nursing profession (Worcester, A. 1949).

Worcester contended that it was "a mistaken idea" that hospital training such as that at the Massachusetts General Hospital or Boston City Hospital was sufficient for neighbor nursing (Worcester, A. 1925, 1027). He was keenly aware that most graduate nurses practiced in people's homes. The problem with graduate nurses, said Worcester, was that people of little means, such as the immigrants and factory workers in industrialized Waltham, could not afford to hire a nurse, and those who could afford nursing services were unable to locate a nurse. The Boston Medical Library's directory of nurses addressed the latter problem so successfully that doctors and patients found nurses easily and the fees that nurses paid dissolved the Library's debt. By 1912 as part of their organizational efforts nurses would develop their own Central Directory.

The nursing services that the WTSN provided the community differed from those of graduate nurses and, as well, from those offered by the innovative Boston Instructive Nursing Association that Phoebe G. Adam and Abbie Howes founded in 1886. The BIDNA nurses went into homes to care for the sick poor, most of whom were immigrants, and to instruct them in hygiene. Boston philanthropists, who equated sin with sickness, underwrote these services as part of their mission to teach immigrants American ways, and thereby, protect the city's health and morality.

Worcester's WTSN contrasted with its contemporaries at the MGH (1873), BCH (1878) and Massachusetts Memorial Hospital (1883) and with the BIDNA. The WTSN was not associated with a general hospital nor with philanthropy. It was a free-stand-ing school where pupil nurses paid tuition, cared for patients in Waltham, Lincoln, Auburndale, Concord, West Newton, Newtonville, Watertown and Belmont and collect-ed fees for their services which were turned over to the School. The WTSN's uniqueness would eventually become its downfall.

In the meantime, the number of hospitals grew and training schools proliferated. Each promised a nursing education but exacted the cheap labor of their pupil nurses. Medicine staunched the proliferation of hospitals and Rockefeller millions subsidized the reformation of medical education. The hospital ward became the classroom where medical students stud-ied the cause of disease and learned to make exact diagnoses. The pupil nurse became more essential as the hospital replaced the home as the site of care. The reformation of nursing education would have a prolonged and troubled journey.

Worcester feared for medicine's art of practice as doctors focused on science. His solution was to make nursing medicine's art. As was his wont, he did so without collaborating with nurses who were on another path. They hoped that path led to nursing as a distinct profession with its education separate from a hospital's labor needs. Their efforts came to naught in 1903 when they were unable to persuade Simmons College in Boston's Fenway to create a program preliminary to clinical nursing.

During this same time, as Harvard Medical School erected its magnificent buildings on Longwood Avenue, Worcester turned to his alma mater to institutionalize his concept of nursing. It did no harm that Worcester held three Harvard degrees and was the son-in-law of former President Thomas Hill (1862-1868). President Charles Eliot (1869-1909) looked with favor on Worcester's proposal for a nursing school at Harvard. The necessary large endowment was readily promised but the benefactor's portfolio took a hit on the stock market. As Worcester put it, "Obstacles...wrecked the enterprise before its start" (Worcester, 1949 [6]). Harvard's interest in nursing changed during President A. Lawrence Lowell's (1909-1933) administration. The University declined the honor of implementing the-recommendations of the Rockefeller Foundation's study of nursing [Goldmark Report, 1923]. Yale University accepted and established its nursing school.

Worcester had taken some comfort in Eliot's promise: "Neither you nor the Waltham Training School for Nurses need have the least fear of their [Massachusetts State Nurses Association] hostility" (Worcester, 1949, [6]). For their part, the nurses stayed focused on education as the criterion for training schools. During the same ten years that the number of training schools increased from 35 to 432, nursing's leaders created: a superintendents society (1893); training school alumnae associations (c. 1893); a national nursing organization of the alumnae (1896); and, the *American Journal of Nursing* (1900). Then, along with other state associations throughout the United States, Massachusetts' nurses began a drive to gain laws to regulate the practice of nursing.

From 1903 to 1910 they sponsored *House Bill #564: An Act to Regulate the Practice of Professional Nursing of the Sick* in the Massachusetts Legislature. That bill sought an all nurse-board of registration and mandated graduation from a training school in a general hospital. The severity of the opposition earned for the Massachusetts's bill the distinction of having been the most virulently resisted. The men nurses, most of whom had trained in specialty hospitals like the McLean Hospital, were not eligible for registration according to the bill's criteria. Rightly, they feared that their earning power would suffer if registration were passed. Many of them joined doctors and hospital administrators against the nurses. A valiant few did not and these are listed in 1910 among the first registered nurses in Massachusetts. The doctors supporting the nurses were vocal but their voices were too few. When a much watered down bill was passed, nurses had won the educational criterion but the governor appointed a doctor to head the Board of Registration in Nursing.

Two years before his death at ninety-six Worcester summed up for the *Harvard Medical Alumni Bulletin* (1949) what registration of nurses meant: "All went well with us [WTSN] until the graduates of Hospital Schools obtained the political and legislative control of nursing. [The 1910 law] made the WTSN diploma worthless" (Worcester, 1949). In 1919, when Worcester was president of the Massachusetts Medical Society (1919-1921) the Massachusetts State Nurses Association's secretary, Mary E. P. Davis, wrote him that his training school graduates had lost their eligibility for membership in the MSNA because: pupil nurses were sent out to care for patients without being fully trained; the employment of pupil nurses was unfair to graduate nurses; and, earnings of the pupil nurses belonged to them and not the WTSN.

That year after the nursing registration success, 1911, Whitcomb and Barrows of Boston published Linda Richards' autobiography, *Reminiscences of America's First Trained Nurse*. Worcester persuaded Richards to write the autobiography and called on a convalescent living with the Worcester's to edit the text. Two of Richards' former associates, Edward Cowles, M.D. with whom she developed the training schools at the Boston City and the McLean Hospitals, and John Berry M.D. with whom she had created the training school in Kyoto, Japan testified in the introduction to Richards's preeminence in the Training School Movement. Most likely Worcester suggested the title but he added nothing to the introduction. This is a strange omission given their long relationship having first met in 1883 when he was a medical student and Richards was at the BCH. Stranger still was the absence in a book about the first trained nurse of any encomiums from nurses. Worcester later relished the praise nursing's leaders gave the volume unaware of his part in its existence (Worcester, 1949). Strangest of all, Richards never revealed the story behind her story.

If the nursing leaders claimed Richards as the symbol of the trained nurse, Worcester claimed her as America's Florence Nightingale. Worcester was deferential to Florence Nightingale to the point of obsequiousness. His arguments supporting the WTSN were buttressed with Nightingale's positions to the disparagement of American nursing. Important *what ifs* occur at this point. What if Worcester had chosen to forge relationships with Massachusetts' nursing leaders? And, what if the nursing leaders were able to persuade Worcester that their concept of nursing was a more valid response to American needs than Nightingale's? But he did not, nor did they, and the struggle continued. Worcester persisted in his adulation of Nightingale and flaunted his preference for British nursing. He hired her favorite nurse, Angelique Pringle, for a two-year stint at the WTSN. Then he was offended when Massachusetts's nurses were "indifferent to Miss Pringle." Nor could he win over Massachusetts' nurses with his opinion that their mandating a nurse to teach nursing was a "ridiculous requirement" (Worcester, 1949). He had started his WTSN without any nursing input and continued to dismiss the need.

Worcester remained an Anglophile as far as nursing was concerned. At the same time, he was justifiably proud of being a Son of the American Revolution. He vaunted the heritage of having heard his grandmother's eyewitness account of the battle in Lexington between the Red Coats and the Minutemen. His patriotism was American born and bred. Perhaps his antipathy to American nursing rested in his memory of his parents and neighbor nursing that remained so precious he could not tolerate any criticism of it. Here the evidence is silent. Nonetheless, history was important to Worcester. He was a charter member of the Waltham Historical Society, Incorporated. He valued the past and was sensitive to how the future would look back on its past. In 1930 he created an historical moment that served him more than it did its subject. In the last month of her life, Worcester had Linda Richards transferred from the Frances Willard Homestead in Northborough, Massachusetts to the New England Hospital for Women and Children. Private nurses had cared for Richards during the five years since she suffered a stroke 17 March 1925. Richards spent her last month on this earth in the hospital where she had earned nursing's first diploma. Nursing students of her alma mater relieved her private nurses and shrouded her body when Richards died 16 April 1930 in her eighty-ninth year (Eaton, L. August 31, 1989). Worcester had his symmetry but his sympathy for the frail old lady must be questioned.

One month later, on 16 May 1930 more than eight hundred registered nurses and nursing students gathered for the Massachusetts State Nurses Association's memorial service at Boston's Old South Church. Worcester, then Harvard's second Henry K. Oliver Professor of Hygiene (1925-1935) led the eulogists with inflated claims that Richards and Florence Nightingale knew each other well. The truth was they had met once over lunch at Nightingale's home in May 1877, a visit MGH's Martin Brimmer had arranged in gratitude for Richards rescuing the faltering Boston Training School in 1874.

Lucy Lincoln Drown, BCHSON (1884) who succeeded Richards as superintendent remembered Richards when she was full of hope, energy and enthusiasm. Mary Riddle, BCHSON (1889), the first chair of the Board of Registration of Nursing spoke of the light that Richards had cast on the care and comfort of patients. Then, as the Memorial drew to a close Annie Goodrich trumpeted nursing education. It must have cost Worcester a twinge or two as he listened to the Dean of the Yale School of Nursing (Memorial, 1930, 781-2). His wish for nursing's connection with Harvard was history as his WTSN soon would be.

The WTSN closed in 1935 in its fiftieth year having graduated seven hundred and seventy-six nurses. The elegant u-shaped WTSN building that Robert E. Glancy of Watertown built in 1899 with its front parallel to the Charles River and its rear facing Christ Church Episcopal at 760 Main Street was sold to the Rhineheart Functional Handwriting System. Various owners succeeded Rhineheart through the years until the building came to rest most recently with Fred Kimberk. Architect Kimberk who is rehabilitating the building celebrates its small foot-print and its wood, brick and stone structure. His commitment to Waltham's history is evident in his designating rooms on the building's first floor for exhibits of the Waltham Historical Society, Incorporated. There, Co-presidents Sheila FitzPatrick and Wayne McCarthy mount displays from the documents and artifacts the Society has collected and preserved since 1913. The Society's efforts have made it possible to tell the story of Worcester's contentious relationship with Massachusetts' nurses.

Waltham Training School for Nurses Class of 1889
Superintendent is most likely Mary Hackett
Photo by Waltham Historical Society, Inc.

WORKS CITED

Eaton, Louise, (31 August 1989). Correspondence with Mary Ellen Doona,

Newsclipping. (18 May 1887). Alfred Worcester Box, Waltham Historical Society, Incorporated,

No author. (1930). The Memorial Service for Miss Linda Richards. *American Journal of Nursing.* 30:781-782.

Worcester, A. (21 August 1919). Address: Fiftieth Anniversary of the New England Hospital for Women and Children. Alfred Worcester Box, Waltham Historical Society, Incorporated.

Worcester, A. (26 November 1926). Home Nursing. *New England Journal of Medicine.* 215: 1027-1029.

Worcester, A. (1949). The Shortage of Nurses: Reminiscences of Alfred Worcester '83, *Harvard Medical Alumni Bulletin.* Alfred Worcester Box, Waltham Historical Society, Incorporated.

EARNING PRESTIGE AT THE BETH ISRAEL HOSPITAL SCHOOL OF NURSING: 1918-1967

(originally published June 2009)

When the BIHSON closed in 1967, primary sources were discarded or displaced. Ethel Mascioli Ryan mined the archives that alumnae held in their memories. These oral histories are recorded in Ryan's *Recaptured Memories* (2001). She and the Alumnae of the BIHSON have preserved an essential part of the profession's narrative. By the time the Beth Israel Hospital School of Nursing opened (November 1918) the 45 bed hospital at 45 Townsend Street in the Roxbury section of Boston was almost two years old. If the hospital was new, the idea of a Jewish nurse was still more novel. In 1918 Boston had only six Jewish registered nurses. By the time the BIHSON closed in 1967, it had graduated 1264 nurses, only a sprinkle of whom were not Jewish.

The new hospital and its nurses aimed to help the sick without regard to class, color or creed. That was how Boston's poor Jews had been treated at the Massachusetts General Hospital, St. Elizabeth's Hospital and the Carney Hospital where they counted as 10% of the charity patients. The Boston City Hospital, specifically designed to care for the poor, excluded those who had not paid the poll tax which automatically excluded Jewish immigrants. Those few Jews who were treated at the BCH feared that the food compromised their dietary obligations. More worrisome was the horror of dying in a non-Jewish setting.

Lack of English was still another problem: A Yiddish-speaking Jew conveyed his problem to an English-speaking doctor who could not understand nor converse with the patient. To cite one of many consequences of such communication problems, a doctor researched a cluster of symptoms that Jews presented, namely, neurasthenia, pain, apprehension and constipation;

diagnosed it as "Hebraic debility;" and, published his paper in 1907 in the forerunner of the *New England Journal of Medicine*. Such an attempt to medicalize a social problem limited debility to Jews when it must have been the situation of others who were also poor, sick, frightened and misunderstood.

Some in the Jewish community proposed that BCH should create a Jewish ward where Jewish doctors and nurses knowing the culture and speaking the language could care for Jewish patients. This proposal was rejected outright, pleasing proponents of Jews taking care of their own as Catholics did at St. Elizabeth's and Carney Hospitals, and Protestants did at the New England Deaconess and New England Baptist Hospitals. Critics of this proposal argued that this would further segregate the Jew already shunned for his "otherness" because of his religion, culture and language.

Jewish women were at the forefront of resolving this impasse when in 27 August 1911 they organized themselves into autonomous auxiliaries throughout Boston: West End, South End, Roxbury, Dorchester, East Boston, Blue Hills, North End, Men's and Junior's. Later narrators of the origins of the BIH credit these women and their fund raising prowess with bringing the hospital into existence. Ironically, this feminine activism occurred before women had the vote—they got suffrage in 1920—or had careers beyond the home. Of the 231 signers of BIH's articles of incorporation 6 December 1915, 202 were women. On the fourth of February 1917, the BIH admitted its first patient—Mrs. Fannie Levine (Linenthal, 1990, 102-127). A dream had become a reality.

The next year as influenza raged throughout the world and invaded the wards at BIH, ten applicants crossed over the threshold of the BIHSON into the nursing profession. They and their successors chose the BIHSON for a variety of reasons. Some wanted to reconnect with faith and to get back to their roots. Sometimes the BIHSON was a second choice, the applicant having been rebuffed at other schools because of anti-Semitism. Boston offered a special attraction especially to girls living in rural areas. And, a few chose nursing because they lacked money for college. Parents also played a part. Some decried the choice of nursing for their daughters while other parents beamed with pride. Mrs. Berman hoped her daughter, Sheila Berman Greeley '66, would find "Mr. Right" expecting that if he were in the BIH community he would be "Mr. Jewish Right" (Ryan, 237). She did not but Elaine Fierberg Josephson '46 found a profession and a husband. "I love nursing," she said. "[BIHSON] was probably the best thing I ever did next to marrying my husband 47 years ago" (Ryan, 136).

Like other hospital programs, the BIHSON provided room, board and laundry services with the understanding that students' nursing care paid for their training. Whether care-as-tuition was equal to the labor expected is a question the profession still asks. The fact was the students were the nursing staff and also part of the domestic help. Once patients were cared for, they scrubbed bedpans, cleaned the utility room and mopped floors.

High standards and strict discipline kept a tight rein on these young women during their three years. Control of their behavior reached even to the TPR charts where students such as Selma Michelson Swartz '42 had to connect the dots with a ruler pocketed alongside her bandage scissors (Ryan, 111). Though complaints were many, they were seldom voiced though students at the BIHSON as did their counterparts at other schools did mimic the familiar litany: "we did not ask you to come," and "the door swings both ways." Such statements of not needing students and their labor were a sham for the economy of the hospital depended on the cheap student labor and the training school's ever-renewing supply of it.

The experience of being immersed in a milieu where competence was expected was as educational as what was said in the lecture halls. Students saw nurses deal with complex clinical situations and over time gained a similar mastery. Each challenge met and then mastered added another layer of confidence. "The responsibility was scary but I rose to it and really loved what I was doing," said Caroline Ober Kitkov '41 (Ryan, 108). Being alone on the night shift, said Doris Issokson Shumrak '48, "taught me responsibility and decision-making and to be constantly aware of what was going on around me and to be adaptable in many different situations" (Ryan, 165). Doris Bienstock Soreff '57 said with pride, "There was not a situation that happened that I could not handle" (Ryan, 215). Students were in charge on the evening and night shifts. At times they filled in for an off duty head nurse as did Jacqueline Shiffer Abrams-Lelyveld '38 (Ryan, 85). Students gained prestige at no cost to the hospital.

"We just had a good time all the time. We worked like dogs, but we were close," remembered Edith Levine Krantzman '48 (Ryan, 171). That camaraderie in the dorms also marked their time on the wards. A shift ended not after eight or ten hours but only when the work had been done. When students completed their shift, they went from floor to floor to help classmates to finish their work, said Charlotte Factor Yarrow '42 (Ryan, 113). They confided in one another, cheered successes and commiserated over difficulties. They were often exhausted but commitment to their choice of nursing bolstered their endurance. What is more, discovering powers within themselves amazed as well as invigorated them. Doris Bienstock Soreff '57 confessed, "I stumbled into something I was good at, that I had a feel for, a talent for" (Ryan, 214).

Youthful exuberance trumped fatigue as students focused on fun beyond hospital walls. Cleverly, students discovered how to evade the matron at the sign in and out desk by going out the back door. They had few dollars but had ingenuity in abundance. During the World War II era, students borrowed the uniforms of their Cadet nurse classmates. "We wanted to be in uniform like everybody else," remembered Ruth LaVine Corbert, '47 (Ryan, 144). That uniform meant free passes at the theatres where Broadway bound musicals were trying out. The ersatz Cadet nurse had to pay only the tax. Dressed in a borrowed uniform, Doris Donovitz '45 went to the Parker House roof and Doris Issokson Shumrak '48 to the Jewish Welfare Army and Navy Club near Kenmore Square to meet young men in uniform (Ryan, 124, 165). Throughout all the years the successors of the first Women's Auxiliary hosted teas with lots of pastry and treated students to other social events.

Rituals marked professional milestones: the candlelight capping ceremony ended probation. Banding ceremonies added black stripes to the cap. The day they "went into white" student days were done. They donned the starched long sleeved, multi-buttoned uniform and exchanged the thin black bands of the student cap for the one inch black band of the graduate. No longer needed, the thin black bands were given to younger students. Once this was done, the new graduates served a breakfast of bagels, cream cheese and lox to the entire school. Then they paraded through the hospital in their white glory to receive the accolades of the entire hospital community. Anne Adams Peters '66 aptly termed the maturation from probie to graduate "earned prestige" (Ryan, 244).

Down through the years from Townsend Street (1918-1928) to Brookline Avenue (1928-1967), the soul of the hospital was reflected through nurses, as Dr. Wilinsky told the BIH Nurses Alumnae Association (Ryan, 27). They shone their bright light on Jew and non-Jew alike and respected each person's culture, creed and language. Their three years together on the wards, in the dorms, during affiliations, and at play imprinted them forever as BIHSON nurses whose cap, as Adele Herwitz '40 said, was their "passport" (Ryan, 103). "Those were good days," remembered 95-year-old Anna Sidel Tofias '24. "We worked hard...but looking back on [those years] they were the best years of life" (Ryan, 330).

Beth Israel School of Nursing Pin

REFERENCES

Linenthal, Arthur. 1990. *First a Dream: The History of Boston's Jewish Hospitals 1896-1928.*
    Boston: BIH and Countway Library.
Ryan, Ethel Mascioli. 2001. *Recaptured Memories: 1918-1967.* Boston: BIHNAA, 2001.

BOSTON COLLEGE SCHOOL OF NURSING: THE ANTECEDENT YEARS (1945-1947)

(originally published March 2007)

Nineteen-hundred-and-forty-five was filled with event. Vice-president Harry S. Truman advanced to the presidency with the death of Franklin Roosevelt, the leader who had lifted the country out the Great Depression and mobilized it during World War II (1941-1945). Hitler committed suicide in April, the Germans capitulated in May, Truman dropped the atomic bomb on Hiroshima and Nagasaki in August and trials began in Nuremberg that would pass judgment on Nazis and their concentration camps.

If 1945 marked the end of hostilities, it also celebrated creativity. Alexander Fleming and his colleagues accepted the Nobel Peace Prize for the discovery of penicillin. *Harvey* and *Carousel* opened on Broadway, the first a light-hearted fantasy of a man and his invisible rabbit; the other, a lyrical Rogers and Hammerstein musical of doomed romance. *Lost Weekend's* portrayal of alcoholism flickered across movie screens as did Noel Coward's tale of illicit romance in *Brief Encounter*.

Rationing ended and food, clothing and gas became available again. Short skirts made necessary by war-time rationing of cloth were abandoned in favor of Dior's New Look with its extravagant use of fabric and a hemline well below the knee. Automobiles hit the road again once gas was released from military purposes. With pockets filled with G.I. loans, veterans left cities for houses in the suburbs causing a major shift in the demographics of the United States. Class boundaries tumbled as veterans surged onto college campuses, their G.I. loans giving them access to an education once open only to the privileged few.

Having soldiered with men and women of different origins, races and faiths, veterans had little patience with the restrictive categories of the past. Decades before *thinking outside the box* urged expansive views, post war America was putting the concept into practice. Nurses were among the first to take advantage of the new vistas that opened up. Those who had served in Europe and the South Pacific were not willing to return to Boston's hospitals and their constraints. Many of these demobilized nurses opted for advanced education in New York City, their independence made possible by the G. I. Bill.

Their choice made other choices necessary. One particularly sensitive to nurses' changed attitude was Richard J. Cushing (August 24, 1895-November 2, 1970) Boston's recently appointed archbishop. The South Boston native was an Eagle and a half having graduated from Boston College High School in the South End and completed two years at the Heights before entering St. John's Seminary across Commonwealth Avenue from Boston College. That relationship would become pivotal in the Archbishop's quest to renew nursing in archdiocesan hospitals.

These hospitals and others across the country were the reality behind the statistics: the number of staff nurses had dropped 43 per cent between 1941 and 1944. Personnel rushed in to fill the gaps at all levels-staff, head nurses, supervisors and faculty-were inadequately prepared to do the job. Eighty per cent of hospital care rested in the hands of student nurses but these were also in short supply. Nurses' low salaries and hospitals' stretched staffing did not appeal to high school graduates. The Cadet Nurse program, enacted into law in 1943, would increase the number of students but their impact would be on the future and not on the current crisis. The American Nurses Association stated unequivocally in 1945, "The quality of nursing care [is] dangerously low."

The Archbishop tried unsuccessfully to persuade Mary Gilmore (later Helming) and Mary Macdonald (1918-2000) to leave their posts at the Massachusetts General Hospital School of Nursing for leadership roles at St. Elizabeth's Hospital. At the beginning of their long careers in nursing leadership, these two nurses represented many others who recognized that advancement to leadership roles in Catholic hospitals was rare. With faculty, administrative and supervisory positions filled with the nursing orders such as the Sisters of St. Francis at St. Elizabeth's Hospital and the Daughters of Charity at Carney Hospital, nurses found their paths to leadership blocked. Worse, as a contemporary assessment concluded, unless steps were taken to change this situation, Catholic nurses would never determine policy but would be forced to travel paths laid out by others.

The war had made authoritarian hierarchies and protocols of etiquette then existing in civilian hospitals relics of a past age. Symbols of authority had no power over nurses who had seen the worst that war could do to a human being. Shaped by caring for young soldiers, nurses had discovered that nursing was a matter of professional judgment and not a knee-jerk response to dictates from above. So focused were these nurses on getting on with their lives and careers, they did not notice that they were writing the first lines in the obituaries of hospital training schools and student labor as a hospital economy.

Sensitive to the signs of the times, the Archbishop was determined to create a college education for nurses. Regis College in Weston and Emmanuel College in Boston's Fenway were ideally structured to accept students of a woman-dominated profession. Sister Olivia Gowan, the dean of the nursing school at Catholic University in Washington, D. C., however, recommended a university setting for the proposed nursing school.

It would not be unreasonable to assume that the Archbishop with so many other issues demanding his attention was getting tired of the nursing problem. First, his attempts to re-organize the nursing department at St. Elizabeth's Hospital had hit a brick wall and then the obvious choice of women's colleges for a women-dominated profession hit another. At the same time the urgency of the nursing shortage would not allow solutions to be delayed. The Archbishop solved his problem by giving it to his beloved Boston College.

There were problems here too. Boston College, like every other Jesuit school, college and university was open to students of all nationalities, races and faiths. Church policy had thwarted their efforts to include women in these student bodies. Long-standing decrees against modern science and liberal democracies banned co-education as false and harmful. President William Keleher S.J., already immersed in expanding Boston College to deal with the blitz of veterans invading the campus, found himself caught between restrictive policies of a passing age and an Archbishop whose inclusive strategies anticipated the reforms that would sweep the Church two decades later. In the event, Keleher reported to his Jesuit superiors 3 December 1945 that the Archbishop said that the nursing school at Boston College was a "must". He showed the Jesuits a middle ground between the ban against coeducation and Jesuit education for nursing. Boston College could put the proposed school at the In-town School on Newbury Street, a short distance from the all male campus at Chestnut Hill.

If 1945 ended with this decision made, the next year opened with more decisions to be made. By August 1946 Keleher appointed Anthony Carroll S.J., a veteran of World War II and a chemistry professor at Boston College, to head "our nursing school". His catalogue description announced that the new school would offer "the practical study of nursing linked with the lasting values of the humanities informed by the distinctly Jesuit method of teaching the whole person." This was no little matter. Jesuit education aimed to graduate a nurse "trained to cope successfully with even the unforeseen problems of life...equipped with the professional knowledge and technical skill which [would] enable her to take her place among the leaders of the nursing profession." Significantly, Boston College education for leadership would not be an exclusive post-graduate course for nursing administrators and educators. Boston College would educate all nursing students for leadership.

Boston College refused the Archbishop's quest to have one of the local nursing sisterhoods assume the deanship. Instead, Mary A. Maher (1902-1982), would head the nursing school, and by doing so, became the first woman dean of an undergraduate school at Boston College. A graduate of the Rhode Island Hospital School of Nursing, with a certificate in public health nursing from Simmons College and a bachelor of science from Columbia University, Maher was an experienced teacher herself. After positions at the Rhode Island Hospital and the Massachusetts General Hospital Schools of Nursing, Maher progressed to become the supervisor of the Commonwealth's nursing schools, even as she continued serving as the regional consultant to the United States Children's Bureau. Her professional stature and political savvy were known and respected. More important, she had a reputation for courage, personal integrity and intellectual honesty.

Maher chose Rita P. Kelleher, then the director of nursing at the Quincy Hospital School of Nursing, as the first faculty. A graduate of the Faulkner Hospital School of Nursing, Kelleher had degrees from Columbia University and Boston University, as well as teaching experience at the Clinton Hospital, the Massachusetts General Hospital and at the Quincy Hospital Schools of Nursing. She specialized in teaching science for nurses. At the time of her appointment in 1947, Kelleher was the president of the Massachusetts League of Nursing Education, her peers having acknowledged by their votes her leadership in nursing education.

Boston College recognized Maher and Kelleher's nursing expertise but the philosophy of pragmatism they had studied at Columbia was suspect. Philosophy was the "capstone of a Jesuit education," wrote Charles F. Donovan S.J., the late historian of Boston College. Not even the war-time emergency that accelerated the undergraduate program could make philosophy courses unnecessary. Philosophy would be required for the new dean and her faculty, as well. Their friendship for one another supported their mastering the material every Saturday morning after a full work week of creating the curriculum and developing clinical placements.

The School continued to take shape. A nursing library of sorts was in place, Carroll having bought $200 worth of nursing books, texts, histories, a bound set of the *American Journal of Nursing* and a subscription to the *Lady's Home Journal*. The great research library, the Boston Public Library, was just a short walk away and Bapst Library at Boston College was accessible by trolley. Once Carroll secured the services of Mary L. Pekarski (1925-1988), the nursing library was in good hands. The Emmanuel and Simmons College graduate traveled from Lawrence into Boston and day by day created a nursing library that sixty years later has only admirers and no equal.

Her appointment was still to come in October 5, 1946 when the *Pilot* headlined that Boston College was opening a school of nursing. As is usual in human affairs the official announcement lagged far behind the word of mouth already on the street. The school would be Boston's second collegiate nursing program, the first being at Simmons College. Chartered in 1899, Simmons opened its undergraduate nursing program in 1933. With the Yale University School of Nursing founded in 1923 to implement the recommendations of the Rockefeller Foundation-funded *Goldmark Report*, New England now had three collegiate nursing programs. To say that nurses welcomed Boston's new school hardly conveys their enthusiasm.

Nurses returning from military duty and walking away from nursing as usual set off a series of events that eventuated in the establishment of the Boston College School of Nursing. A photo taken at the gala tea held February 3, 1947 captures a moment in the shift from hospital training schools to university education. As Sally Johnson, Director of Nursing at the Massachusetts General Hospital, presided over the silver tea service, she epitomized the long history and stellar reputation of that school founded 74 years before. Mary Maher hovering solicitously at her elbow personified respect for the past while at the same time it announced the university's inclusion of nursing as a valid academic discipline. In the background is Matthew Donovan S. J. who represented Jesuit education.

On January 27, 1947 just the week before the tea, the Spring semester began. Thirty-five registered nurses stepped over the threshold into Boston College. That fall, 25 high school graduates followed the path laid out by the RNs and took their step over the threshold into Boston College. The choice that these 60 women made in 1947 has been repeated in the choices of their successors over the past 60 years.

Behind these 60 students and 60 years are the unknown soldiers and their nurses who redefined nursing during World War II. They changed the course of nursing history and laid the first stones of the School's foundations. Their names were long ago lost to history but–the practical study of nursing linked with the lasting values of the humanities and shaped by the Jesuit method of teaching the whole person-is their enduring monument.

Credit: School of Nursing Records, University Archives, John J. Burns Library, Boston College

REFERENCES

Donovan, Charles F.; Dunnigan, David R. & FitzGerald, Paul A. 1990. *History of Boston College: From the Beginnings to 1990.* Chestnut Hill, MA: The University Press.

Doona, Mary Ellen. 1997. *Boston College School of Nursing: 1947-1997.* Chestnut Hill, MA: BCSON.

Kelleher, Rita P. 1987. *Memoirs: Boston College School of Nursing: 1947-1987.*Privately printed.

FAMOUS NURSES

CLARA BARTON AND SARA E. PARSONS:
TWO NURSES FROM OXFORD, MASSACHUSETTS

(Originally published June 2005)

Oxford was the home of two Massachusetts women whose deeds spread much distinction on American nursing. Clara Barton (Clarissa Harlowe Barton 1821-1912), the more famous of the two, was born in North Oxford to farmers Stephen and Sarah Barton. Sara Elizabeth Parsons (1861-1949), by contrast, came to Oxford as a young girl when her mother married into the Wellington family. Barton and Parsons' pioneering work in nursing would take them far from the little town nestled in the Blackstone Valley. When their lives were done, their bodies were returned to Oxford where their bones now mingle with those of their family in local graveyards.

Long after their deaths, their deeds live on, adding to Massachusetts nursing's long history. The papers that document their lives are in the Library of Congress (Barton's) and the Massachusetts General Hospital School of Nursing Collection at the Countway Library in Boston at the ready for scholars and researchers. Most know Clara Barton as the "Angel of the Battlefield" celebrated for her heroic services to wounded men during the Civil War (1861-1864). She was forty years old when the first shot was fired at Fort Sumter April 1861. Barton had been in Washington, D.C. for a bit more than a decade working as a copyist at the Patent Office when the War broke out. By the time the last shots were fired, 660,000 men had lost their lives in the service of national unity. Two thirds of these martyrs died from disease, the other third in brutal slaughter. By the War's end, Barton was hailed throughout the country for her heroic services.

Barton began her service to these men and their families as a volunteer bringing supplies to the war hospitals in Washington nearby her work. Her first direct nursing care of soldiers was bandaging the wounds of the Sixth Massachusetts Regiment when it arrived in Washington.

By August 1862 these efforts expanded into direct care of men on the battlefields. She was not the only woman on the battlefields. Many volunteers had been supplied by the United States Sanitation Commission that President Abraham Lincoln had created June 3rd, 1861. The Commission also distributed supplies to the worker's battlefront, provided food and potable water, as well as transport for the wounded.

If not the only woman on the battlefields, Barton's long-term commitment to the soldiers during the war marked her as unique. After the War, she continued that commitment when she joined with others in locating missing men, marking graves of men hastily buried and corresponding with their grieving families. Still later that commitment was directed towards creating the American Red Cross after her first-hand experience with the International Red Cross during the Franco-Prussian War (1870). This woman from Oxford changed the world of military nursing.

After the War, Americans spent their best efforts to honor their dead. Statues of Civil War soldiers erected during this post war period grace many town commons throughout Massachusetts. By 1877 the State's capitol had its own monument created by Martin Milmore, a Sligo, Ireland native who was raised in Boston. The magnificent Soldier and Sailor monument with its statue of Liberty at its peak proudly graces Flagstaff Hill on Boston Common. The granite pillar is flanked by four statues: a sailor, a soldier, Peace and Clio, the Muse of History (this statue is the logo for "Clio's Corner" that appears in the *Massachusetts Report on Nursing*).

The monument is further decorated with four bas-reliefs depicting: Fort Sumter, men leaving for Fort Sumter, men returning from the War and Boston's Sanitation Commission. The newspapers of the day reported that among the thousands thronging to the dedication of the monument in 1877 were 25,000 Civil War veterans.

Even as Massachusetts was paying tribute to the dead, it was also looking for ways to use what had been learned from the War. Out of this study came the decision to transform civilian nursing as the Civil War had changed military nursing. Nurses training was the key. Nurses had been graduating from the New England Hospital for Women and Children since 1873. That year, too, socially prominent women whose fathers, husbands and brothers were on the staff created their nursing school at the Boston General Hospital (precursor to the Massachusetts General Hospital). Before long Boston City Hospital established its training school.

The three training schools made Boston a mecca for nurses training. What is more, the presence of the trained nurse at the bedside gave evidence that the hospital had changed from a place to die to a place where a person might be treated and regain his health.

Oxford, Massachusetts nurtured the two women who were leaders in nursing's post-war transformation. As so many other young women did in post war America, Sara Parsons turned to nursing. She left Oxford for nursing education at the Boston City Hospital where Linda Richards, the first graduate of the New England Hospital for Women and Children and was nursing superintendent. It is reasonable to assume that Parsons chose the Boston City Hospital training school because of Linda Richards' preeminence as nursing's leader.

An early evaluation of Parsons' first days at the training school questioned her maturity and wondered at her ability to complete the program. The subject was moot for almost before she began, Parsons had to return to Oxford where her mother was seriously ill. Within weeks Parsons' mother was dead and Parsons had to mother her two half-sisters, run the household as well as do farm chores. Parsons had little time to grieve her mother's death and even less time to grieve the loss of her own aspirations. Years passed before Parsons was free to resume her own life.

She returned to Boston, this time, to the Boston Training School (precursor to the Massachusetts General Hospital School of Nursing). This time there was no question of her maturity. She excelled in exams and her practical expertise surpassed that of her classmates. She served as head nurse for a year after graduation and then enrolled in the McLean Hospital Training School. During her tenure there, first as a student and then as a head nurse, the hospital moved from Somerville to Belmont, Massachusetts. Their bright cap and white apron, more visible than nursing diplomas, signified that the trained nurses were a necessary part of hospital care. The trained nurse would also be a necessary part of the movement to "hospitalize the asylum," that is, to go beyond housing patients to treating their diseases, researching the causes of the diseases and educating the next generation of professionals.

Parsons was among the leaders of this effort. Indeed her first position after completing her course of study at the McLean Hospital was to establish a nurses' training school at the Butler Hospital on Blackstone Boulevard in Providence, Rhode Island. Within three years she had established the nursing department and prepared three classes of trained nurses.

Oxford, Massachusetts gave Clara Barton and Sara Parsons to nursing. Barton's care of soldiers during the Civil War created an ideal of nursing that caught the public's imagination. That ideal served to invigorate society's reform of care in civilian hospitals. By 1873, the reformation of hospital care stimulated the creation of the trained nurse. Sara Parsons exemplified the new nursing ideal, the trained nurse that had its origin in Clara Barton's care of wounded soldiers during the Civil War. Oxford, Massachusetts nurtured the two women who were leaders in nursing's post-war transformation.

MARY ELIZA MAHONEY: A FORCE FOR JUSTICE

(originally published in June 2007)

The gentle and diminutive Mary Eliza Mahoney (1845-1926) is an iconic nurse who earned her place among the giants of the profession. She epitomizes a professional ideal that nursing is a service to humanity. She also represents a dark chapter in nursing's master narrative when the profession closed its doors to nurses of her color.* She has been lying in her grave at the Woodlawn Cemetery in Everett, Massachusetts for eight decades. In death as in life her message to nurses is humanity is an inclusive term.

Mahoney's nursing journey began 23 March 1878 at the New England Hospital for Women and Children's School of Nursing (NEHWCSON) in Roxbury. For sixteen months, garbed in a calico dress and felt slippers, she learned nursing while caring for people with medical and surgical problems and women during their confinement. As much as her program was educational it was equally, if not more so, a field of paid labor. For her first six months as a pupil nurse Mahoney received one dollar a week. This increased to two dollars a week the second six months and to three dollars a week during the last four months.

On graduation 1 August 1879, Mahoney was able to command fifteen dollars a week when she signed on to the nurses registry at the Boston Medical Library (founded in 1805 and since 1964 part of the Frances A. Countway Library of Medicine in the Longwood Medical Area). This was at a time when women who worked providing personal services or in trade and manufacturing were earning an average of five dollars and ten cents a week.

Mahoney alluded to this earning capacity when she addressed the National Association of Colored Graduate Nurses (NACGN 1908-1951) gathered in its first convention in Boston during three hot and humid August days in 1909. Founded only the year before, the NACGN aimed to:

> advance the standards and best interests of trained nurses;
> break down discrimination in the nursing profession; and,
> develop leadership within the rank of Negro nurses.

Mahoney was eligible for membership in the new organization. Her school had an alumnae association, and thereby, she could belong to the American Nurses Association (ANA). Registration was the standard as nursing professionalized in 1908 and would be the standard for the NACGN as well. Mahoney became a registered nurse in 1910 when Massachusetts established its Board of Registration of Nursing. One of more than five thousand nurses grandmothered in, she then met all the requirements for membership in NACGN. The Association had already honored her with a life-time membership.

The NACGN accepted Mahoney and her friend Dr. John Hall's invitation to come to Boston for its first convention. Mahoney welcomed the twenty-six nurses at the Twelfth Baptist Church and then presided over a tea at the NEHWC. Sometime during the festivities, Mahoney rose to praise her nursing school. She was thirty years from her pupil nurse days and knew from experience how her training had opened opportunities to her. Excellent evaluations that her patients had given of her care validated the high quality of her training. Other colored nurses had not been so fortunate. The record shows that many of them had inferior training and others faced barriers when they tried to enroll in the better schools. Mahoney declared her nursing school was different. The NEHWC's nursing school did not exclude pupils because of their race. Succinctly, she said, her nursing school "was not selfish."

Ironically, as Mahoney spoke out against the profession's injustices, she did not mention that the correction of another injustice had created the opportunity for her to rise from being a domestic at the NEHWC to being a pupil nurse in its nursing school. In 1878 the Hospital denied admission to Dr. Caroline V. Still, the daughter of Philadelphians William (1821-1902) and Letitia Still of Underground Railroad fame. The uproar this caused prompted the NEHWC to consider how far it had strayed in fifteen years from its founding principles of 1863. Once excluded themselves by medicine's misogynist bias against women doctors, the founding feminists had slipped back into the prevailing social norms and excluded a qualified doctor because of her color. The "feminist showplace" as historian Virginia Drachman called the NEHWC, seized the opportunity to renew its commitment to fitness, not race, creed or nationality, as the only test for applicants. At this point Mahoney was invited to apply to the nursing program.

In a fashion similar to the NEHWC feminists, nursing's social activists, Lavinia Dock and Lillian Wald, deplored the racial injustices being perpetrated within the nursing profession. "This anti-social feeling," said Dock as the NACGN was established, had entered nursing as it expanded. She and Wald decried the barriers that the profession had erected and vowed that those injustices would not infect nursing's education or its licensure procedures. Their determination was not matched by results. Schools routinely excluded colored applicants. From 1908 through the dire years of the depression to the post World War II dissolution of NACGN, Negro nurses struggled against exclusion, and after that, with discrimination.

Biases were not just about race but about creed and nationality as well. Catholics and Jews were politely advised by many nursing schools that they would be happier elsewhere. As harsh as this was for Catholics and Jews, it was not as severe as the denial of opportunity that Black Codes threw in the way of colored nurses and their patients.

During NACGN's s first decades Mary Eliza Mahoney attended conventions and inspired NACGN members as they asserted their right to practice nursing. The 1921 convention in Washington, D. C. was the last she attended. Seventy-six years old at the time, she was already ill with the breast cancer that would claim her life five years later. Impoverished by her lengthy illness she returned to the NEHWC with her month-long hospitalization paid by the Hospital, alumnae and friends. She died Monday morning, 4 January 1926. She would have been eighty-one years old in May. Mr. Willard O. Armes, a Boston cotton broker, who claimed he owed his life to that "dear soul" prayed over all that remained of Mahoney as she was lowered into her grave.

Death claimed her body but not her spirit. The petite Mahoney only grew in stature. At the 1935 convention in New Orleans, a newly reorganized NACGN institutionalized her spirit when it established the Mary Mahoney Award. The recipient would have to:

show outstanding contributions to the profession and the community,
work towards improving the professional status of the Negro nurse and thereby,
improve inter-group and interpersonal relationships within the nursing profession.

When the NACGN met the next year in New York City, it awarded the first Mary Mahoney Award to Adah Thoms, a Virginia native and a graduate of New York City's Lincoln Hospital School of Nursing. Thoms had served as president from 1916-1923 during World War I (1917-1919) and the lethal influenza pandemic (1918-1922). Desperate for nurses to replace those felled by the flu, the Surgeon General rescinded his adamant rejection of colored nurses and asked them to care for all the soldiers at Camp Sherman in Ohio and Camp Grant in Illinois.

Not least of Thoms' service to the profession is: *Pathfinders: A History of the Progress of Colored Graduate Nurses* that added this important chapter to nursing's master narrative.

The Mary Mahoney Award became an ANA responsibility when the NACGN dissolved in 1951. Seventy-eight years passed and thirty-two medals were awarded before a Massachusetts nurse was recognized. The recipient, Mary F. Malone, had established ODWIN (Opening Doors Wider in Nursing—1964) in Dorchester at the centennial of Lincoln's Emancipation Proclamation and the passage into law of the 1964 Civil Rights Bill. Malone and her colleagues identified potential nursing students, prepared them to compete for admission into nursing programs and supported their success. ODWIN also reached out to nursing faculty and educated them on the special health care needs of black patients. Six years after Malone received the Award, Dimock Community Health Center (successor to the NEHWC) named its Youth and Family Services building after Mary Eliza Mahoney.

In conclusion then, Mahoney came to prominence as a symbol of colored nurses excluded from the mainstream of nursing. The NACGN pulled her from obscurity and placed her as a symbol of justice before the profession. Tiny in size but large in influence, Mahoney continues to remind the profession that humanity is an inclusive term.

Mary Eliza Mahoney, front row fifth from the left, at the first national convention of the National Association of Colored Graduate Nurses held in Boston, August 1909

REFERENCES

Doona, M.E. "Glimpses of Mary Eliza Mahoney (7 May 1845-4 January 1926)." *Journal of Nursing History* (1, 1986): 20-34.

---. Mary Eliza Mahoney (1845-1926). *The Massachusetts Nurse* (1984): 8-9.

Miller, Helen Sullivan. (1986) *Mary Eliza Mahoney 1845-1926 America's First Black Professional Nurse: A Historical Perspective.* Atlanta: Wright Publishing Co.

Staupers, M. K. (1961) *No Time for Prejudice.* New York: Macmillan.

*Terms used throughout this paper are those contemporaneous with the account and follows *The Chicago Manual of Style.*

STELLA GOOSTRAY: A TINY PRINCIPALITY OF POWER

(Originally published June 2006)

S tella Goostray was devoted to nursing's history and knew the dearth of nurses' first person accounts of their times. Thus when Mary Ann Garrigan asked Goostray to record her own memories, she was more than willing to comply. Her Memoirs, published in 1969, made it possible to give this account of her leadership of the National Nursing Council for War Services.

6172 registered nurses and 1429 students attended the May 1940 convention in Philadelphia where the national nursing organizations—the American Nurses Association, the National League for Nursing Education and the National Organization of Public Health Nursing—gathered under the theme: "Nursing in a Democracy." A pageant celebrating the fortieth anniversary of the *American Journal of Nursing* opened the convention. Remarking on the Journal's keeping nurses in the United States and in 62 other countries informed, ANA's president, Julia Stimson, a Worcester, Massachusetts native, said the Journal was "our mirror as well as our mouthpiece—our handbook and our pride" (Roberts, 1940, p.673). Thanks to the foresight and indomitable spirit of the *Journal's* founders, editor Sophia Palmer and business s manager, Mary E.P. Davis (Massachusetts General Hospital School of Nursing Class of 1878), nursing had a *Journal* to celebrate.

Then the convention got down to business. Papers on leadership were presented, raising membership dues was considered, new committees were formed and reports of standing committees were accepted. A new section of Men Nurses was created that LeRoy Craig, a graduate of the McLean Hospital School of Nursing in Belmont, Massachusetts, chaired. The new section campaigned unsuccessfully to get military rank for male nurses. The status of colored* nurses was considered a "vital question" as indeed their exclusion from full participation in the profession surely was. Since 1916 ANA membership was contingent on State membership. Such were the times; colored nurses were excluded from membership in many southern states. Some delegates at the convention spoke out against such practices and proposed that any nurse who met the qualifications for United States citizenship should be entitled to membership in state and national associations. Other delegates referred the matter back to the states respecting states' rights policy, but in doing so, maintained the status quo. The matter was sent to the Committee on Constitutions and Bylaws for further consideration. Eight years later, the ANA began to deal with membership for colored nurses by applying pressure on state associations in the South.

The National League for Nursing Education dealt with the matter in a different fashion. It revised its by-laws while at the convention. Negro nurses excluded from the American Nurses Association, the NLNE stated, but who were members of the National Association of Colored Graduate Nurses could join the NLNE as individual members. The NLNE's recent experience at its 1939 convention in New Orleans seems to have prepared the way for this action. NLNE officers, Stella Goostray of Boston's Children's Hospital, and Nellie Hawkinson, a Webster Massachusetts native, protested to the management when Negro nurses had to use the service entrance into the hotel. Goostray and Hawkinson got little satisfaction from the manager who said he was following the standard rule of hotels in the South. Years later Goostray remembered being sickened at how colored nurses were treated. It is interesting to note the concurrence of the NLNE's changing its by-laws about membership of colored graduate nurses and Stella Goostray's being elected president of the National League for Nursing Education at the same 1940 convention. As she later said, "A wall began to tumble" but did not reveal what part she might have played in making that wall fall (Goostray, 1969, p.111). Goostray epitomized the leader who "girded with moral purpose [was] a tiny principality of power" (Burns, 1986, p.457).

The convention's theme "Nursing in Democracy," was appropriate for the historic Philadelphia location at any time but especially so in 1940 with war looming over the Nation. Indeed, the possible loss of freedom was on everyone's mind. As Mary Roberts editorialized in the *AJN* following the convention, democracies were falling overseas and there was destruction everywhere (Roberts, 1940, p.673). Germany had invaded Poland the September before, France would fall the month after the convention and in July rockets would begin raining on Britain presaging the eminent collapse of democracy. Prudently, the Nation responded to Hitler's tyranny when Congress passed the Selective Training and Service Act drafting men aged twenty-one years through thirty six.

Nurses began to prepare their profession as well. While still at the convention ANA's House of Delegates wrote to President Franklin Delano Roosevelt:

To the President of the United States:
WHEREAS, this is a time of unusual anxiety and concern to the [N]ation and of Great responsibility for the President of the United States, therefore, be it, *Resolved,* that we, the delegates of the American Nurses Association, and members of the National League for Nursing Education, now assembled in Philadelphia, wish to offer the support and strength of our organizations in any nursing activity in which we can be of service to the country ([Roberts] 1940, p .678).

Returning from the convention, nurses looked at how nursing was positioned if the war continued. Isabel Stewart, professor of nursing at Teachers College at Columbia University in New York City, conferred with Stella Goostray. This was not the first time that Stewart and Goostray had put their heads together over a nursing problem. They had met at Teachers College when Stewart was on the faculty and Goostray was a student earning her baccalaureate degree in 1926. They met often in NLNE committee work as they bent their best efforts towards advancing nursing education. Stewart thought that nursing should not wait until the Red Cross Nursing Service got in touch with nursing organizations. Further, Stewart envisioned national commission that represented the profession as a whole. The primary objective of the organization she envisioned would be to meet the demand for the supply of nurses while at the same time prevent any dilution of hard-earned standards of nursing education. The leaders were anticipating opportunists who would use the national emergency as the excuse to water down nursing education and fill nursing vacancies with inadequately prepared nurses and non-nursing personnel.

The first person Goostray remembers consulting was her Boston colleague, Sophia Nelson. Goostray admired Nelson as one of nursing's "best thinkers" and knew of her vast experience with the Red Cross in developing nursing services for refugees in Europe during World War I and for providing much needed services during the economic depression of the 1930s when she was president of the National Organization of Public Health Nurses. In 1940 Nelson was heading the services at the John Hancock Insurance Company that provided nursing care at home to its insurees. If Nelson was able to provide a perspective from a nursing practice point of view, Nellie Hawkinson, then located at the University of Chicago, added a perspective of wisdom acquired from her executive leadership of the NLNE and her leadership in nursing education in the mid-West.

Stewart, Nelson and Hawkinson agreed with Goostray's suggestion that Julia Stimson, as president of the American Nurses Association, should be the one to call nurses together. Accordingly, July 19, 1940 Goostray wrote Stimson stating that there should be a committee which would represent our three national nursing organizations . . . and also represent the whole profession in working with all federal government groups, the American Red Cross, and any national committee representing other professional groups.

Notwithstanding the urgency of the times, the fact that a group could be convened so quickly speaks to the close working relationships among the participants. More than likely what nursing would do if there were a war had been the topic of many conversations at the Philadelphia convention. In any event these nurses were not unprepared. On July 29, 1940, ten days after the letter was posted, a meeting was held at ANA headquarters in New York City. Present were: Julia Stimson and Ella Best from ANA, Mary Roberts, the editor of the *American Journal of Nursing*; Stella Goostray, Isabel Stewart, Claribel Wheeler, Blanche Pfefferkorn and Ella Taylor (a statistician) from the NLNE; Grace Ross and Ruth Houlton from the National Organization of Public Health Nursing; Mary Beard from the American Red Cross; Sister Olivia Gowan from the Association of Collegiate Schools; and Alta Dines who was doing a survey of nurses.

And as Goostray records, "By the end of that day, the National Council for National Defense was on its way" (Goostray, 1969, p.117). The Council preceded by three months the Sub-committee in Nursing of the government's Health and Medical Committee established in November 1940. Stimson served as chair of the Council and Alma Scot, the executive secretary of the ANA provided the same services for the Council. Even as the ANA provided leadership for the new Council, it also offered office space. Initial funding came from the pooled resources of the Council members, which consisted of: the ANA, the NLNE, the NOPHN, the ACS and the National Association of Colored Graduate Nurses. The American Red Cross Nursing Service, the Army Nurse Corps, the Navy Nurse Corps, the US Public Health Service Nursing Service, the Veterans Administration Nursing Service, the Bureau of Indian Affairs and others such as the Childrens Bureau were asked to appoint directors or superintendents to the Council. Later, the Council expanded to include other standing members. The American Hospital Association insisted on more than membership in the Council. It wanted, and got, a joint committee with the Council (Roberts, 1959, p.355). The Council's functions were:

determine what role nurses would play in national defense;
unify nursing activities related to national defense;
study, plan and increase nursing's resources;
ensure continuance of high quality nursing education and service;
act as a clearing house regarding nursing and national defense.

Knowledge of nursing's history shaped the creation of these functions. Nurses knew how nursing's training schools had proliferated once hospitals saw the training schools as an ever-renewing supply of cheap labor. From the four nurses training schools in 1873, the numbers of schools had grown to 1,129 in 1910 to 1,775 in 1920, to 2,255 in 1926. Quality was sacrificed to quantity so that most were schools in name only. With pupil nurses doing the nursing care in the hospitals, there was little need of graduate nurses. Their numbers overwhelmed private nursing so that large numbers of nurses were out of work long before 1929 when the bottom fell out of the stock market and the Nation's economy collapsed.

In the years before 1940, nursing superintendents had bent their best efforts trying to regain control of nursing education. They had managed to create a standard curriculum, form a proto-accreditation process that eliminated some schools and get laws enacted that said who could call her/himself a registered nurse. In the nine years prior to the convention the numbers of schools had decreased from 1800 to 1300 and the quality of nursing education in these schools had improved. The new Council was aware of nursing's history and was not about to let the profession's hard work of reforming nursing education be undermined by those who would argue from expediency that dire circumstances required lowered standards. Most especially they would not allow the numbers of schools to be increased without a commensurate increase in educational facilities and faculty. Neither would they allow the standards they had created for student selection to be lowered. As Goostray advised in her NLNE presidential address in 1941, "Do not let us do anything that will jeopardize the improvements in nursing education which we have made" (Goostray, 1941, p.746).

The war was no longer confined to Europe on Sunday morning December 7, 1941 when the Japanese attacked Pearl Harbor. The issue about having sufficient nurses for both military and civilian needs took on an added urgency. "Nursing's good friend" as Goostray calls Congresswoman Frances Payne Bolton, pushed through funding for nursing education to the amount of $1,250,000 in 1941 and $3,500,000 in 1942. Funding for the Council was also an urgent matter but proposals to the government had been rejected. The Kellogg Foundation came through for nursing and agreed to support the Council if it was incorporated. Accordingly, the Nursing Council for National Defense became the National Nursing Council for War Services, held an election for president as incorporation mandated and elected Stella Goostray. At first reluctant to take on the added task, the 54-year-old Goostray acquiesced once she was reminded that it was her wartime responsibility (Goostray, 1969, p.120).

Goostray (July 8, 1886-May 8, 1969) was eminently well qualified for the leadership position. She was a first generation American. From her English-born father, Job Goostray and Scotch-Canadian mother Jane Wylley Goostray she got her logical mind and sense of humor, according to Muriell Vessey, her successor at children's hospital, and freedom from petty personal judgment and personal competitiveness that her nursing colleagues would later prize.

Goostray was 29 years old when she enrolled in the Childrens Hospital School of Nursing in 1916 inspired to serve her country as World War I blazed. From that point to the end of her life she was committed to nursing. Even a bout of typhoid fever contracted as a beginning student and lengthy convalescence could not dissuade her from her mature choice of nursing. With $300 for tuition, she left a writing career with her Episcopal Church. She would gift nursing with her writing skills authoring journal articles, reports and books, among them: *Materia Medica: Drugs and Solutions* (1924), *Introduction to Materia Medica* (1939), *Mathematics and Measurements in Nursing Practice* (1963), *Applied Chemistry for Nurses* (1924, 1966) and *A Textbook on Chemistry* (1966). History was a special interest that she shared with her father and like her writing skills she used this interest for nursing. Among her historical studies are: *Fifty Years of the School of Nursing, the Childrens Hospital Boston* (1941*),* *Memoirs: A Half Century of Nursing* (1969), biographies of Linda Richards and other nurses for *Notable American Women* (1971). She used her leadership position to urge nurses to preserve nursing's primary documents (Goostray, 1965).

Goostray was associated with the Childrens Hospital for her entire nursing career except for five years in Philadelphia General Hospital School of Nursing while she was earning her degree at Teachers College. She began as a science instructor and ended as the School's educational director. Along with the joint responsibilities of nursing service and nursing education at Childrens Hospital, Goostray earned a graduate degree at Boston University. She was an active member on state and national committees associated with nursing education, accreditation and licensure. In many cases she rose from membership to president. She served on the Board of Directors of several health care organizations especially ones devoted to children such as the White House Conference on Child Health and Protection. She was a member of the Board (1925-1927), secretary (1928-1930) and then president of the *American Journal of Nursing* (1931-1937); president of the National League for Nursing (1940-1944); director of the Nursing Council for National Defense (1940-1942) and president of the National Nursing Council for War Services (1942-1946).

Goostray was a gregarious woman as well as a leader dedicated to the advance of nursing education. She gloried in working with professional associates many of whom testified to her gifts of critical intelligence, integrity and joy in leadership. She loved the hustle and bustle of being with others and enjoyed the clash of ideas and argument. Confident of her own gifts she was quick to acknowledge those of others. She was genuinely tolerant of opposing views and sharp enough to recognize traps that undermined nursing's priorities and progress. She had established a nursing department at Childrens Hospital noted for its excellence in care and education. Her leadership team, especially Mary Norcross her childhood friend, Childrens Hospital School of Nursing classmate, colleague and companion permitted Goostray's professional activities. It was a mutually enhancing relationship: Goostray shaped national nursing policies and Childrens Hospital benefited from her national reputation. Multi-tasking is a 21st century term but at mid-twentieth century it was Stella Goostray's everyday practice. She simply enjoyed to the fullest the life she had chosen for herself.

She brought all these skills with people, organizations and ideas to her leadership of the National Nursing Council for War Services. As the country had to sift through its young men to create a fighting force, nursing also had to determine the number of nurses that were available. A national survey was undertaken but until these numbers became available, the Council worked with what it had. Projecting that 55,000 nursing students would be needed, the Council looked over the numbers of nurses who had graduated in 1936 and the number who were expected to graduate in 1940. The Council then estimated that 26,000 nurses would graduate in 1941. These numbers fell far short of the 55,000 nursing students that were needed. Adding to the shortage was the fact that nurses left nursing once they married. In light of the national emergency something had to be done to entice these women, they were mostly women, back to the bedside to fill the staffing vacancies that occurred when nurses enlisted in the armed forces.

Then, whether or not nurses should serve with the armed forces was sketched out according to whether or not they were essential to civilian nursing services. Essential nurses were those working as administrators, staff, supervisors and educators in hospitals that had nursing schools and in public health nursing. Nurses who did not meet the criterion of being essential to the running of hospitals and public health services; those who were less than forty years of age and single; and, those working in offices, doing private duty nursing and other non-nursing activities were expected to enlist in the armed forces (Kalisch & Kalisch, 1986, p.509).

As neat as these categories were, they did not take into account how the increase in manufacturing for the war effort would lure women who might have chosen nursing towards the higher paying jobs in industry. These wartime jobs also had an impact on health care. The automobile industry's conversion to making tanks, for example, made many new jobs but also increased the number of industrial accidents and admission to civilian hospitals (Kalisch & Kalisch, 1986, p.520-522). Essentially, nursing already stretched too thin had to meet these changing demands. One unexpected consequence of nurses having to use volunteers and auxiliary help in hospitals was defining what patient problems required a skilled nurse and what nursing services could be given by non-nurses.

As urgent as sorting out nurses for the military was creating a cadre of nurses to fill civilian positions. The 80-year-old Annie Goodrich (1866-1954), retired from the deanship at Yale

University School of Nursing in Washington, D.C. during the nursing shortage of World War I. In 1940 she was for reopening the School to meet the crisis of having to add 55,000 students to the nursing pool. The Surgeon General squashed this idea saying nursing education was a civilian matter not a military one. Rumors flew around that Goodrich belittled Goostray and Council colleagues as inadequate to lead nursing education. Goodrich also separated herself from those in the Council who were of her World War I vintage, especially ANA President Julia Stimson, a veteran of World War I nursing services in France and Goodrich's successor at the Army School of Nursing. Stimson was opposed to Goodrich's idea of reopening the School because it was too expensive and in 1940 there were other venues open to educating nurses that did not exist in 1918.

Goodrich was not dissuaded. She pursued the Army School of Nursing idea by going directly to Congresswoman Frances Payne Bolton, as she had done two decades before when the Army School of Nursing proposal was rejected. Then Bolton arranged for a special meeting of Goodrich and the Secretary of War Newton Baker who reversed his position and accepted the proposal. In 1940 Goodrich's tactic was not so successful. The Secretary of War and the Surgeon General rejected the idea of re-opening the Army School of Nursing (Kalisch & Kalisch, 1986, p.501). The Council was happy that its position had been validated. At the same time, the Council was sensitive to Goodrich's situation. What is more, the Council wanted her on its side. They dealt with both aspects of the issue by asking Surgeon General Parran to invite Goodrich to Washington, D.C. as a consultant. Thus the Council helped Goodrich to save face and had the services of her vast experience. Goostray remembers this incident of intergenerational conflict and concludes, "The times called for a new approach" (Goostray, 1969, p.121).

The new approach required strengthening the existing schools of nursing. The Council had to accept the reality that it could not produce 55,000 nursing students. Yet all was not lost. Goostray and her colleagues were not unaware that working with the government's manpower agencies lifted nursing into the upper levels of national planning (Roberts, 1959, p.356). She was more than equal to the exalted tasks especially so when she realized that the Nation was coming to see nursing as an essential force in the Nation's life. The Civil Defense and Surgeon General joined nursing in its concern with the nursing shortage but it was Congresswoman Bolton and Senator Thomas who put a bill before the Congress. Goostray, as president of the National Nursing Council for War Services and of the NLNE, testified on the bill's particulars before Congress. She reported that the NLNE was not opposed to an accelerated nursing program. Then she joined Bolton, Thomas, and the president of the American Hospital Association in a broadcast to the Nation on the need to persuade young women to enroll in nursing schools and become a member of "a proud profession." Without one dissenting voice, the bill passed into law (Public Law 74) in June 1943 and the United States Cadet Nurse Corps was born.

The Council served as a clearinghouse fielding thousands of requests for more information. Of the 169,443 women who joined the Cadet Nurse Corps, 124,065 had graduated by 1948 more than doubling the numbers needed. The Council helped 2,000 Negro nurses enrolled in the Cadet Nurse Corps. By 1951 the numbers of schools admitting Negro women was more than 300 whereas prior to the Corps only 76 schools admitted Negro nurses (Roberts, 1959, p.447). In an interesting comparison with Goodrich's World War I's Army School of Nursing which graduated one third of the students it enrolled, the Cadet Nurse Corps graduated two thirds of its nursing students. The Cadet Nurse Corps proved to be more than a new approach. It was a successful approach.

The Corps provided tuition, uniforms and a monthly stipend to the students. As president of the Council, Goostray co-signed with Surgeon General Parran on payment for the uniforms. In return for their education, clothing and stipends, the students pledged:

In consideration of the training, payments, and other benefits, which are provided me as a member of the United States Cadet Nurse Corps, I agree that I will be available for military or other Federal, governmental, or essential civilian services for the duration of the present war (Piemonte, 1987, p.15).

The US Cadet Nurse Corps accelerated students through the usual 36-month program in 30 months. The American Hospital Association resented not having nursing students for the additional six months for this was when they were of the most benefit to hospitals. From the clear vantage point of six decades later, nursing students were obviously pseudo-employees of hospitals. Federal funding of the US Cadet Nurse Corps gave nursing education a "lift" as would the post war federal funding of the GI Bill that supported veteran-nurses as they headed to college campuses and became the leading edge of nursing's inexorable, if slow, movement to self-determination.

Even as the Nation was trying to deal with the civilian nursing shortage and trying to recruit more nurses into the military, it ignored a group of nurses who were eager to serve their country. There were an estimated 7,000 Negro nurses in 1940 but the Army Nurse Corps maintained a quota system and had accepted only 160 Negro nurses by 1943. These few were assigned to hospitals, which cared for Negro soldiers, segregated from their white counterparts. By 1943 the quota was raised to 250. Other applicants received letters saying, "Your application for appointment to the Army Nurse Corps cannot be given favorable consideration as there are no provisions in Army regulations for the appointment of colored nurses in the Corps" (Carnegie, 1986, p.169).

The National Association of Colored Graduate Nurses was a member of the National Nursing Council for War Services in which Goostray said, "their association was a participating organization ... on exactly the same terms as any other participating group" (Goostray, 1969, p.113). Not content to just register being "seriously disturbed" by the exclusion of the Negro nurses, Goostray led the charge to right this wrong. First the Council wrote to the Surgeon General of the U.S. Army Medical Corps and the Surgeon General of the U.S. Navy Medical Corps. The question the Council asked was: "Why are Negro nurses not accepted on the same basis as any other American nurse who met the requirements?" The Navy acknowledged reception of the Council's letter but took no action. The Army requested data which Goostray submitted of Negro and white nurses working side by side in hospitals throughout the country. Six months of silence followed.

The Council created a special committee to address this impasse. The president of the Council appointing herself as its chair indicated the committee's importance. No longer content with corresponding with the Surgeons General, Goostray sought a face-to-face meeting. She was already a frequent commuter to Washington, D.C. because of her Congressional testimony and her work with the Cadet Nurse Corps. She remembers trains crowded with servicemen. One night was especially memorable for a young man using her shoulder as his pillow. She never disturbed the young soldier apparently realizing that her service as a pillow was part of her wartime responsibility. She carried a thermos of coffee and a flashlight with her once she realized coffee might be unavailable and blackouts could make walking along the train's passages a hazardous feat. Foresight was one of Goostray's great strengths.

Once in Washington, she met with the assistant to the Surgeon General of the Medical Service of the Army and the Surgeon General of the Navy. In both meetings, Goostray and her colleagues Anna Wolf and Elmira Wickendon asked, "Why are negro nurses not being appointed to the Nurse Corps of the Army and Navy on the same basis as other American nurses who meet the qualifications." Goostray summed it up, "We got no encouragement, and my impression of the Surgeon General of the Navy was that we might as well have been talking to a stuffed shirt" (Goostray, 1969, p.124).

Having had no satisfaction from the respective Surgeons General, the Council decided the time had come to "tell the world." The Council went public and was determined to stay public until the Council achieved its purpose, namely, the enrollment of Negro nurses in the military's nurse corps. The NACGN aided the Council by putting it into contact with other Negro organizations and people who were influential in Negro circles. The General Education Board of the Rockefeller Foundation, for example, financed a unit within the Council to deal solely with this issue. Estelle Riddle Massey, later Osborn, a former president of the NACGN was appointed to head the unit. For the first time in American nursing history, white and black nurses worked together at a national level planning for nursing's future. The Rockefeller

Foundation increased its funding and the Kellogg Foundation added its financial support which eventuated in establishing a collegiate program in nursing at the Hampton Institute (Goostray, 1969, p.125).

The concerted efforts of the Council and its consultants raised the standards in Negro nursing schools so that their students were able to meet the US Cadet Nurse Corps requirements. Integration of some nursing schools that were accepting white and Negro nurses tripled. Financial support, constant hammering at military prejudice and raising standards were central to the success that finally came when 600 Negro nurses enlisted in the Army Nurse Corps. The Council hammered away at the Navy Nurse Corps for two more years. Finally in 1945 the first Negro nurse was accepted in the Navy Nurse Corps. "A wrong [was] finally righted," remembers Goostray (1969, p.123).

Despite the efforts of increasing the number of nursing students filling vacancies in civilian hospitals and opening military opportunities for Negro nurses, the nursing shortage continued. The shortage was especially dire in military settings as the war in Europe wound down and the war in the Pacific continued. Accordingly, the President took the matter to the Nation in his State of the Union speech on January 6, 1945. Acting on the advice of the Secretary of War, the President called for an amendment to the Selective Service Act to induct nurses into the military. The House of Representatives quickly passed a bill to draft nurses. Nurses were re-classified in the hope of gleaning more nurses from the already scarce supply in civilian hospitals.

Goostray, from her position as president of the National Nursing Council for War Services vehemently protested this development. She sent a telegram to the President saying that his call for a draft would have a negative impact on nurses volunteering for the armed forces. She suggested that the President use his press conference to appeal to public agencies, such as, industry, hospitals, doctors, and patients to persuade nurses to enlist at once. She advised Paul McNutt, the chairman of the War Manpower Commission that drafting nurses would be a big mistake and feared that draftees would be drawn from hospitals. She reminded him that nursing schools must maintain their minimum staffs, supporting her position with data that showed in 1944 78% more students were enrolled in nursing schools than had been in 1940 (Goostray, 1969, 127). Sensitive to the urgent needs of wartime, Goostray did not overlook that these nursing students were the supply of future graduates. What is more, these nursing students were doing most of the skilled nursing care in civilian hospitals.

Goostray remembered the six months from January 6, 1945 when the President called for drafting nurses until May 30, 1945 as "nerve-wracking months" (Goostray, 1969, p.127). The President's call for nurses had the salutary effect of rousing thousands of nurses to enlist. Perhaps this had been the President's strategy all along: a threat of a draft could be the necessary catalyst to persuade nurses to enlist. More likely, the President's public statement cut through the confusion that disparate messages had created. Once the need for enlistees was clarified, nurses responded. In any event Goostray's concurrent strategy of going public, as she had done with the issue of the military's exclusion of Negro nurses from the armed forces, won the day. Her own commitment to not letting the urgent overwhelm the important protected the maintenance of quality nursing education and nursing services that was one of the founding functions of the Council she so wisely served.

Contemporaries saw Goostray as a "wise and stabilizing force" overseeing the Council's nearly 50 active committees, which were dealing with various aspects of nursing and the national defense (Roberts, 1959, 356). Soon after the war was over with Germany conceding defeat in June and Japan doing the same in August 1945, Goostray stepped down from the presidency having served from July 1942 through November 1945. The Council shortened its name to the National Nursing Council with Goostray's Boston colleague, Sophie Nelson, serving as president and overseeing its final days until the Council disbanded in November 1948. As Goostray passed the torch, she spoke on how the Council was a unique moment in nursing history for the unity of purpose with which the nursing profession and the public worked together. Then she called on nursing to continue this unity, saying:

> Now is the appointed time to make our choice as to whether we shall go on working together for what is best for nursing, both in its relations to the nursing profession and those whom it serves, or whether we shall be concerned mainly with our own boundary lines or organization.
> She was hopeful that a way would be found if nurses remained open-minded and objective as they pooled their thinking, worked out their plans and put them into operation (Goostray, 1969, p.131).

Goostray was ever mindful of the past even as she made the choices that steered nursing towards its future. She knew how hard her predecessors had worked to rescue nursing and its education from those who exploited its students as a source of cheap labor. She knew how hard she and her colleagues labored to create nursing's standard curriculum to protect nursing students who expected to be trained when they entered nursing schools. She knew how hospitals still controlled nursing and took special glee in having power during the war that the American Hospital Association resented.

The president of the Massachusetts Hospital Association was incensed that the Council would not lower nursing education standards to meet hospital service needs. He laced his remarks to the convention with "cuss" words telling the nurses in attendance what nursing should do. Then he introduced Goostray who in what she hoped was a dulcet tone, turned to him and said, "Dr. _____, I know all those words and can use them as well as you can but I don't think I need to. My arguments need no reinforcement." And, as she recalls, "The crowd roared" (Goostray, 1969, p.131).

The nation's need for the work that the Council was doing gave nursing a power it did not have before. Another AHA leader spoke out about nurses "presuming to dictate all of the adjustments." Goostray shot back that nurses had been in "bondage long enough, and like the Children of Israel [they] were on the march to the Promised Land" (Goostray p.123). That was Goostray in capsule form. She knew and respected nursing's past but looked forward to a future when nursing would be an autonomous profession. Thanks to the Council's work to maintain high standards and thanks to the nurses in the military and at home, nursing was on a world stage. The government's response to the work of the Council had effectively established that nursing was essential to the war effort. A grateful Nation would fund the necessary reforms in nursing education that pushed nursing to the border of the Promised Land of self-determination.

Ever one of Clio's devoted servants, Goostray served on the National Nursing Council Historical Committee chaired by Emma Wickenden along with other members, Marjorie Davis, Alma Haupt, and Boston colleagues, Ruth Sleeper and Sophie Nelson. Hope Newell authored *History of the National Nursing Council* that the National Organization of Public Health Nursing distributed in 1951.

Nurses in Massachusetts can rightly take pride in their predecessor who was chosen by her peers as the nurse to lead nursing through the tumultuous war years. Goostray more than met their expectations by leading nursing to new levels of national prestige. She did this by being a leader whose moral purpose made her "a tiny principality of power."

* Contemporary terms are used, namely, colored and Negro.

© BACHRACH

STELLA GOOSTRAY

From the Stella Goostray collection, History of Nursing Archives at the
Howard Gotlieb Archival Research Center, Boston University

REFERENCES

Burns, James MacGregor. 1978. *Leadership*. New York: Harper Colophon Books.

Carnegie, M. Elizabeth. 1986. *The Path We Tread*. Philadelphia: Lippincott.

Goostray, Stella. 1969. *Memoirs: A Half a Century of Nursing*. Boston: Boston University History of Nursing Archives.

---. 1965. "Nationwide Hunt for Nursing's Historical Treasures," Nursing Outlook (13): 26-29.

---. 1941. "Supply, Demand, and Standards," American Journal of Nursing (41): 745-747.

Kalisch, Philip A. and Kalisch, Beatrice J. 1986. The Advance of American Nursing 2nd ed. Boston: Little, Brown and Company.

Piemonte, Robert V. 1987. Highlights in the History of the Army Nurse Corps. Washington, D.C.: U.S. Army Center of Military History.

Roberts, Mary M. 1940. "The Philadelphia Biennial," American Journal of Nursing (40): 673-680.

---. 1959. American Nursing: History and Interpretation. New York: Macmillan Company.

AGATHA COBOURG HODGINS:
PIONEERING ANESTHETIST

(originally published September 2015)

On May 7, 1915 the luxurious *Lusitania* was nearing the end of its voyage from New York to Liverpool, when the torpedo from a German U-boat exploded into her hull. In eighteen minutes the magnificent ocean liner was at the bottom of the sea, twelve miles off the coast of Ireland's Head of Kinsale. Struggling for their lives in the 55 degree debris strewn waters were men, women, children and babies. Of the 1959 passengers and crew aboard, only 767 survived. As horrendous as Germany's deliberate attack on civilians was, not to be ignored was that Britain failed to provide a protective convoy for her luxury liner, in spite of intelligence that German submarines were active in the ship's path.

One hundred and twenty eight Americans were among the dead but even that loss of life did not lessen the United State's commitment to remaining neutral in Europe's war. A year before, June 28, 1914, the assassination of the heir to the Austrian Hungarian Empire sparked the war that a year later was spreading throughout Europe. By the time it ended, November 11, 1918, the Great War had claimed thirty-seven million men as casualties: seventeen million were dead and twenty million were wounded. Empires – the Ottoman, Austrian-Hungarian, Russian and German - had vanished.

On April 6, 1917 President Woodrow Wilson declared the United States must keep the world "Safe for Democracy" and persuaded Congress to declare war on Germany. Long before that day Massachusetts' nurses were already caring for the sick and wounded at the Western front. Among them was Agatha Cobourg Hodgins (1877-1945), a 1900 graduate of the Boston City Hospital Training School for Nurses (BCHTSN), then under the leadership of Lucy Lincoln Drown and her assistant Mary Riddle. After graduation, Hodgins specialized in anesthesiology training under Dr. George W. Crile at the Lakeside Hospital of Western Reserve University in Cleveland, Ohio.

She and Crile served during the first three months of the American Ambulance Hospital (AAH) in Neuilly just outside of Paris. Dr. Harvey Cushing, who would become a renowned neurosurgeon at the Peter Bent Brigham Hospital, headed the Harvard unit staffing the AAH for its next three months. Try as he might to persuade Hodgins to remain, Cushing was unsuccessful. When her tour of duty was completed in the early months of 1916, Hodgins returned to Cleveland to train registered nurses, doctors and dentists at the School of Anesthesiology she and Crile headed at Lakeside Hospital.

Her decision to train others rather than continue in Europe proved to be one that benefitted traumatized soldiers. The nitrous oxide with oxygen technique that she and Crile had perfected was a success in anesthetizing these men and preventing operative shock. It proved successful as well with men who had been compromised by the grey-green clouds of chlorine gas that the enemy wafted over the trenches. With their eyes, noses, throats, and lungs damaged by that "horrible weapon", nitrous oxide and oxygen was superior to chloroform and ether that were then in use. The first graduates of Hodgins' program in 1916 numbered eleven nurses, six doctors and two dentists. Many of the anesthetists, who served during World War I, especially once the United States joined the effort, could count Hodgins as their teacher.

In June of 1931, Hodgins organized the alumnae of her program into the National Association of Nurse Anesthetists (the precursor of the American Association of Nurse Anesthetists). Perhaps as she did so, Hodgins recalled her student days at the BCHTSN when Riddle and Drown were organizing graduate nurses. Their efforts culminated in 1903 in the establishment of the Massachusetts State Nurses Association, the precursor of the American Nurses Association Massachusetts. Riddle was its first president and Drown its first historian. More certain evidence of Hodgins' continuing ties to Massachusetts was her Chatham home that she bought in 1919 several years after the Great War was over. She retired there in 1934, and when her life was over, March 24, 1945, the pioneering anesthetist was laid to rest in Chatham's Union Cemetery.[1] The United States was again at war, and the Great War had been retitled World War I.

Virginia Gaffney. Agatha Cobourg Hodgins: "She only counted shining hours," *AANA Journal* April 2007 97-100.

ANNIE MCKAY: MASSACHUSETTS' FIRST SCHOOL NURSE

(originally published December 2009)

On a hot August forenoon only days away from the opening of schools throughout the Commonwealth, the Massachusetts School Nurses Organization gathered with associates, friends and officials at 1521 Washington Street at West Brookline Street in Boston's South End for the unveiling of a commemorative plaque. In 1905, this was the address of Annie McKay (1867-1944), Massachusetts first school nurse. Dorothy Keeney, school nurse (ret.) and historian of the MSNO, told the gathering that McKay left her home each day to care for children attending the Josiah Quincy, Way Street and Andrews Schools. She taught them basic health practices that kept them well so that they were able to learn. This was no easy task because these children lived in the South End, then one of Boston's most congested areas in a pre antibiotic time when infectious diseases were a leading cause of death.

Keeney related how McKay's teaching of the children in the schools and in visits to their families before and after school prevented illness and reduced absenteeism. As Mary Ellen Doona commented, in keeping children healthy and in school, McKay gave these children a future. MSNO President Mimi Stamer, who represents McKay's successors throughout the Commonwealth, reported that there are now 2100 school nurses caring for the Commonwealth's 1.1 million children.

Such dedication to children's health merits appreciation. Accordingly, Congressman Michael Capuano sent his congratulations. More locally, Mayor Thomas Menino proclaimed August 25, 2009 Annie McKay Day in Boston. Mary Smoyer, a founding member of the Women's Heritage Trail, celebrated Annie McKay's stature as one of Boston's outstanding women. William Lenihan, the South End's City Councilor added a personal note remembering that his grandfather had lived in the South End and wondered if his path ever crossed McKay's. Diane Gallagher brought the greetings of the History of Nursing Archives where the papers of the MSNO are archived. Linda Grant, M.D., Director of Health Services to Boston Schools was still another speaker admiring the history of Massachusetts' school nurses.

In a program replete with compliment and accolade, no tribute was more fulsome than that of Dr. Alfred DeMaria of the Massachusetts Department of Public Health. School nurses are health care's unsung heroes, said DeMaria. He spoke of their critical role in public health. This was no little praise as the HINI (Swine) Flu epidemic looms on the horizon with children as an especially susceptible target.

Thus do infectious diseases threaten children in 2009 as they once did in 1905. Unknown in McKay's time, however, are the 20% of school children who bear a medical diagnosis, some of them severely debilitating with the health record of a few children bearing a DNR directive. MSNO's past president, Katherine O'Neill and Beth Thomson were among the many school nurses applauding as the plaque honoring Annie McKay was unveiled. Thanks to Thomas Geraghty, Jr. who currently owns the Stanford, everyone entering and leaving the building will be able to read of Annie McKay's pioneering work in 1905 that created the template for school nursing and the nurse who gave her successors a past to celebrate as they make their own history caring for the Commonwealth's children.

Annie McKay (Photo by Beth Thomson)

See also: Doona, M.E. (2005) The Emergence of the School Nurse [Annie McKay]. *The Massachusetts Report on Nursing*, September 12-15.

CARRIE M. HALL (1873-1963):
PIONEER AT THE PETER BENT BRIGHAM HOSPITAL

(originally published March 2009)

On 25 June 1998, alumnae of the Peter Bent Brigham Hospital School of Nursing gathered with administrators of the Brigham and Women's Hospital for an exhibit in the Carrie M. Hall Building, named for the Brigham's first Superintendent of Nursing and Principal of its nurses training school. Leading into the Carrie M. Hall Conference Rooms were photographs and awards among which were the Florence Nightingale and Edith Cavell Medals that Hall received for her leadership in Europe during World War I.

The first of John and Caroline (Rogers) Hall's three children, Carrie May Hall (1873-1963) was born in Nashua, New Hampshire 5 July 1873. She began her life the same year as nursing's first diploma was awarded to Linda Richards (1841-1930). Thirty-one years later in 1904, Hall accepted her own nursing diploma from the Massachusetts General Hospital Training School for Nurses (MGHTSN). During the next nine years, Hall gained administrative experience at the MGH (1904), the Quincy Hospital (1905) and the Margaret Pillsbury Hospital in Concord, New Hampshire (1906-1911). Along with these early positions, Hall served as president of the New Hampshire State Nurses Association (1911). While at the Brigham (1912-1937) she was president of the Massachusetts States Nurses Association (1921-1925) and then, president of the National League for Nursing Education (NLNE-1926-1928).

But all that was still to come, as Hall returned from Teachers College in New York to Boston in 1912. There she found that Boston's medical community had anticipated the reforms of the Flexner Report (1910). In 1906 the Harvard Medical School had relocated from

Boylston Street (now the site of the Boston Public Library's Johnson building) to Longwood Avenue on twenty-six acres of the Ebenezer Francis estate. (The name endures in the Brigham and Women's Francis Street address). The Boston Psychopathic Hospital had just opened on Fenwood Road bringing psychiatry back from rural hospitals to the center of medical education and research. Nearing completion was the Peter Bent Brigham Hospital on Huntington Avenue that restaurateur and real estate baron, Peter Bent Brigham (1807-1877), had funded for the care of "sick persons in indigent circumstances."

Hall agreed to assume the nursing leadership at the Brigham provided the nursing department could open six months before the hospital did. Lost to the shadows of nursing's history is how Hall considered the proposal. It is reasonable to assume that she consulted with Sara E. Parsons (1864-1949), an 1893 graduate of the MGHTSN and since 1910 the leader of nursing at the MGH. Hall and Parsons would have met during MGHTSN alumnae association meetings. Given their positions as leaders of the new profession, it is likely that both attended the Boston convention of the American Society of Superintendents of Training Schools for Nurses and the Associated Alumnae in Boston in 1911 when they became, respectively, the National League for Nursing Education and the American Nurses Association.

What is known for certain is that Hall opened the Peter Bent Brigham Hospital School of Nursing 7 November 1912 with five students and Sally Johnson (1880-1957) a 1910 MGHTSN graduate as her assistant. Hall believed that good nursing education derived from good nursing care. She used the power and prestige of her position to advance nursing. She urged the visiting team of the Rockefeller Foundation to include hospital nursing in its study of nursing. The Foundation's Goldmark Report (1923) incorporated Hall's concerns but for some time to come nursing education continued to be the servant of the hospital. By 1926 she had to conclude that the "needs and purposes of the hospital and the school of nursing do not always run in parallel lines" (1926). If nursing education suffered, nursing care was excellent then, as it continues to be in 2009, as Brigham's nursing department nears its centennial.

As a twenty year old, Hall was dazzled by the brilliance of the new electric lights at the 1893 World's Fair in Chicago. Thirty-three years later as president of the NLNE founded at that Fair, Hall called on colleagues to carry the "bright torch of their principles and ideals ever higher and higher" (1926). The economic crash of 1929 darkened nursing's path yet by the time Hall retired (1 July 1937), 729 women had graduated during her tenure. More would follow until 1985 when the School closed. Among the many gifted graduates were Martha Ruth Smith and Lillian Goodman, the first deans respectively, of the Boston University School of Nursing and the University of Massachusetts at Worcester. They pioneered nursing education at the university as Hall had once done at the Peter Bent Brigham Hospital.

REFERENCES

Hall, Carrie M. 1926. "Taking Courage: The Presidential Address-1926," *American Journal of Nursing* (26): 547-550.

JOSEPHINE ALOYSE DOLAN
(JULY 27, 1913-DECEMBER 4, 2004)

(Originally published March 2005)

Josephine "Jo" Dolan, nursing's historian, died December 2004 in her ninety-first year. Jo was the expert guide for generations of nurses as they journeyed to nursing's past. She helped nurses discover predecessors and find inspiration for their own professional lives. A similar journey had also brought Jo to nursing's history.

Jo was the middle child between an older sister, Mary, and a younger brother, Tom, born to Thomas J. and Josephine (Tynan) Dolan in Cranston, Rhode Island. From birth to death Jo remained a New England woman. She was raised in Lawrence, Massachusetts, educated in Lawrence, Lowell and Boston, taught nursing in Connecticut and retired to Holliston, Massachusetts. Rooted in a small area of the northeast section of the United States, Jo nonetheless traveled to far off places in search of nursing's history. She chronicled that history in seven editions of her book, *Nursing and Society: An Historical Perspective*.

The acute illness and then sudden death of her father changed Jo from a carefree adolescent into a serious student. Out of that sad moment Jo found in a nurse caring for Mr. Dolan a model for her own life. Following graduation from the Sisters of Notre Dame's St. Mary's High School in Lawrence, Jo enrolled in the Daughters of Charity's St. John's Hospital School of Nursing in Lowell. As so much nursing education was in those days, that which Jo experienced was more labor for the hospital than lectures for a profession. And, as so many other students had done, Jo collapsed under the load. She took a three-month respite during which she traded the hospital's rigor for her mother's care. Jo rebounded, finished her nursing program and in 1935 graduated into the economic depression that had been going on since the crash of Wall Street in 1929.

After a brief period of private duty nursing, Jo enrolled at Boston College's Intown Center at Newbury Street. There, Jo came under the prescient guidance of Elizabeth Sullivan (1890-1941) who was a rarity in the mid-nineteen-thirties. She was a nurse with a doctorate. As nursing education supervisor for Massachusetts, Sullivan was at the forefront of nursing reform. She advised Jo to enroll at Boston University where collegiate nursing education was beginning to take root. There, Jo met one of Sullivan's colleagues, Mary Maher, whose public health nursing perspective broadened Jo's view of nursing. These and other teachers were at the leading edge of academic nursing education and their students were in demand. In 1944, even as Jo continued on to graduate studies (she earned the master's degree in 1950), she accepted a faculty position at the University of Connecticut at Storrs. Caught up in establishing herself as an educator, Jo had little opportunity to reflect on how life-changing a decision UConn was nor to foresee how that decision would lead to her preeminence as nursing's historian.

That was still to come when Jo began her academic career. There at UConn, as in hospital schools of nursing, nursing history was a distinct part of the curriculum. Jo was not on the faculty very long when Dean Caroline Ladd Widmer asked her to teach the nursing history course. The request was like else of nursing's move from the hospital onto campuses, a moment by moment response to changing needs. As anxiety-provoking as this was, it provided a milieu in which creativity could flourish. Everything was thrown up into the air and came down in different places. Jo landed in a different place but one that she soon made her own.

She was fortunate in her dean. Through her grandfather, Cyrus Hamlin, a missionary in Turkey, Widmer was linked to modern nursing's prime event, the Crimean War (1854-56). She treasured her grandfather's sketch of Florence Nightingale as a "quiet, self-possessed, interesting, intelligent lady." A nursing history enthusiast herself, Widmer provided the necessary infusions of energy as Jo assumed her new role and mentored Jo until she got a steady footing. The rest, as the cliché goes, is history. In deference to Widmer and in keeping with her own ideals, Jo would feature Florence Nightingale in telling nursing's history. Jo did more. She also celebrated the many unheralded nurses from preliterate times to the electronic twentieth century.

Jo and her course became popular throughout the campus attracting non-nursing majors and expanding her reputation beyond the confines of the nursing school. Much of this was due to Jo's engaging style that invited people into her warm orbit. Her growing expertise in nursing's history recommended her to others. Medical historians at Yale, for example, invited her to their sessions. She was especially honored when UConn's history department invited her to attend the lecture by its visiting scholar, medical historian, Richard Shyrock. By this time (1958) Jo had established herself as an author, having revised the late Minnie Goodnow's (1871-1952) history of nursing text. Jo was pleased when Shyrock lauded her achievement, and later was astounded when he told her he would not revise his *The History of Nursing: An Interpretation of the Social and Medical Factors Involved* (1959) now that Jo had written hers. Sister Charles Frank of Catholic University at Washington, D.C. decided not to do a third edition of her Foundations of Nursing (1959), leaving nursing's history to Jo.

Preeminence in so short a time was a sort of praise. More was to come. Jo was invited to serve on the National League for Nursing's Historical Source Materials Committee. From 1965-1971, she served as its chair. There Jo worked with such nursing stalwarts as Mary Roberts (1877-1959), the editor of the American Journal of Nursing and author of American Nursing (1954), Anne Austin (1891-1986) author of the History of Nursing Source Book (1957) and Isabel Stewart (1878-1963) who with Austin updated into one volume A History of Nursing (1962) that had evolved over the years from M. Adelaide Nutting (1858-1948) and Lavinia Dock's (1858-1956) four volume A History of Nursing (1907-1912). Austin not only mentored Jo, she also shared anecdotes about Nutting and Dock. These stories helped Jo put flesh on the bare bones of professional biographies.

The combination of seasoned elders and nurses just reaching their peak made the Committee a creative force. One of Jo's fellow committee members was Boston Children's Hospital's Stella Goostray (1886-1969). Each had had the benefit of Elizabeth Sullivan's mentoring at the beginning of their nursing education. Like Jo, Goostray was devoted to nursing's history and made educating nurses about their source materials her mission. Along with directing nursing service and education at Childrens Hospital, Goostray chaired the Massachusetts League for Nursing's Historical Source Materials Committee and wrote a biographical sketch on Linda Richards for *Notable American Women,* the biographical dictionary published by Radcliffe College's Schlesinger Library. Goostray cheered on her colleague, Mary Ann Garrigan (1914-2000), the founding curator of the History of Nursing Archives established in 1966 at Mugar Memorial Library at Boston University.

If this national experience with nursing's leaders broadened Jo's commitment to nursing's history, her relationship with colleagues in the humanities at UConn shaped her in a different way. They taught her to appreciate how art was more than works of beauty. Art also conveyed social attitudes. These faculty had a ready student in Jo. She toured European museums with them, and with their guidance, studied works of art extracting their message for nurses. She collected images that showed nurses as a significant part of various societies down through the ages. Before long, she had amassed a vast library of slides of nurses and nurse-figures caring for the sick. She used these visual aids to help students in the lecture hall and readers of her text to connect with the story she was telling.

For example, by juxtapositioning images of first century saints caring for the sick-as-Christ with images of twentieth-century nurses in patient centered settings, she pointed out that nursing evolved over time from a religious duty to a secular profession. She also underscored the sick's privileged position and society's enduring obligation.

St. Irene, for example, was one of her favorite images. St. Irene cared for St. Sebastian after he had been shot with arrows for his Christian St. Paula, a disciple of St. Jerome, who founded a hospital in Palestine where she nursed the sick.

If these saints were the elite individuals of their societies, the monks and nuns who followed were a corporate response to the moral imperative that society should care for the sick. In the preface of the fourteenth edition of her text, Jo wrote:

> Religious influences played a significant role in emphasizing the plight of the sick and poor and the need for human dignity, in elevating the status of women, in encouraging men to select nursing as a career and in stimulating the emergence of dynamic nurse leadership.

Even as her eye was trained as a result of studying great works of art, Jo's use of images in her classroom lectures and in her text trained the eyes of her students and readers. She connected them with an aesthetic world found in the Metropolitan and the Frick Museums in New York City, the Museum of Fine Arts and the Gardner in Boston, the National Gallery in Washington, D. C., the Peabody Museum at Yale, and the Museum of the American Indian to list only a few sources of her images.

Nurses depicted in stained glass windows in churches, monasteries and abbeys were still another source of images. The stained glass window in the National Cathedral in Washington, D.C. featuring the life and work of Florence Nightingale had an honored place on the cover of the fourteenth edition of Jo's text. Artistic renderings of the window graced each chapter heading. Art on the more everyday level of postage stamps showed how various cultures throughout the world privileged the role of the nurse in their respective countries. That delighted Jo, the philatelist, almost as much as it pleased Jo, the nurse.

Jo also collected artifacts associated with caring for the sick. She had a large collection of feeding cups, the precursors of the glass straw. Some were fine china while others were crude crockery. The utensils spoke volumes about class distinctions of the past that had not dissolved as the students she was teaching knew all too well. Jo splurged her salary on such artifacts. She bought early nineteenth century pharmaceutical chests with bottles neatly enclosed. Doctors serving on board ships had need of their portability and compactness. These and many other items were finds that Jo picked up as she haunted second hand shops and antique stores, and dickered with dealers. During one excursion, she spotted a field lamp like the one that Florence Nightingale carried in Constantinople. The candle was surrounded by an oiled-cloth cylinder that allowed light to shine through while preventing breezes from snuffing out the flame. When not in use, it could be collapsed into a small circle that was easily carried. Ironically, Jo knew more about the lamp than the shop owner. Right there in the shop she gave the man a lesson on what the device was and who may have used it.

Jo put these and other artifacts to good use in her classroom at UConn and as illustrations for her text. The artifacts were put to another use when Jo became a television "star" in 1965. Over a period of three years, while still teaching at UConn, Jo presented her lectures before a television camera. Remote television hook-ups were still in the future, so Jo had to travel from Connecticut to Minnesota each week. She taped her lectures over the week-end, and these were later telecast to seven nursing schools in the twin cities of St. Paul and Minneapolis. During the lectures, Jo held up various artifacts and showed her watchers how nurses of the past had used them in their care. If not dramatic, these performances certainly made the primitive nursing technology more real for viewers. The tapes of the television programs have preserved for posterity instances of Jo, the teacher.

So crowded with incident was her career as nursing's historian and her life as a colleague on UConn's campus, Jo's working life sped quickly by. The sudden illness and subsequent death of her dear sister, Mary, with whom she shared a home in Storrs only underscored what Jo already knew. It was time to plan the next phase of her life, that of closing the door on the classroom and opening the door on to retirement. Her brother, Tom, and his lovely wife Claire urged Jo to return to Massachusetts to be near her family. She had been at UConn from 1944 through 1976 and thus Storrs had become her home. Yet, Massachusetts had its own appeal. Tom and Claire and their daughters would be nearby. Blood won out. Jo wrenched herself away from her academic family in Storrs and moved to Holliston, Massachusetts.

Once settled in Holliston, Jo welcomed nurses to her beautiful home and entertained visitors in her sunny sitting room with its windows looking out onto the surrounding countryside. She mentored nursing history's next generation as she herself had been mentored. All the while, she was amazed at how quickly the years had passed since she was the one being mentored. In her frequent visits to Storrs she picked up with old friends where she and they had left off. From 1976 through 1985 she was a visiting lecturer, as well as a welcomed visitor at UConn. The Mu chapter of Sigma Theta Tau, nursing's national honor society at UConn was especially welcoming. Jo had helped to establish Mu at UConn in 1953 and she led it as president from 1962-1965. In 1986 Mu created the Josephine A. Dolan Award for excellence in nursing scholarship. "Healers and Sustainers of Health" was Mu's guiding motto, one that mirrored Jo's sentiments completely.

The Connecticut Nurses Association established the Josephine A. Dolan Award in 1980 honoring her long service to nursing organizations in the Nutmeg State. At each convention since, the award is given to a nurse who has made an outstanding contribution to nursing education. Then in 1983, Jo's alma mater, Boston University's School of Nursing, presented her with its Outstanding Alumna Award. A decade before in 1974 Rhode Island had honored its native daughter. Rhode Island College conferred on nursing's historian a doctor of pedagogy citing Jo for being a master teacher. She proudly appended the Pd.D. to her name and her nursing credentials.

While Jo was settling into retirement in Holliston her nursing colleagues at UConn were planning a special tribute. They designated a room on the third floor of Storrs Hall, the nursing school building that would honor Josephine A. Dolan, UConn's first professor of nursing and illustrate the history of nursing. Here in the Josephine A. Dolan Room, nursing students would study nursing while being surrounded by the history of their past as represented in the many artifacts Jo had collected over the years. A mid-nineteenth century hospital bed, a wicker, wheelchair, a wooden, walker, a wooden baby tender and a crutch from America's Civil War (1861-1864) are among the many patient care artifacts that rotate through the exhibit space. Even the most self-absorbed students could hardly fail to notice the story that surrounds them. It would be as if Jo, although far away in Massachusetts, were still a presence for UConn's young nursing students.

Meanwhile, Jo continued to present nursing's history. The graduating seniors at Boston College, for example, listened to Jo during their "pinning" ceremony on the lawn outside the Burns Library. There with the icon of Wisdom over the door to the Burns Library at her back, Jo recounted nursing's privileged passage through the world to young women and men on the verge of putting their own stamp on nursing's history. Friends and families of the graduating seniors gained a new perspective on the antiquity and richness of the profession their graduate had chosen.

By this time, Jo was missing UConn less and was becoming more comfortable with her transition to Massachusetts. She reached out to the proposed Wellness Center in Holliston sharing with its founders, expertise from her nursing colleagues. She became a communicant of St. Mary' Church, who reached out to her with its generous and genuine hospitality. She often hosted lunch at the family restaurant in Holliston where everybody really does know your name.

Then, another community beckoned to her. Boston College opened its heart to its former student, a heart that had never really been closed. Jo returned to Boston College where once she had read Shakespeare, memorized poetry and grappled with the intricacies of dialectics before Elizabeth Sullivan advised her to enroll at Boston University. Both Boston College's Intown Center and Elizabeth Sullivan were gone, their history was now part of Boston College's ongoing present that was stretching into the future.

Mary Pekarski (1923-1988), the founding librarian of the Boston College School of Nursing Library, had long admired Jo's Nursing in Society. The Librarian had studied history while at Emmanuel College where Jo's sister, Mary, had also studied. Once she committed herself to nursing, Mary Pekarski read widely in nursing history and helped nurses do the same. She wanted to go to Storrs to meet the author she so prized but servicing the urgent present of the users of her nursing library wrecked such wishes over and over again. The annual meeting of the Nursing Archives Associates at Mugar Memorial Library at Boston University solved the difficulty. Jo, dressed in sunshine yellow, as befitted the beautiful spring day, was in the audience. So, too, was Mary Pekarski. There in spirit though ailing in Marblehead was Mary Ann Garrigan, the dynamic force who had created the Nursing Archives. Hovering in the ether, one might surmise, was the ghost of Stella Goostray. Clio's Massachusetts devotees were, for once, all in the same place at the same time.

Jo and Mary Pekarski seized that moment, and the many that followed during which they discussed nursing's history. Both had been raised in Lawrence and with only a ten year difference in their ages, they knew many of the same people. Their reminisces about Lawrence served to bring them closer, though truth be told, it was as if they had always known each other. Then, Mary Pekarski hosted a small reception at Boston College's O'Neill Library to which she invited Thomas O'Connor, a professor in Boston College's history department. Pekarski and O'Connor were old friends on the Boston College campus having met in the Intown Center years before. She tried to entice O'Connor to research nursing but with no primary sources, nursing was a fallow field. Pekarski tucked away that fact as she created the Rita P. Kelleher History of Nursing Collection and planned for a future when there would be primary sources.

Jo's friendship with O'Connor picked up where it had left off twenty years before. In 1968, Jo had invited O'Connor to address the issue of history's significance for nursing at the Intercollegiate Conference held that year in Lenox, Massachusetts. Jo was intent on attendees seeing nursing within an historical context so that they might realize the special relationship between nursing and the humanities. Over lunch, with Mary Pekarski presiding, Jo and O'Connor remembered their long ago efforts as they renewed their old friendship.

Then, Boston College announced how much it loved its former student. In 1987 at the fortieth anniversary of its nursing school, the University conferred on Jo an honorary doctorate in nursing. Standing with President J. Donald Monan S.J. and facing a field full of graduates, families and friends Jo heard:

> Distinguished educator and renowned authority on nursing history; role model whose name graces prestigious awards for outstanding contributions to nursing education and nursing scholarship; admired woman who enhances rigorous professionalism with a profound regard for faith's role in the nurse's heritage. Your authoritative text, Nursing in Society, the keystone of your scholarly reputation, traces the evolution and emergence of nursing from a simple practical skill of antiquity to the complex humanistic science of the late twentieth century, revealing with equal discernment the roots of promise unfulfilled, and the seeds of triumph yet to come. With admiration for your unfaltering dedication to the advancement of your profession and your learned discipline, Boston College happily declares you Doctor of Nursing Science.

Jo had attended the University's dinner for the honorees the night before. Like her fellow honorees she gave a brief talk on her journey to this moment at Boston College. Jo gloried in recounting nursing's rich history for the other honorees: Ireland's Taoiseach, Garret Fitzgerald, Science's Walter Massey, chief executive, John Elwee, statesman, Vernon Walters, and the Jesuit humanist, Rev. Francis Sweeney S.J. After the conferral ceremony the next day, she and her invited guests: her brother Tom, her sister-in-law Claire, her niece Deirdre, Mary Pekarski and myself dined with the other honorees and their families and friends. Forty years after leaving Boston College, Jo had become a full-fledged member of the Boston College community. Her brother, Tom, who had completed two years at Boston College when World War II began, was glad to be back at the Heights on the much changed Boston College campus.

Jo often spoke of her trips to Ireland, especially to Leitrim and Tipperary, the land and counties of her ancestors. Now she decided that part of her history of nursing collection should be preserved at Boston College, the University that Jesuits founded in 1863 to educate the sons of Irish immigrants denied access to other colleges because of their race and religion. Boston College's roots remain Irish but the trunk, branches and leaves have grown into a national university that welcomes students of many national and international origins, of different races, and of the two genders. Jo wanted part of her collection to be at this University with its goal of excellence, and which in 1947, created a nursing school where women and men might be educated in the excellent care of the sick.

On the twentieth of March 1988, only three days after St. Patrick's Day, Mary Cronin, the University Librarian and Mary Sue Infante, Dean of the School of Nursing, presided over the formal acceptance of the Josephine A. Dolan Collection. Among the items in the Collection are correspondence, film, videocassettes of the television series, publications, artifacts, letters of Florence Nightingale, and some of Nightingale's correspondence with Alice Fisher. Other correspondence, articles, proceedings of nursing organizations, personal papers, manuscripts, publications, photographs, and administrative records are preserved in the Thomas J. Dodd Research Center at UConn.

Fittingly, the Boston College ceremony took place in the magnificent British Catholic Authors Room of the John J. Burns Library of Rare Books and Special Collections. That same room provided the backdrop for taping Jo's story for posterity. On September 29, 1987 Professors Joellen Hawkins and Loretta Higgins, leaders of the Heritage Committee of Alpha Chi Chapter of Sigma Theta Tau, interviewed Jo. Interestingly, Jo had been a member of Sigma Theta Tau's Heritage Committee from 1979 through 1983 and had overseen the taping of nursing leaders who had preceded her. Now, she was the subject. Weeks later, among those viewing the finished tape with Jo was Rev. Charles F. Donovan S.J., the former Academic Vice-president, and in 1987, the University Historian. He was pleased that Jo's story was now a part of Boston College's story. Jo was pleased that nursing's history was being honored.

In 1989 Jo attended the première performance of *Immortal Diamond: A Jesuit in Poet's Corner* at Boston College's Robsham Theatre at the centennial of Gerard Manley Hopkins' (1844-1889) death. The one-man play was a blend of Hopkins' poetry and the dramatist, Van Etten Casey's prose. A contemporary of Florence Nightingale, Hopkins like her, was blown by the turbulent winds of the Oxford Movement. Nightingale decided not to join the Roman Catholic Church though she admired it for the place it gave to women's work. Hopkins not only joined the Church, he also joined the Society of Jesus.

Among the many things the Jesuit poet graced with his words was the relationship between the person needing care and the person giving care. Jo heard the actor-Hopkins reciting "Felix Randal." On hearing of the thirty-one-year-old Randal's death, Hopkins remembers watching how the muscular blacksmith wasted away from tuberculosis, the scourge of mid-nineteenth-century. Hopkins recalls how dear the blacksmith became to him as he visited him over the course of the illness. Reflecting on Randal's death, Hopkins realized that the vigil had made him dear, too. Such a realization occurs to nurses as they care for their patients.

Honors continued to come Jo's way. Long before in 1972, the National League for Nursing had chosen her as the first recipient of its Distinguished Service Award. In 1992 at its annual convention, the Massachusetts Nurses Association honored Jo with its Lucy Lincoln Drown Nursing History Society's award. Once the formalities were over, members of the

Massachusetts Student Nurses Association swarmed around Jo. They peppered her with questions, to be sure, but mostly they beamed their pleasure at being in her midst. A rosy scenario indeed which Jo's rose colored dress charmingly enhanced. Jo was with students again, her preferred place.

Jo's last years were filled with knowing that she was a prized person. Her spirit was as indomitable as ever but she was becoming increasingly fragile. She left her beautiful home in Holliston for residence at The Willows in Westboro. The assisted living setting soon bore Jo's unique stamp. As ever, by her chair, there was a stack of mail along-side a stack of stationery and stamps waiting for her attention. Tom and Claire again lived nearby. And the residents at The Willows were being drawn into Jo's warm orbit.

If Jo was making new friends, she was ever mindful more and more that she was losing treasured old friends. Her beloved mentor, Anne L. Austin died in 1986 but not before Jo had written a praise piece on her for the *Journal of Nursing History* (1985). Mary Pekarski, ten years Jo's junior, died in 1988. Their relationship in spirit would continue after their deaths. All the nursing collections in the John J. Burns Library of Rare Books and Special Collections are preserved in its Nursing Archives named for Mary L. Pekarski. One of those nursing collections is the Josephine A. Dolan Collection. It rests securely in this safe spot, as once Jo rested in Mary Pekarski's warm heart. Robert K. O'Neill, the Burns Librarian, ensures that Jo's collection is accessible to nurses, scholars and researchers.

At the time of Jo's birth in 1913, nurses were mostly women who did not have the vote and were exploited as an ever renewing supply of cheap labor. When Jo died as 2004 ended, nursing was an independent profession firmly situated in the university. Throughout her career, this New England woman kept her light shining on nursing and how necessary it is to society. She told nurses the story of their profession from pre-literate antiquity to the highly technological present. Jo taught nurses that if they are to understand their present, they must know their past. She challenged nurses to treasure this rich inheritance and to keep the light glowing on nursing's history.

REMEMBERING JULIA ANN SULLIVAN, RN, PhD
(1923-2005)

(originally published December 2005)

The nursing community mourns the passing of Julia Ann Sullivan RN, PhD, whose many accomplishments included shaping colleagues and students when she headed the baccalaureate program at the Boston University School of Nursing. Such was Julia's integrity and force of personality that the degrees, experience, awards and honors she accumulated over her long commitment to nursing never defined her. As significant as these accomplishments were, Julia knew they pointed to nursing's importance. Essentially, Julia already knew she was good. Indeed no one could hold her to a standard higher than the one she had set for herself. This adamantine commitment to excellence inspired a generation of students and colleagues. During a time when personal celebrity often trumped professional purpose, Julia's authenticity became a beacon. It is little wonder that she is so mourned.

Julia died July 31, 2005 after a brief illness in Newport, Rhode Island where she had been born August 30, 1923 eighty-two years before. The third child of three daughters and one son born to Edward C. Sullivan and Bridget Dennehy Sullivan, Julia was a first generation American. The Sullivans lived in the Ward 5 Irish-American section of downtown Newport created years before by immigrants who had worked as cooks, maids and gardeners in the Newport's mansions built during America's Gilded Age.

The first sounds Julia heard were the soft brogues of her County Kerry, Ireland-born mother and County Cork, Ireland-born father. She bore the same name as her paternal grandmother which gave her a special link to the family's past. If Julia was conscious of her Celtic heritage, she was equally immersed in the promise of America. Indeed, because her roots reached so deeply into Irish soil, they provided her with a stability that held her fast as she reached out and took advantage of America's opportunities. She and her siblings Cornelius, Honora, and Mary—enjoyed the special ambiance that comes from growing up in two cultures. Her parents shaped the family's values. Mrs. Sullivan created the nurturing environment and Mr. Sullivan supported the family as Captain of the Newport Police Department.

The soaring sea birds and Atlantic Ocean that bordered Julia's home were constant reminders of unbounded horizons. Throughout her career, Julia would keep her eyes on the horizon even as she was immersed in the present. Her vision was sharpened by education. Following her schooling at St. Augustin's grammar school and St. Joseph's high school, Julia trained at the Rhode Island Hospital School of Nursing. Following graduation, as so many nurses of her World War II generation did, Julia joined the war effort. Given that the United States Navy was as present as the ocean in Newport, it was only natural that Julia chose the United States Navy Nurse Corps. She was one of 12,239 nurses to do so.

This choice made Julia part of nursing's transformation. Military nursing broke the iron grip that hospitals had on nursing education, where students were visible but not vocal. To their credit these programs provided ready access to patients and clinical material which, once mastered, instilled confidence in young students. At the same time that these nurses were dealing with life and death decisions, however, they were constrained by rules of etiquette that enforced conformity. Students were called professionals but were treated as children. As so many other young nurses did, Julia must have scoffed at this contradiction. The exuberance that always characterized Julia would not have allowed her to take such inanities seriously.

There was etiquette and structure in the Navy Nurse Corps but rather than constraining nurses as hospitals did, Navy protocol enhanced professional autonomy. Julia was expected to make her own judgments and accept the consequences of her decisions. Such change was anxiety-provoking, but for Julia, as for so many other military nurses, this expectation was invigorating. Nursing's horizons had been expanded and began to live up to Julia's ideal.

Once the war ended, Julia mustered out of the military and matriculated into academia. With Elaine Frato Newsome, her friend from Rhode Island Hospital School of Nursing days, and using her G.I. benefits, Julia ventured to Syracuse University in upper state New York. The two friends chose this program because it offered a dual degree: nursing and education. Much later in her career Sigma Theta Tau, nursing's honor society, and Pi Lambda Theta, education's honor society, would elect Julia into their membership. Those honors were in the future when on December 5, 1956 Julia received her baccalaureate degree and became one of the pioneers who pulled nursing education onto college campuses. The War had done what the profession had been trying to do since 1903.

How much of this Julia realized at the time is hard to assess at this remove. What can only be known for certain is that Julia was immersed in making nursing's future even as she was grateful for what she had gained from its past. Following graduation she headed the orthopedic clinic at Grace New Haven Hospital in Connecticut. Then she proceeded on to Boston University. Its basic nursing program was just over a decade old and its graduate program still younger. Nonetheless, BUSON was already a leader.

Federal funding poured into the School as the nation, grateful for how military nurses had cared for its soldiers, tried to remedy the nurse shortage and reform nursing education. Grants supported innovations that challenged accepted practices. To be sure these changes created tension but the tension also fostered creativity. This was fine as far as Julia was concerned for she was ever ready for new things. The profession's quest for collegiate education for nursing was not fully achieved at this point but it was nearing the end of the beginning. Intent on meeting the new challenges of her post-war life, Julia little realized the significance of the revolution of which she was a part, nor that she was now in the vanguard of the next phase of nursing's long and troubled journey to becoming a profession in deed as well as in word. Essentially, Julia was making nursing history even as she was being pushed around by nursing history. After completing course work and her master's thesis: "A Study of Medical-Surgical Patients' Expectations of Nursing Care" on August 25, 1958 Julia received the master's degree. Her next decision conveys her agreement with the Brown Report's manifesto (*Nursing for the Future*, 1948) that nurses were a social necessity and education for nursing should take place in institutions of higher learning. Julia left Boston University for a series of academic positions at the University of Rhode Island, Cornell and Tate University in Brooklyn, New York. Each experience added to her growing expertise on nursing curricula as well as helped to hone her teaching skills. She was already an expert clinician.

The advancement of nursing education depended on curriculum change. Julia never let her enthusiasm for change overrun her judgment. The judgment that she had learned as a child in the Sullivan home had been tested as a Naval officer and refined by scholarship. This judgment along with her clarity of vision enabled Julia to separate the essential from the trivial. Her capacity for critical thinking would become especially important when Julia returned to Boston University as the seventies ended.

Before that happened, Julia enrolled in Martha Rogers' doctoral program at New York University at Washington Square. By this time federal funding that had supported nursing education's revolution in the two decades following WWII had created a cadre of scholars who were exploring every facet of nursing. Theories of nursing proliferated and generated an expansive nursing literature. At one time the indexes of nursing journals such as the *American*

Journal of Nursing were the only way to access the nursing literature. Virginia Henderson changed all that when she compiled nursing's literature from 1900-1959 in her four volume Nursing Studies Index. Then like other professions, nursing got its own index to its literature. Once computers arrived on the scene, data bases exploded and nursing's expanding literature was accessed in a flash.

Julia was no laggard in contributing to nursing's knowledge explosion. She chose NYU because it was one of the few doctoral programs offering a concentration in nursing. The choice for her research demonstrated how Julia had expanded her ideas of medical-surgical nursing from a focus on the individual hospitalized patient to patients and their families. Using Roger's theory of the unitary person and a selection of intact families with children as her subjects, Julia investigated how the suffering of a person with a chronic disease, in this case multiple sclerosis, affected each member of a family and the family's functioning as a whole. Soon after receiving her degree, Julia accepted a position at the State University at Downstate New York.

After years of being away from the Ocean State, Julia sought a position that would be nearer her Newport home and family. In 1976 Julia returned to Boston University School of Nursing as Associate Dean for Baccalaureate Affairs under the deanship of Linda Amos. Although no one knew it at the time, John Silber, the president of the University, would close the School twelve years later. But that was still to come as Julia established herself with new colleagues. Her enthusiasm for the task inspired others to follow her lead. Young faculty naturally gravitated towards Julia. Her love of nursing, her scholarship and her stature as a professional were magnets to nurses cherishing the same ideals. Ever the leader, Julia encouraged faculty to take on nursing's challenges, to center their energies on nursing and to not let the buzz of "queen bees" distract them from nursing.

Sarah Pasternack, then a faculty member at the BUSON and now at Childrens Hospital Medical Center, remembers Julia as a wise leader who was ever mindful of her nursing identity. Pasternack describes Julia as "an admired role model and mentor." Julia also put her mark on the Massachusetts Nurses Association where she served on the Board of Directors of MNA's District V. The grateful Association acknowledged her loyalty as a member of District V and honored her excellence in nursing education. As with all the honors Julia received throughout her career, Julia used these to highlight the profession and its members.

Julia spread her influence beyond the confines of the BUSON and the MNA. Her expertise with nursing curricula made her a sought after consultant locally, nationally and internationally. Ever the ready traveler, Julia welcomed these new ventures, especially those that took her to far off places. She served as consultant at universities in Saudi Arabia, East Jetta and

Liberia. While British professors advised about history, literature and the sciences, Julia addressed nursing issues.

Julia was a busy academic but she was never too busy to make new friends. Even as she was mentoring undergraduate faculty, she made alliances with faculty in the graduate program. When Arlene Connolly served as the interim Associate Dean for Graduate Affairs, she had many occasions to work with Julia. If Julia was serious about her obligations, she was fun once the work day was done. Connolly remembers Julia in party mode after Commencement activities. She "loved escaping the city and BUSON and just relaxing after the big to-do of the morning," recalls Connolly, the hostess in Concord for post-Commencement relaxation. "We always managed to have a very enjoyable time and we both looked forward to the pleasure of being away from the crowds, the students, the noise and the exhaustion of the big day."

Katharine McCarty, of BUSON's maternal-child program got to know Julia after both had retired. Julia came up from Newport to Boston for Kathy's Christmas parties. The gregarious Julia was glad to see everyone. She sat in one of Kathy's heirloom chairs, a straight-back formal chair, in preference to the more cushioning chairs in the room. She probably chose this chair because of her back problems. No one but Julia ever sat in this chair. In any event the chair was so situated that Julia saw everyone as they entered Kathy's home. These friends, former colleagues at BUSON, were as happy to see Julia as she was to see them. Before long, the party-goers christened Julia's preferred chair the Dean's Chair.

The same kind of camaraderie happened when people in Boston visited Julia and her family in Newport. They were always welcome as were her Newport friends who knew that any time Julia was home they could drop in between one and five o'clock. There was talk galore, as her Irish people would say, as well as plenty of hospitality. Like Julia herself the good talk and fine food were laced with elegance. There were petit fours, decorated sugar cubes and gifts so beautifully wrapped it was a shame to open them.

Julia began her tenure at BUSON during America's Bicentennial Year when history became the vogue throughout the country. The American Nurses Association was no exception and themed its convention that year: "A Past to Remember/A Future to Shape." BUSON was a conspicuous presence at the convention in large part due to Mary Ann Garrigan (1914-2000). In 1966 she had established the History of Nursing Archives at what is now BU's Howard Gotlieb Archival Research Center. Garrigan headed the committee that established ANA's Hall of Fame which made its debut at the Bicentennial convention. Nurses of 1976 heard about nursing's early leaders who had preceded them such as Clara Barton, Dorothea Lynde

Dix and Louisa May Alcott of Civil War (1861-1864) fame and Linda Richards, Sophia Palmer and Isabel Hampton Robb who established nursing education and nursing organizations.

Sarah Pasternack, the present president of the Nursing Archives Associates remembers being at that convention at a table of BUSON faculty just behind Julia. In retrospect that propinquity proved to be prophetic. As leader of the undergraduate program Julia now held the same position that Mary Ann Garrigan had held before she established the History of Nursing Archives. In 1990, after Julia had retired as professor emeritus, she became president of the Nursing Archives Associates. A decade later, Sarah Pasternack assumed the presidency. In retrospect it seems obvious that Julia should receive Theta Chapter of Sigma Theta Tau's Mary Ann Garrigan Award.

Nursing's history now claimed Julia's devotion. As with any other task she undertook, Julia bent her best efforts to implementing the goals of the Nursing Archives Associates. From childhood Julia had a special feeling for the past and how it shaped the future. The History of Nursing Archives was almost twenty-five years old and was a treasure trove of primary documents about nursing education. Some hospital training programs closed as baccalaureate programs increased in number. More and more hospitals' training schools closed following ANA's 1965 Position Paper that said education for nursing should take place in institutions of higher education. Thanks to Mary Ann Garrigan's presence and persuasion the papers of those schools were deposited in the History of Nursing Archives. As the president of the Nursing Archives Associates Julia effectively protected the profession's memory.

Julia invited MNA's Lucy Lincoln Drown Nursing History Society to co-sponsor the annual meetings with the Nursing Archives Associates. That relationship brought a new group of nurses to the Archives. This mutually beneficial sponsorship of the Nursing Archives Associates and the Lucy Lincoln Drown Nursing History Society continued until the Spring of 2001, when MNA disassociated itself from the American Nurses Association. Mary Ellen Doona, MNA's historian until the disaffiliation and member of the Nursing Archives Associates Board, remembers the elegance and intelligence that Julia brought to her presidency. Doona says that Julia's great sense of humor made serving on the Board of Directors during Julia's tenure a pleasant as well as a productive experience.

Anne Donovan, a retired Navy nurse who knew Julia at various times at MNA, the Nursing Archives Associates and the Navy Nurse Corps Association activities, loved serving on committees with Julia. She was "fun and made a contribution," says Donovan. Many in the profession know the reality behind Donovan's brief encomium. There are more than a few nurses who join committees to fluff up their own resumes and then do little if any work.

Nursing and the Navy Nurse Corps were the twin poles of Julia's professional career. She did not abandon them in retirement. She became a hospice volunteer for Newport's Visiting Nurse Association. With more free time, she was able to increase her activity with her Navy colleagues. She attended meetings of the Navy Nurse Corps Association and helped in raising funds for scholarships for Navy nurses.

Julia stood out from most other nurses not so much for her height and elegance—though they were considerable—as for her undeviating commitment to nursing excellence. She sought the best as a clinician and an academic, and enthusiastically sought colleagues who had the same vision of nursing. With them she kept her eyes on nursing's horizons and tried to prevent the urgent from overwhelming the important. Julia's idea of collegiality was grounded in the ancient belief that two are always better than one to see and do a thing.

Julia had a gift of friendship and lived what Aristotle said: "Friendship was one of those things which life can least afford to be without."1 Her sister Mary says Julia prized her relationship with friends and colleagues. Distance might separate her from her friends but the friendships remained intact. Jane Barry, a Newport native and fellow Navy nurse, met Julia while both were on the faculty of the University of Rhode Island. Later they were on the faculty at BUSON. Barry remembers her academic colleague as a "good and excellent clinician." When she describes Julia's friendship Barry is more profound, saying Julia was a "good and loyal friend."

Julia's friends knew that she had been troubled with back problems from spinal stenosis with related neuropathy that increasingly slowed her down and lessened her trips to Boston and Navy Nurse Corps Association meetings. These friends were shocked when they heard Julia had had a stroke. All had been as usual the day she suffered the stroke. Julia had been to the hairdresser with Jane Barry and given her a birthday gift. That evening she said good-bye to her sister Mary who was off to a cousin's graduation.

Julia was alone when the stroke hit. The first words she said on being found were typical Julia. "What's new?" she asked. The news was not good. After a few weeks of being able to talk with her loved ones, Julia lost her ability to speak, and then, her ability to process what was being said. There were no extraordinary measures taken in keeping with Julia's prior wishes. Julia had seen too many lives prolonged at a biological level when the person had already faded away. That was not for Julia. She had always eschewed the technological imperative that said because there was technology, there was an obligation to use it. In keeping with her Catholic tradition, Julia knew there was a time to live and a time to die.

Sad as her family, friends and colleagues are, they are comforted in knowing that Julia was well-cared for during her last six weeks on this earth. After a funeral Mass at St. Augustin's Church, a contingent of police from the Newport Police Department escorted Julia to her grave. Her parents had died years before but the police remembered their former captain as they honored his daughter. Julia met her parents' expectations that she be a good and decent person. She rose to positions of prominence and pulled those positions up to her own high standards. She had a sharp eye as befitting the Irish meaning of her last name—*O'Súileabháin*—keen eyed. She saw that nursing was good and kept her eyes focused on its horizons.

Julia's Irish tradition says the dead are never far away. They continue to walk this earth, felt but not seen. As nurses remember Julia and honor her uniqueness, they will feel her presence, especially when they keep their eyes focused on nursing.

REFERENCES

Thomson, J.A.K. 1971. *The Ethics of Aristotle*. Baltimore: Penguin.

HELEN C. FAGAN AND NURSING'S HISTORY
(1929-2011)

(originally published December 2011)

Nursing's "urgent nows" shaped Helen C. Fagan as they do all nurses. She was present: as a young registered nurse caring for patients on St Elizabeth's Hospital's nursing floor known as St Cosmos; later as a teacher passing on her knowledge at the Hospital's nursing school; and still later as the School's administrator directing its nursing faculty." She responded to the intensity of these moments, ever mindful of Solomon's insight that our time is a very shadow that passes away. Helen knew that time and tide waited for no one.

Knowing how quickly the present fled into the past, Helen made sure that the urgent nows of individuals long dead informed the present. Foremost in her memory were: Ann McElroy, Ann Dolan, Margaret McInerney, Elizabeth Carling and Ann Doherty. These five women saw other women in desperate need of care, and opened St Elizabeth Hospital for Women in the South End of Boston in the autumn of 1868. Helen's nursing care was centered abound compassion grounded in competence. She anchored others during times of crisis as well as calm, standing with them in their situation until once again they could stand alone.

Helen stood out for her concern for nursing's history. When she closed the door on the School in 2000, she ensured that its story would not be forgotten by establishing the St Elizabeth's Hospital School of Nursing Collection in the Mary L. Pekarski Nursing Archives in the Burns Library at Boston College. In this Archive, the School's documents from its founding in 1895 through to its closing in 2000 are preserved including records, photos, catalogs, lectures and ceremonial programs and a DVD recorded April 25, 2010 in which graduates from across seventy years of the School's history shared their lived experiences as nursing students. They told how the lessons they learned continue to influence their compassion and competence.

Helen taught that present moments—nursing's urgent nows—pass quickly into the past, but before they did they were to be grasped in all their intensity and must remain so inflamed that they lighted the next moment as it moved into the future. Helen accepted the task of being keeper of St. E's institutional memory and narrative; truly one of Clio's devotees...a servant of this muse of history. She kept a scroll of fame in which she wrote the names of the more than 2000 nurses who had graduated from SEHSON telling the deeds of St E's nurses and the nursing history they had made. She added particulars on others' bare accounts of long hours and hard work, reminding everyone that nursing students also had lots of fun, and made life-long friendships. She made sure that graduates of the last four decades of the School knew the story of the Sisters of St. Francis who had led St E's from 1883-1963. These religious women were committed to excellent nursing care, and great examples of women in positions of power long before the days of women's liberation.

Helen died in her Needham home Tuesday August 30, 2011 while reading the newspaper after a busy morning of volunteer work. The SEHSON Alumni gathered together October 16, 2011 at an annual Mass of Remembrance for all the alumni who have died; this year's Mass dedicated to the memory of Helen C. Fagan. Born on Christmas day 1929 this gift to nursing's history taught by example that the past is alive if present moments are grasped in all their intensity. Janet Pizzi SEHSON 1981 spoke for many when she said, "We have all been graced by [Helen's] presence and she will live on in each of us as we care for our patients and live her legacy every day." The baton must now pass to other alumni whose responsibility is to ensure sure that the history Helen made of her urgent nows at St. Elizabeth's does not fade from memory nor flicker into oblivion.

MEMORIAL MOMENT: ALICE MARIE (HOWELL) FRIEDMAN

(originally published June 2014)

Clio's loyal servant, Alice Marie (Howell) Friedman (17 February 1922-14 January 2014), died in Amherst, Massachusetts one month before her ninety-second birthday from the sequellae of a fall. Nursing's history was the air Alice breathed while a student at the Massachusetts General Hospital School of Nursing (1941-1944). She learned that Linda Richards, "America's First Trained Nurse," rescued the flailing Boston Training School that later became the MGHSON. Alice also learned that Richards' students, Sophia Palmer and Mary E. P. Davis, were the founding editor and business manager of the *American Journal of Nursing* founded in 1900.

As grounded as she was in her School's contribution to nursing's history, Alice kept her eye on the future. Her goals were to have a college education and to be a public health nurse. Alice's goals flew in the face of the Massachusetts General Hospital School of Nursing's (MGHSON) insistence that she continue at the school following graduation. Alice's dream that had long before determined her path into nursing trumped such authoritative demands. She left MGHSON and continued her education at Teachers College (1947) in New York City. While there, she cared for families at the famous Henry Street Settlement House in New York's lower east side. By the time Alice returned to Boston, nursing's scene was much changed. Nurses had become a national treasure because of their service during World War II. A thankful country funded nursing education that then began its migration from hospitals to college campuses.

Alice was part of nursing's renaissance. During her first years back in Boston as a public health nurse with the Visiting Nurses Association, Alice cared for families in Boston's South End. Caring for families required many of the same skills Alice had learned as a child as her military family moved from base to base: moving into new neighborhoods; meeting new people; and, assessing their needs while establishing herself as their nurse. Along with these nursing duties, Alice got involved with a resurging professional organization and continued her nursing education. By 1965 when the American Nurses Association decreed that nursing education should take place in institutions of higher education, Alice was at Boston University earning a graduate degree in Public Health Nursing (1967). She was among the newly minted specialists who were much in demand as registered nurses descended onto college campuses. Her academic career that began at Boston College continued at the University of Massachusetts at Amherst where after eighteen years she retired as an emeritus.

Alice was a multi-tasker long before the term was invented. She spent a year at the University of Kent at Canterbury as an honorary research associate. Alice was busy that year meeting with educators in universities at Edinburgh, Manchester and Wales but not too busy to find nurses who were researching the profession's history. They welcomed Alice into their group and into their deliberations on professional autonomy. What is more, they published Alice's research on Hannah Porn, a midwife in Gardner Massachusetts, whose successful practice fell victim to the medicalization of childbirth as the nineteenth century came to a close (Maggs).

These relationships that were forged during her year in Britain provided a template for helping students to see that nursing was an international profession. She lost no time on her return from Britain in creating an exchange program between UMASS/Amherst School of Nursing and the nursing program at the University of Wales in Cardiff. This proved only the beginning. Its success paved the way for similar opportunities in Ireland, Jamaica, Puerto Rico and Ghana. More important than expanding their horizons, she taught her students to make the most of their time as students.

Alice's trick of managing time played a large part in her being able to be a professional woman as well as wife to her beloved Harvey who predeceased her, and mother to Joel, Suzanne, and Elizabeth. Only because she was such a master at managing time was she able to fulfill her commitment to professional organizations, serving as vice-president of the Massachusetts Nurses Association 1964-67, chair of its Economic and General Welfare Committee and member of the Board of Directors of MNA's District One. She also served on the local Board of Health and Amherst's Health Planning Committee. Serving as secretary to the MGHSON Alumni Association suggests that Alice had forgiven her alma mater that once had tried to jettison her nursing career.

Alice's knowledge of Massachusetts's contribution to community health nursing is evident in "Nursing in Massachusetts during the Roaring Twenties," as her love of nursing's history is in her organizational efforts (Doona). She was a member of the Nursing Archives Associates at the Mugar Memorial Library at Boston University and served as its president in 1985. She also held membership in the American Association for the History of Nursing, the Society for Nursing History and the National Oral History Association. Answering the clarion call of Stella Goostray and Mary Ann Garrigan to preserve nursing's history, Alice did an oral history of Mary A. Maher, the founding dean of nursing programs at Boston College and UMASS/Amherst. Before long, Alice herself became the subject of oral histories. One such oral history done by Mary Ellen Doona is archived at the Burns Library at Boston College, while the W.E.B. DuBois Library preserves Dr. Robert Cox's interview of Alice's career at UMASS/Amherst. Already gracing the shelves of the library is the history of the nursing program that Alice helped to write for its fortieth anniversary.

At its centennial in 2003 the MNA interviewed Alice on her pioneering efforts for collective bargaining in 1964. At that time Boston nurses were earning $86 a week, the same as beauticians in the area. Medical records librarians and medical social workers in hospitals earned $106 and $107 respectively, while dieticians earned $98 and physical therapists earned $94. Only lab and x-ray technicians among those working in hospitals earned less than nurses (Robinson). Teachers who had summers off were earning $5,735 annually while general duty nurses dealing with life and death issues year long earned $4,080 (Robinson).

Alice chaired the Economic and General Welfare Committee and remained an advocate for nurses controlling nursing throughout her career-long association with the MNA. As collective bargaining became more and more certain, the MGH and probably other hospitals as well, raised nurses' salaries.

Alice was a contributing co-editor with Joellen Hawkins and Loretta Higgins for the *Dictionary of American Nursing Biography* that Martin Kaufman guided into publication in 1988. Hawkins remembers that Alice's:

long term perspective on leaders and innovators in the profession plus her personal knowledge of so many of those leaders were invaluable to inclusion of those who created the profession of nursing in its evolution from a trained occupation to a profession…. Her contributions to nursing and especially to preserving our history will continue to inform scholars as well as those new to nursing.

With the same dedication, Alice Friedman served on the executive committee of MNA's Lucy Lincoln Drown Nursing History Society. She was part of making sure that Linda Richards and Mary Eliza Mahoney were inducted into the National Women's Hall of Fame at Seneca Falls, and that Sara E. Parsons was inducted into the American Nurses Hall of Fame. Among her many joys in 1996 was personifying Lillian Wald, her public health nurse ideal, in "Ethics, Nursing and a Century of Revolution: Contributions to Personal Health Care," a panel discussion that the Lucy Lincoln Drown Nursing History Society presented at ANA's centennial convention in Washington, DC.

Alice "lived her life with kindness and courage" remembers her friend and colleague, Ann Sheridan. Fittingly Rabbi Benjamin Weiner prayed, "May [Alice's] presence continue to be felt by those who loved her and now carry her memory." Alice helped nurses to make those who had preceded them a presence in their practice.

REFERENCES

Doona, Mary Ellen, Joellen W. Hawkins, Ursula Van Ryzin, Alice H. Friedman and Loretta P. Higgins. "Nursing in Massachusetts during the Roaring Twenties." *Historical Journal of Massachusetts* (23): 133-164.

Maggs, Christopher, ed. (1987). *Nursing History: The State of the Art.* London: Croomhelm.

Robinson, Betty. (1983). "Nurse Control of Nursing: The Professional Association and Collective Bargaining." Ph.D. Diss. Boston University, 27-194

JOANNE MARIE GARVEY
(1954-2008)

(originally published March 2008)

Joanne Marie Garvey (1954-2008), one of Clio's loyal servants, died at the Beth Israel Deaconess Medical Center on January 3, 2008, succumbing to the renal cancer that had been diagnosed in November 2005. Born in Dorchester, Massachusetts Joanne was the third daughter and youngest of six children born to the late Stephen and Mary (Kelly) Garvey. Nursing colleagues gathered at her wake on Sunday January 6, 2008 to share their sorrow with Joanne's family. The next day they attended her funeral mass at St. Elizabeth's Church in Milton and her burial services at the Milton Cemetery. Friday, January 11, 2008, Joanne would have marked her fifty-fourth birthday.

If the years of Joanne's life were short, she made the life in those years count much to the benefit of nursing in Massachusetts. By the time she was appointed to the executive committee of the Massachusetts Nurses Association's newly formed Lucy Lincoln Drown Nursing History Society in 1983, Joanne had graduated from the Boston City Hospital (BCH) School of Nursing (1974), Northeastern University (1979) and was nearing the completion of her master's program in nursing administration at Boston University. Doctoral studies at UMASS/ Boston were still in the future.

As so many other nurses do, Joanne continued to practice as she earned these degrees. Her preferred arena of nursing was the acute care setting, first in positions as staff nurse and head nurse at the BCH, per diem positions at the BCH and in staff and administration positions at the Brigham and Women's Hospital. From the beginning, she was known for being an excellent nurse. "She was good at every level," said her BCHSON classmate, Kathy Henderson Byrne. Peggy McCarthy Mogan who worked with Joanne at the BCH and the B&W added Joanne was the "most honest person I ever knew. She was genuine."

The executive committee quickly discovered what many in Massachusetts nursing organizations already knew. "Her work ethic and insightfulness were impressive," reported one nurse who had worked with Joanne on a by-laws committee. The same was true of her commitment to the Society's executive committee. Her practitioner's perspective and her sharp intellect clarified the task. If she connected with the work at hand, she connected more so with her fellow committee members. This, as time would show, was Joanne's strong point, in life with her family and friends and in her profession with patients and colleagues. Being connected with others counted above all.

Joanne's fellow committee member, Janet Wilson James (1918-1987), the late professor of women's studies at Boston College and scholar of nursing's pioneer historian, Lavinia Dock, admired Joanne's style and admitted her to the pantheon of good nurses. Joanne and Janet worked together to create the Guidelines for Preservation of Nursing School Record that MNA distributed to nursing schools throughout Massachusetts. The professor and the nurse also worked on a process whereby .Massachusetts nurses could participate in National Women's Week activities. Such work fit into Joanne's position that nursing must be connected to the larger world.

In keeping with duties as committee member and MNA's First Vice-president, on May 12, 1986 Joanne attended the Waltham Hospital's celebration of Florence Nightingale's birth. The next month, on June 11, 1986 Joanne represented MNA and the Lucy Lincoln Drown Nursing History Society at the centennial of the St. Barnabas Guild at Trinity Church in Boston's Copley Square. Joanne congratulated President Ellie Kolman and all the successors of the ten Episcopal nurses who had established the Guild in 1886. Once the formal part of the program was concluded, Joanne moved out into the reception to greet the celebrants and their guests, among whom was the St. Radegonde Guild founded in 1909 at Boston College then across Harrison Avenue from BCH. Joanne greeted Annetta "Nettie" Romano, the president of the Guild and caught up with BCH news with fellow alumnae. Joanne gleefully celebrated the presence of Dolina McInnes, who began her training at BCHSON in 1923, a decade after Lucy Lincoln Drown had retired as its superintendent.

Joanne was among the panelists at MNA's 78th convention in 1985 when it presented a program on the 75th anniversary of the Board of Registration in Nursing. As she had earlier reported on the St Barnabas Centennial, she did the same for "The Diamond Jubilee of Nursing Registration in Massachusetts: Where are the Diamonds?" keeping nurses unable to attend the convention connected with what had occurred there. She summarized the remarks of panelists Phyllis Magliozzi, Alice Friedman, Mary Ellen Doona, Debbie Manning and her own review of the struggle for licensure laws in Massachusetts. Joanne concluded that Massachusetts' precious diamonds were all its nurses caring for patients.

Joanne admired the work of predecessors and celebrated Massachusetts' early and enduring role in nursing's development. She was partial to the BCHSON Alumnae Association founded in 1896 and served many years on its Board. In her mind, nursing's past, present and future were a connected whole. It was a belief grounded in her concrete experience within the four generations of the Garvey Kelly family. Her nursing career was grounded in a similar connectedness. Service to others followed naturally. She started this during her years at Cardinal Cushing High School working with the elderly at Marion Manor in South Boston. Then she followed her sister Patricia, eight years her senior, into nursing and into the BCH once fondly called the hospital of Boston's poor.

It was at BCH that Joanne first connected with homeless men and women. She learned nursing skills in the nurse run clinics at the Pine Street Inn and social activism in the City's first Walk for Hunger in the 1970s. Her connectedness to these men and women was not a quick work but one that grew and developed over the years. She "did" Easter at the Pine Street Inn with a group of friends, nurses and family under the leadership of Denise Sullivan. Some cooked hams at their homes; others made raisin sauce and still others cooked sweet potatoes. Car after car laden with the moveable feast arrived at the Inn where the "chefs" served it to the 650 plus men and women with more than enough for seconds and even thirds.

The labor of this and other dinners was lightened by the camaraderie of the "chefs" and their joy of seeing the unique person behind the homeless label. Joanne's outstanding traits were "her goodness and brilliance," says Denise Sullivan who adds, "Anything I asked Joanne to do or she asked me to do for the homeless was done. We worked together." "I was just a little kid," remembers Catherine Kelly Atkinson when Joanne took her along on these expeditions to the homeless. She did not fully understand who the homeless were and what Joanne and her friends were doing. Catherine only knew she always wanted to be with her Aunt Joanne. At the B&W, Joanne would "rally the troops," remembers Peggy McCarthy Mogan. Among them was Barbara Perron who declares, "It was the one of the best things I have ever done."

In spite of a busy career in nursing administration, Joanne's connectedness to homeless men and women remained a constant. She served on the B&W's Homeless Committee (1998-2000), coordinated B&W's Food Group to Pine Street Inn (1988-1999), and chaired the Committee to End Homelessness Golf Tournament (2002-2005) held at the William Devine Golf Course at Franklin Park. Nor did these homeless men and women fall from Joanne's attention once she started her doctoral studies at UMASS/Boston. Now she used research methods to translate personal commitment into reasoned discourse to share with the profession. She presented the findings from her study: "Combating Homelessness through Supportive Services for Low Income Elders" at UMASS/Boston's Research Day May 2003.

Fun with family and friends filled her life and replenished her energies. Early on, vacations were summers with nurse friends in rented cottages at Humarock enjoying sunny days and then traveling up to BCH for night duty. Skiing and golfing were later enthusiasms. Travel to Europe, Alaska and Florida was vacation but other trips were professional obligations. She presented "The Future of Nursing" in Fukoka, Japan (1990); "The History of Western Nursing" in Moscow (1995); and, "Ethics in Nursing Care" in Moscow (1996). If the venues were exotic, the method was familiar. Joanne was the agent connecting nurses in these nations with nurses at the B&W.

Ironically, perhaps one of Joanne's most significant contributions to nursing was her own journey from health to illness and from illness to death. The November diagnosis began that journey that became a window on nurses' privileged position at the patient's side providing a glimpse of nursing in Boston from 2005 to 2008. Joan Garrity who calls herself a friend-on-the-stairs marveled at Joanne's upbeat attitude and big smile every time they passed each other at UMASS/ Boston. What she was witnessing was Joanne's operating principle. Joanne decided that she could not control the cancer but she could control her attitude towards it. "She didn't get a sick persona" says Gail Gall a UMASS/Boston colleague whose chatty style was a perfect complement to Joanne's quiet manner. She wanted to go on as usual making plans, supporting her fellow PhD candidates and working on her dissertation. She would give details of her illness to strangers but spared her friends and family, essentially caring for them and keeping connected with the healthy part of her life.

When she began to get sicker, she had to reschedule her trip to Vienna with her niece Ann Marie Rogers-Madden from October to Spring 2008. Friends hovered nearby wanting to do something but respecting how Joanne wanted to proceed. Finally, Peggy McCarthy Mogan insisted, "Tell me something real that I can do-like shopping or something." Joanne responded, "You can stay with me at night when I move to Quincy." Cheryl Ventola, Joanne's friend from the B&W, then made sure there was someone with Joanne every night. "Everyone wanted to help," she said, "It made my job easier." Among those who signed on were: Kathy Byrne, Maryann Glynn, Ellen Leary, Peggy McCarthy-Mogan, Barbara Perron, Linda Samia, Cheryl Ventola and Katherine Kelly Atkinson.

Determined as she was, Joanne had to concede that she lacked the energy to finish her doctoral program. Sessions in her home with Professor Joanne Dalton analyzing research data then came to an end. On November 28, 2007 as Dalton and Velina Batchvarov watched, Carol Ellenbecker, director of the PhD program, presented Joanne with the certificate that Dean Greer Glazer and the Provost of UMASS/Boston created. It recognized Joanne's "outstanding contributions to the profession of nursing and to the College of Nursing and Health Science, and for her exceptional achievements as a candidate for the PhD in Nursing." Now the balance that Joanne nimbly maintained between her personal and professional obligations tipped away from nursing in favor of family and friends.

She wrote her Christmas cards early so that everyone would have her new address. Charlotte Byrne helped her get to the Quincy post office so that she could personally drop cards into the mail slot. Hope blazed in such messages as, "Maybe we can get together when I get back from Florida. I hope to be feeling better by then." On December 18, 2007, her sister, Maryann Garvey Rogers, helped Joanne negotiate the icy parking lot to shop at Anderson's Jewelry in Wellesley for gift certificates for friends. Joanne always loved the holidays and Christmas most of all. Accordingly, on the 20th she hosted a get together for the friends who had been staying with her at night. Barbara Perron had the sense that Joanne was "doing it for us." Given that Joanne had endured the sudden deaths of two siblings, John (1980) and Patricia (2001), it seems likely that Barbara's intuition was right. In any case, all were amazed at how well Joanne had rallied her strength for this Christmas with friends.

A few days later Joanne was admitted to the oncology unit at the Beth Israel Deaconess Medical Center. She had less than two weeks to live. As she had done throughout Joanne's journey, her sister Maryann stayed with her as family and friends dropped in and out. Kathy Byrne was a special source of comfort and once again Cheryl Ventola created a sign up list. Gail Gall, Debbie Molloy, Vicky Morrison, Linda Samia and Anna Yoder, Joanne's friends from UMASS/Boston; and Ellen Leary, Peggy McCarthy Mogan and Barbara Perron from BCH and B&W signed on. Each knew what good nursing care was and each wanted that good nursing care for the good nurse who was their friend and colleague.

As sad as the duty was, each felt privileged to be with Joanne. Barbara Perron says that she and Joanne talked quite a bit which gave her "the chance right up to the last second of getting to know Joanne." Peggy McCarthy Mogan stayed with Joanne over the New Year's weekend glad for the chance to be alone with her friend from BCH and B&W days. She noted that staff nurses were never too busy to help her care for Joanne. Nursing students did their part. One nurse watching their amazement remarked, "Look at Joanne," she said. "She is still teaching students." A BIDMC supervisor put her face close to Joanne's telling her the two of them had worked together at the B&W. "I know you Joanne," she said trying to penetrate the haze of illness and medication to reach Joanne. Then she reassured her; "We will take good care of you, Joanne." Vickie Morrison of Salem State cared for Joanne the night before she died. Once medication squelched the pain, Joanne was calm and quiet and her breathing became easier. Joanne died the next evening with her sister Maryann, her niece Ann Marie and nephew Kevin Kelly at her side. Her brother Bill had just left.

Pall bearers: Kathy Henderson Byrne, Ellen Leary, Debbie Malloy, Peggy McCarthy Mogan, Vickie Morrison, Barbara Perron, Linda Samia, Cheryl Ventola and Anna Yoder "walked down" with Joanne to her funeral mass. Her siblings, Steve, Bill and Maryann and her aunt Sister Anna Mary CSJ were surrounded by Joanne's nieces, nephews, friends and nurses. The tears shed for Joanne expressed gratitude as much as they did grief. Some of that grief has already become joy, as nurses and family realize how deeply Joanne, the woman of lofty stature and still loftier ideas, touched the lives. The magnificent white hawk that soared above the mourners at Joanne's gravesite seemed a promise that sadness would also lift.

Joanne always tied up loose ends. It is time to do the same. Professor Joanne Dalton will put out publishable information. The first chapter of Joanne's dissertation: "Impact of Formal Nursing Services on Alzheimer's Care Givers' Level of Depression" making sure that Joanne's thinking becomes part of nursing's literature. Obituaries, Steve Garvey's eulogy, the green-covered booklet for the Mass of Christian burial, testimonials from her friends, her curriculum vitae and other documents will be sent to the Lucy Lincoln Drown Nursing History Society Collections in the Burns Library of Boston College and the History of Nursing Archives at Boston University. These sources will be preserved there for the scholars who will come along to study nursing in Boston at the beginning of the 21st century. They will discover how Joanne and her friends exemplified nursing's privileged place at the patient's side.

MASSACHUSETTS NURSES IN ANA'S HALL OF FAME

(originally published December 2012)

Now thirty-six years old, the American Nurses Association's Hall of Fame was established as the nation prepared to celebrate its two hundredth birthday in 1976. Heading the inaugural committee was Mary Anne Garrigan (1914-2000), who had the foresight, ten years before to establish the History of Nursing Archives at Boston University. As the Bicentennial Year began, the ANA Hall of Fame Committee announced its charter members with Dorothea Lynde Dix (1802-1881), the untiring advocate for the mentally ill and Superintendent of Women Nurses for the Union during the Civil War (1861-1864), representing pre-training school nurses.

Other Massachusetts nurses honored in that inaugural year were: Linda J. Richards (1852-1912) and Mary Eliza Mahoney (1845-1926), both graduates of the New England Hospital for Women and Children (NEHWC): Richards in 1873, and correcting an injustice that had excluded Colored* women from nurses training, Mahoney in 1879. Another charter member was Sophia F. Palmer (1853-1920), an 1878 graduate of the Boston Training School for Nurses (later the Massachusetts General Hospital School of Nurses, MGHSON) and in 1900 the founding editor of the *American Journal of Nursing (AJN)*. Stella Goostray (1886-1969), Director of Nursing at Childrens Hospital was also inducted into the inaugural Hall of Fame. She led the National Nursing Council for War Services during World War II. More historically minded than most, Goostray advocated that nursing's documents be preserved, taught nurses about their heritage and applauded the opening of the History of Nursing Archives in 1966.

At a subsequent convention Mary E. P. Davis (1858-1924), Sophia Palmer's classmate at the MGH, was inducted into the Hall of Fame for her success as the business manager of the *AJN*. Davis was the mastermind in establishing in 1903 the Massachusetts State

Nurses Association [later Massachusetts Nurses Association] that continues since 2001 as the Massachusetts Association for Registered Nurses.

Much of Anna C. Maxwell's (1851-1929) status as a Hall of Famer is for her career in New York City that was built on experiences in Massachusetts at the NEHWC as student and matron, training at Linda Richards' program at the Boston City Hospital and directing the Boston Training School for Nurses at the MGH. As Maxwell did, Sara E. Parsons (1864-1949) served during the brief Spanish American War (1898) but her early focus was the care of the mentally ill, following her studies at the McLean Hospital. She returned to her alma mater at the MGH in 1910 as its Director of Nursing. During World War I, she led the nursing department of MGH's Base Hospital Number Six in France, and later testified in Congress that nurses serving in the military should have rank.

World War I established Julia Stimson's (1881-1948) credentials as a Hall of Famer. Born in Worcester, MA Stimson directed nursing services for the Expeditionary Forces in France towards the end of World War I. When Congress granted relative rank to nurses in 1920, Stimson became nursing's first major. She was ANA's president in 1938-1944.

Anne Hervey Strong (1876-1925), born in Wakefield, MA practiced public health nursing in the historic Henry Street Settlement House in New York's Lower East Side. While still in New York, Strong gave classes for nurses at Boston's Instructive District Nurses Association [precursor of Boston Visiting Nurses Association]. She returned to Massachusetts when the School of Public Health Nursing was established at Simmons College in 1918. Strong became its first Director.

The ANA Hall of Fame recognized Dorothy M. Smith (1913-1997), a graduate of the Quincy Hospital School of Nursing, for creating the nursing program at the University of Florida/Gainesville that integrated practice, education, and research. Similarly, Frances Reiter (1904-1977), taught and practiced in Boston from 1942-1945 at Boston University and the MGH and then implemented nursing's best practices as dean of the Graduate School of Nursing in New York Medical College. She chaired the ANA Committee that created ANA's position paper that all those who were licensed to practice nursing should be prepared in institutions of higher learning (*AJN*, December 1965). Her paper, "The Nurse-Clinician" in the *AJN* (February 1966) introduced the idea of the clinical specialist.

The latest Massachusetts nurse inducted into ANA's Hall of Fame is the late Josephine A. Dolan (1913-2004) of Holliston, MA. With a diploma from St. John's Hospital School of Nursing in Lowell, MA and a master's degree from Boston University, Dolan taught at the University of Connecticut. In the classroom, on television and in her books Dolan documented nursing's long history of humanistic care. Boston College awarded Dolan an honorary degree in 1987 as it celebrated its nursing school's fortieth anniversary. Given the history to date, it is almost a certainty that Dolan will not be the last Massachusetts's nurse to grace ANA's Hall of Fame.

*term used in Mahoney's lifetime

NURSING IN MASSACHUSETTS

REMEMBRANCE AND REGISTRATION

(originally published December 2004)

When humanity followed an agricultural calendar of sowing, growing and reaping, this time of year marked the earth's death. The days shortened and the nights lengthened as the year ended and winter began. The sun seemed to be leaving the earth as the year headed into its dark half. The Celtic year began during this time. The first day of the new year was Samhain (pronounced saween) which occurred from dusk of October thirty-first to dusk of November first. Interestingly, during the night as the old year became the new year, a crack in time happened which permitted the dead to return to the earth. Although there had been pain and sorrow at the time of death, the relationship between the living and the dead person had not ceased. The return of the dead from the otherworld celebrated this continuity. Thus doors were left open, fires were left burning on the hearth and food was set out on the table to welcome the dead as they returned to be with their families once again.

Samhain was suppressed but not supplanted when Christianity imposed its system on the pagan world. All Hallow's Day (All Saints Day) was superimposed on Salmhain. The holy day recognized all good people who had died, but who were not on the Church's roster of Saints. In sharp contrast with the continuity between the Celtic living and dead, Christians separated the living from the dead. The dead were morphed into saints or demons and resided in heaven or hell, to be rewarded or punished as their deeds on earth mandated.

Samhain survived, though it did so in a much reduced form. On Halloween, All Hallow's Eve, doors are once again opened for creatures seemingly from another world. They receive a happy welcome and lots of sweet goodies. Some carry Jack-o-lanterns, their contemporary version of the turnips that ancient Celts hollowed out to hold the candle that would illuminate the darkness.

If the season of darkness and death was sorrowful, it also provided time free from agricultural duties for contemplation. Reflecting on one's continuity with people from the past yielded new insights for the living and was a stimulus for renewal, The season of darkness and contemplation would endure for several more months but hope arrived in late December, with the Winter Solstice. With the night at its longest and the sun at its lowest point it seemed that the sun was about to leave the sky forever. But then the solstice occurred. As the word conveys, the sun stood still. The conquest of the night was over. From this moment forward, the day would begin to lengthen. People celebrated the returning day, burning huge oak logs that imitated the warmth and brightness of the sun. Thus was born the Yule log. The log was decorated with ivy, holly and other evergreens that kept their color when the rest of the earth turned brown. These greens represented life's strength. Especially sacred to the ancient pagans was the mistletoe with its golden beads of yellow fruit that reflected the sun.

Other cultures had their own festival of lights at mid winter. Ancient Romans celebrated a seven day festival of misrule at Saturnalia in mid December in honor of the god of sowing, Chanukah in December remembers the miraculous oil that kept one candle burning for eight nights though there was oil enough only for one night. As the present day descendants of the Macabees celebrate the ancient miracle with their families over the eight days of the feast, they light candles in the menorah and give gifts to children. The star over Bethlehem marks the birth of the Christ child and His promise of Light. And in January Kwanza, still another festival with roots in an agricultural culture is celebrated with candles and gift giving. These human festivals at the Winter Solstice are moments of hope and joy as the lengthening day masters the dark night.

If each holiday serves to maintain the continuity of generations, the Winter Solstice provides the occasion for Massachusetts nurses to consider how like the bright sun they are to patients dealing with the darkness of disease and illness. It is also an opportunity for Massachusetts nurses to remember their connectedness with all the nurses who have come before them. Like the saints in the Church's calendars, celebrated at All Hallow's Day, these nurses are not mentioned in nursing's history books, Although lost in the shadows, they remain an essential part of nursing and should be remembered,

Linda Richards, Sophia Palmer and Mary E. P. Davis spent their best efforts to protect the rights of such nurses, During a season of darkness at the beginning of the twentieth century they labored to get a law enacted that would differentiate the trained nurse from those who would pose as trained nurses. By 1910 Massachusetts had laws that registered the trained nurse and protected the public from frauds. Nine decades later RN was not only affixed after a nurse's name, it became part of the title of their organization, the Massachusetts Association of Registered Nurses, in short, MARN. During this season of darkness, as MARN approaches the Winter's Solstice it seems especially appropriate to remember the nurses who saw to it that nurses and the public they served were protected.

Foremost among the trio of nurses was Linda Richards (1841-1930). She was born during a time when nursing was part of a woman's domestic duty to her family and began nursing as it became a world of paid work for women and men. Richards was born in Potsdam, New York (now Watertown, New York) to Vermont parents and grew to adulthood in rural Vermont at the edge of the Canadian of the border. She was like many other post Civil War (1861- 1865) women eager for a life beyond the domestic sphere. She left her rural home for Massachusetts where there were more opportunities due to its industrialization during the War, Richards migrated to Foxboro, Massachusetts, now the home of the champion New England Patriots; but then, the center of the straw hat industry, Tradition has it that relatives had convinced Richards to relocate to Foxboro. Apparently she favored Foxboro, for after a lengthy career in nursing she returned to Foxboro when she retired.

A massive fire destroyed a large part of the straw hat industry with all its personnel documents that might have opened a window on Richards' employment history. The little that is known of this phase of her life is found at Harvard's Houghton Library in documents about her five year stint as a missionary nurse in Kyoto, Japan (1885-1890). The reason this much is known about Richards and almost nothing is known of so many other nurses of her era is that Linda Richards became popularized in the new profession as "America's First Trained Nurse."

Her autobiography, published as she retired in 1911, recounts among other things her student days at the New England Hospital for Women and Children (precursor to Dimock Community Health Center) in Roxbury, Massachusetts. Being the first of her small class of five students to finish the yearlong program, Richards graduated in 1873 at a moment when nurses training schools were being established in New York, Connecticut and Boston, The thirty-two year old trained nurse found herself in demand. She declined an offer to lead the Boston Training School for practice under Sr. Helen at Bellevue. A year later she returned to Boston and the leadership at the Boston Training School at the Massachusetts General Hospital.

Richards may have been by nature a restless person or merely delighted that her position of prominence provided so many opportunities for travel. A more likely explanation is the new nurses training schools wanted her services and students wanted to learn nursing in the nurses training schools she headed. Two such students were Sophia Palmer (1853-1920) and Mary E. P. Davis (1840-1924) who studied with Richards in the class of 1879 at the Boston Training

School. Palmer was a New England woman. Her lineage in the United States went back to 1621 when a year after the arrival of the Mayflower William Palmer arrived in Cape Cod from London. By the sixth generation the Palmers were settled in Boston and held degrees from Ivy League colleges. Their sons, Sophia Palmer's father and uncles, held medical and law degrees while the daughters of this family entered the professions through marriage,

Sophia Palmer broke with this tradition. Her typical Brahmin family was aghast when Sophia chose to enter the Boston Training School. So adamant were they against her choice they refused to visit her during her student days. Undeterred by family or by custom, Sophia Palmer earned her nursing diploma at the same time as did her Canadian-born classmate, Mary E. P. Davis. Davis was an immigrant to the United States. She traveled the same migratory route that so many other Canadians followed as they left St. Johns, New Brunswick for work in Boston. The daughter of a former captain in the British army, Davis had a mixed heritage from French, Scotch, Welsh and New York Knickerbocker predecessors. The two women graduated from Richards' program in 1879. Within a year following graduation each had left the Massachusetts General Hospital for private duty nursing. Few graduate nurses remained in hospital practice. With pupil nurses doing the work, there was little need for graduate nurses.

The two women would become formidable partners in professionalizing the field they had chosen. Even while they were students they realized that the nurses training school was being co-opted by the hospital for the free nursing services of its students. Part of the problem was that the nurses training school had been grafted onto the hospital's housemaid services. In fact, ward maids were dismissed and the student nurses given their tasks. The salary of the maids then became the stipend of the nursing student. With so many student nurses, the hospital had little use for graduate nurses. Furthermore, the popularity of nursing attracted women to the nurses training schools which ensured an unending supply of this cheap labor. Before long, the nurses training school became a necessary part of the hospital economy. This process was already established as early as Palmer's and Davis' student days. It would only worsen as the years went by.

Palmer and Davis would shed their bright light on the problem and give it their unflagging energy. Joining with others they tackled the problem. First they gathered together the graduate nurses dispersed throughout the Commonwealth caring for patients in private homes. They gave these nurses an alumnae association, pulling them together into an energetic unity while at the same time providing them with a center for socialization. They linked these Massachusetts' alumnae associations with others throughout the United States. Then they helped to organize national societies, namely, the American Society of Superintendents of Training Schools for Nurses (1893) and the Associated Alumnae of the United States and Canada (1896). At the 1911 conventions in Boston, those organizations were renamed, respectively, the National

League for Nursing Education and the American Nurses Association. The next year public health nurses would organize the National Organization of Public Health Nurses.

Once the nurses were gathered into alumnae associations and national associations, Palmer and Davis gave them a place to read what was happening in the profession. October 1900 arrived and with it the first issue of the American Journal of Nursing (AJN), Sophia Palmer served as its editor and Mary E. P. Davis as its business manager. Among the editorial department heads (, was Linda Richards who wrote on - training schools and hospitals, The AJN was also a forum for graduate nurses. They exchanged ideas about caring for patients or, as they would say, their "cases." The most remarkable part of all this activity was that within a short period of time, Richards, Palmer, Davis and their colleagues had gathered dispersed nurses together into a coherent group, organized them into alumnae associations, created national organizations and published a professional journal that nurses owned and operated.

Seemingly, Palmer and Davis knew that the new profession would be advanced if it had a human face. So it was that the two classmates promoted their former teacher as the icon of the new profession. Linda Richards was installed as the first president of the American Society of Superintendents of Training Schools for Nurses and in doing this, they kept Boston as the center of the new profession. Isabel Hampton Robb who became the first president of the Alumnae Association of the United States and Canada ensured that Johns Hopkins in Baltimore, especially after its influx of Rockefeller money following Flexner's analysis of medical education, would be another center of nursing power. Hampton and her associate M. Adelaide Nutting found Palmer and Davis to be worthy adversaries. The new profession could only flourish with so much energy invested in its development.

When nursing sought to have a similar study of nursing education as had been done on medical education, Nutting, representing the National League for Nursing Education's interests was refused by the Carnegie and the Rockefeller Foundations. Gertrude Peabody who lived with her professor father on the edge of Harvard and who was one of the women philanthropists with the Boston Instructive Nurses Association (precursor of the Boston Visiting Nurses Association) wrote to John D. Rockefeller. This was not the first time she had been in contact with the head of the Rockefeller family. She and her family and Rockefeller and his family vacationed together each year in Maine. As can be expected, the Rockefeller Foundation respected this friendship and responded favorably to nursing's request for a study of its education.

The findings of the study, the Goldmark Report (1923) was institutionalized at Yale establishing the Yale School of Nursing at the fiftieth anniversary of the trained nurse, Harvard had declined the Rockefeller Foundation's desire to have the school founded in Cambridge. This milestone in the history of nursing education occurred after Palmer had died of a cerebral hemorrhage in 1920, a year before the eighty-four year old Davis died in 1924 and while Richards was in declining health. That milestone in nursing education was still to be reached when Palmer and Davis were trying to free nursing education from the grip of the hospital economy. In 1903 with Palmer editorializing in the AJN, Davis heading the committee in Boston and Richards speaking at meetings, they proposed a preliminary course in nursing taught at Simmons College. A wealthy clothing manufacturer, John Simmons, had established the College for the "utilitarian education for girls." This seemed to fit with nursing's practical nature. As important, Simmons College was in the Fenway near hospitals —the Beth Israel, Childrens and Peter Bent Brigham Hospitals—now referred to as the Longwood Medical Area. That effort came to naught. Years later nursing was established at Simmons College in its School of Public Heath Nursing.

During the same time that Mary E. P. Davis in Boston and Sophia Palmer in New York promoted the cause of nursing education, they also sought the help of state legislatures throughout the country to enact laws to protect the trained nurse's earning power and the public she/he served. Human nature being what it is, there was bound to be a ready example of what they opposed. They found a dramatic example in Jenny Toppham. She had been dismissed from the Boston Training School at the Massachusetts General Hospital but presented herself as a trained nurse to unsuspecting families in Boston and Cambridge. She cared for a student in his Harvard rooms who was sick with an acute infection. He recovered from her ministrations. Another family of four who had seemed to be recovering from an illness was not so fortunate. They died after Jenny Toppham poisoned them with morphine. At her trial Jenny Toppham boasted of killing a hundred! Jenny Toppham was found non-guilty by reason of insanity and confined to the Taunton State Hospital for the rest of her life. Interestingly, Linda Richards served as superintendent during some of that confinement.

Jenny Toppham became the epitome of what Palmer and Davis were trying to prevent and became the subject of Palmer's editorials during the battle for the registration of trained nurses. Their efforts in Massachusetts were thwarted by medical men who resisted nurses being a separate force, Indeed as Lavinia Dock, nursing's premier historian recounted, nowhere in the United States was nursing registration as vehemently opposed as it had been in Massachusetts, Much of that opposition took place behind closed doors of parlors as well as offices, for many of Boston's medical elite were also Boston's social elite. Some doctors supported the effort towards registration but they were in the minority. Not least of what was opposed was the nurses desire for an all nurse board of registration. Clearly, the opposition resented nurses assertion of autonomy. Given the patriarchalism of the times, this is understandable. Men were the heads of their families and doctors were the heads of hospitals. It was only 1903 and to give still another idea of the times, women were not allowed to vote until 1920. Ironically by that time nurses had cared for the sick and wounded during World War I (1914-1917), as they had in the Spanish-American War (1898), but they had no say in how their country was governed.

The bill: "An Act to Regulate the Practice of Professional Nursing of the Sick" did not even make it to the Public Health Committee. A new bill was written and Davis continued her activities in mustering the support of Massachusetts nurses, She explained that the law would "give nurses a legal status, and set a standard of excellence [for] nursing education [and] prevent the untrained from palming themselves upon the public as duly qualified nurses." The bill moved off the legislator's desk into committee but still did not succeed in being debated. Seven long years passed before the nurses gained a registration law, and then, the final bill that became law was a compromise. Nurses conceded the all nurse Board of Registration in Nursing. The doctor appointed to chair the Board graciously resigned the position in favor of a nurse. His grace notwithstanding, his resignation was from a position of power over nurses. What is more, medicine and hospital administrators continued to exert their power over the young profession.

Richards, Palmer and Davis began their quest for nursing registration as the season of darkness and death fell over Massachusetts one hundred and two years ago. As the days shortened they organized nurses in the Boston Nurses' Club on Boylston Street and the Alumnae Association of Massachusetts' hospitals nurses training schools. As the Winter Solstice arrived, Palmer in the American Journal of Nursing and Davis in Massachusetts kept nurses focused on registration. They were encouraged by one friendly doctor who told them, "to keep at it!" They in turn kept up the spirits of nurses. At the same time they became more savvy about the legislative process and were prompted by proponents of their bill. Davis had the hard task of keeping nurses engaged in the process. It was a difficult task, one made more difficult because the process stretched out from 1903 until 1910.

As can be imagined many of those days were dark and dreary. Richards, Palmer and Davis served as hope as the Winter Solstice does, looking for the light that would end the darkness. They had begun their drive for registration as 1902 headed into the season of darkness and death. They kept hope alive as that season stretched out over eight years. Finally, in 1910 the light shone brightly. The trained nurse was now a registered nurse, an RN. The public who hired registered nurses could expect that the light of their training and the warmth of their compassion would be focused on them as they dealt with illnesses.

It is only fitting and proper that members of MARN living one hundred years later use this season of death and darkness to contemplate what their predecessors have dome, and renew their connectedness with their forebears. Not least of what MARN members should do is remember Linda Richards, Sophia Palmer and Mary E. P. Davis each time they write RN after their names. Such remembrance makes the bond between the past and the present strong and at the same time serves nursing's future. Most assuredly, as they enjoy their membership in the Massachusetts Association of Registered Nurses, they ought to consider their continuity with nurses of a hundred years ago.

Finally, monuments to Richards, Palmer and Davis abound. Each nurse was inducted into the American Nurses Association's Hall of Fame. Richards is remembered in the Linda Richards Building at Dimock Community Health Center (formerly the New England Hospital for Women and Children) which First Lady Hillary Clinton helped to rededicate, and her ashes are enurned at the Forest Hills Cemetery in Jamaica Plain. The Sophia Palmer Library at the American Journal of Nursing Company honors the Journal's first editor. And, the Palmer Davis Library in Ruth Sleeper Hall honors the indomitable classmates who did so much to professionalize nursing. Their most enduring and significant contribution to nurses remains the RN.

Remembering these stalwart founders of Massachusetts nursing provides the opportunity to also remember three colleagues who died this year: Margaret Berrio, Marcella N. Malay and Valerie L. Wright.

A SPOTLIGHT ON MASSACHUSETTS NURSING'S HISTORY

(originally published September 2009)

In the fall of 1983, the Massachusetts Nurses Association (then the constituent organization of the American Nurses Association) established the *Lucy Lincoln Drown Nursing History Society* in response to members' interest in Massachusetts nursing's history. This *Society* made visible the historical perspective that is necessary in all professional action. Every member of the organization became a member of the *Society*. Many dedicated nurses, students, and nursing faculty, were profligate in volunteering their services and creativity. Alice Friedman, Joellen Hawkins, Loretta Higgins, Patricia Tyra and Ursula Van Ryzin were among others who devoted their best efforts to the *Society's* Executive Committee. Shirley Duggan and Sarah Moroney served nursing history and the *Society* with unstinting commitment.

All this energy resulted in nurses from Massachusetts' history being inducted into the ANA Hall of Fame; the National Women's Hall of Fame in Seneca Falls, New York and Women in Military Service to America in Washington, D. C. At the President's Reception in 1983, five *Society* members personified important nurses from Massachusetts: Mary Hickey, a school nurse; Clara Barton of Red Cross fame; Sophia Palmer, the editor of the *American Journal of Nursing*; Rebecca Nurse, of the Salem Witch Trials; and, Linda Richards who earned nursing's first diploma. In 1984, when African-American nurses from across the Nation made their pilgrimage to Mary Eliza Mahoney's gravesite in Everett, Massachusetts, the *Society* was with them.

The 75th anniversary of the Board of Registration provided the occasion for a panel presentation at the state nursing organization's 1985 convention. Among the panelists was a new graduate who had just taken the licensure exam. On February 26, 1993 forty-seven

Massachusetts nurses portraying the long line of their predecessors paraded into Faneuil Hall on its 90th anniversary. Three hundred years of nursing history in Massachusetts from Native American Indian and an Indian Medicine Woman to futuristic space age nurses conveyed the fact that Massachusetts nursing's history had deep roots. A vignette followed the parade. With primary sources as their script, nurses reenacted the debate on the floor of the Cradle of Liberty that resulted in the founding of the Massachusetts State Nurses Association in 1903.

In 1994, the *Society* presented Massachusetts' long history of nursing education at the National League for Nursing when it convened in Boston. The Executive Committee authored "Nursing in Massachusetts in the Roaring Twenties" that the *Historical Journal of Massachusetts* published in 1995. That same year the *Society* attended groundbreaking ceremonies at Dimock Community Health Center (successor to the New England Hospital for Women and Children) where First Lady Hillary Rodham Clinton received the Mary Eliza Mahoney Award. At another ceremony there a few years later, Senator Edward M. Kennedy represented the Federal Government as the site was declared a National Landmark. In 1996 the Executive Committee presented "Ethics, Nursing and a Century of Caring," a broad sweep of nursing's service to humanity from Ancient Athens to the present, at ANA's Centennial convention in Washington, D.C. When the American Public Health Association convened in Boston, the *Society* took its members on a walking tour of their historical sites in Boston's South End and Roxbury. In 1999 the *Society* led members of the American Association for the History of Nursing "In the Footsteps of the Pioneers." They stopped at the New England Hospital for Women and Children and the Forest Hills Cemetery where Dr. Marie Zakrzewska, Dr. Susan Dimock and Sophia Palmer are buried and Linda Richards' ashes are inurned.

Through the years, the *Society* responded to nursing departments for Nurse Day celebrations; served as a resource; created *A Guideline for Preserving Historical Documents*; fielded questions about Massachusetts nursing's past; corresponded with other historical organizations; and accepted their invitations to present with them. When the Schlesinger Library on the History of Women at Radcliffe College asked if psychiatric nursing pioneer, Hildegard E. Peplau, was noteworthy enough to collect, the Society said yes and months later attended the ceremony as Peplau donated her papers. For several years, the *Society* co-sponsored the Nursing Archives Associates annual meeting at the request of Julia Sullivan, then the President of the Nursing Archives Associates. The enthusiasm of nurse members from every level of the Organization made these activities and many more possible.

The *Lucy Lincoln Drown Nursing History Society* ended on March 24, 2001 when MNA separated from ANA. The *Society*'s papers, minutes, annual reports, correspondence, publications and chronology are in the History of Nursing Archives at Boston University. These documents are preserved at the Archives as are those of MARN's first 98 years as ANA-affiliated MNA. Mary Ellen Doona's personal file is with her papers in the Mary L. Pekarski Nursing Archives in the Burns Library at Boston College.

The Massachusetts Association for Registered Nurses (incorporated on March 23, 2001), keeps Massachusetts nursing's frayed thread to its past from breaking. *Clio's Corner* is a regular feature in each edition of the *MAssachusetts Report on Nursing*, keeping Massachusetts nursing's history visible. The MARN Living Legend Award, presented annually at their annual convention brings that history back into the spotlight. This award is for all those nurses who day after day make history as they care for others. That history belongs in this spotlight. MARN members praise the Nursing Living Legend award and the newsletter's *Clio's Corner* in their letters, emails and conversations. Nurses sense that without their history they are disinherited, perhaps even paupers. For historical perspective is nursing's vitalizing force. Stepping into the future requires a backward glance over one's shoulders-whether those shoulders belong to individual nurses or to the professional organization to which they belong.

I hope that when MARN does create its nursing history society, it will be named the *Mary Ann Garrigan Nursing History Society*. Garrigan knew nursing's history. Because of her historical perspective, she was able to step out of the present and into the future. She established the History of Nursing Archives so that others might relinquish the rhetoric of nursing's myths and seek nursing's real story. She did not follow the path blazed by others. She led the way. Knowing nursing's history made that possible.

On April 3, 2009 Phyllis Moore presented Mary Ellen Doona to the Massachusetts Association of Registered Nurses's members and president for its Living Legend Award. Doona accepted the Award from President Toni Abraham at MARN's Awards Dinner held in the Hilton Hotel in Dedham, Massachusetts.

SOPHIA PALMER, MARY E. P. DAVIS AND THE *AMERICAN JOURNAL OF NURSING*

(originally published December 2006)

Sophia French Palmer (26 May 1853-27 April 1920) and Mary E. P. Davis (ca December 1840-9 June 1924) met on the first day of May 1876 when they began as pupils at the Boston Training School (BTS, precursor of the Massachusetts General Hospital School of Nursing). Palmer was an eighth generation American and the fifth of seven daughters and three sons born to Dr. Simeon and Maria Spencer Palmer of Milton, Massachusetts (Palmer, R. 1976). Davis, her classmate, came from a "long line of New England ancestors" but was an immigrant from New Brunswick, Canada, the daughter of Captain John and Charlotte MacFarland Davis (Editor, 1901, 74; Death certificate).

Palmer and Davis attended lectures once a week if they could be spared from the work of the hospital. They wrote up these lectures and answered quizzes which one of the ladies of the Board of Directors corrected. The Directors' cooks taught the pupils "how to make good stuff to eat" remembered Davis, "but not dietetics." Once a week the superintendent of nurses lectured on nursing subjects and doctors oversaw pupils in their nursing practice. This scant nursing theory and practice was submerged in a plethora of other duties. Davis remembered:

> We did the sweeping in all the wards and ward corridors, but not in the main corridors. We washed the bedsteads and bedside tables. If the head nurse was very particular about the looks of her ward, we had to mop it every day except the day it was scrubbed by the cleaners. We did the dusting, we carried the clothes to the laundry, and the poultice cloths and used bandages to the rinse house. After they

were returned to us, washed and dried, we went to the rinse house and ironed them. We washed dishes twice a day, for we had but one maid for three wards. If the ice gave out after the morning supply, we had to go to the basement of the main building and bring more. We realized early in our training that many things we had to do had little relation to nursing. We took the training as a fundamental, not as an incidental occupation, and though the incidentals were many and grievous, we saw the opportunity to get what we were after. Along with it was developed the mental attitude that has placed nursing in the rank of a profession (Parsons, 1922, 44-45).

Their post-graduate career at the Massachusetts General Hospital was short-lived. There were no regrets when Palmer resigned after two months because, it was recorded, her "manner [was] so overbearing." After four more months, Davis also resigned (BTS Collection). Their success elsewhere in private nursing, as superintendents of training schools and in organizational work over the next twenty years speaks to a vision of nursing larger than that at the MGH in 1878.

The BTS diplomas that they had received in 15 July 1878 were the first to appear on parchment. The two graduates would join with other likeminded women to create institutions to make other nursing diplomas worthy of the parchment on which they were written. Palmer and Davis participated in creating the American Society of Superintendents of Training Schools for Nurses (ASSTSN, precursor to the National League for Nursing) in 1893 and in 1896 the Nurses Associated Alumnae of the United States and Canada (NAA, precursor to the American Nurses Association). Their outstanding monument, however, is the *American Journal of Nursing* established in 1900 on which Palmer served as editor and Davis as business manager.

Palmer and Davis valued the hospital as the place to learn and practice nursing. They recognized that nursing education would need the financial support of hospitals for some time to come. Still, they kept their eyes on the horizon when hospitals would no longer use pupil nurses as "the cheapest form of service to their patients" (Palmer, 1900, 98) and "to increase the revenue of the hospital" (Davis, 1896b, 9-10).

At the twentieth anniversary of the trained nurse in 1893, the time had come to go public on the need for a standard of nurses training. Administrators at Johns Hopkins provided the superintendents with a forum at the International Congress of Charities, Correction and Philanthropy at the Worlds Fair in Chicago. The Columbian Exposition's White City blazed with electric lights announcing the end of steam and the beginning of electricity as the nation's energy source. How much of the Fair the nurses took in has not been recorded but to be sure they could not have missed seeing the first-ever Ferris wheel that dominated the fair grounds.

Among the papers the superintendents presented in the Hall of Columbus that June was one by Edith Draper (1893, 645). She argued that professional advancement depended on unity. She also suggested a "medium of a publication" that might keep nurses current with the professional discourse happening at meetings. Joined together that week into the AASTSN, the 18 superintendents deferred Draper's suggestion of a journal until graduate nurses could be organized, first into alumnae associations, and then, into the NAA. Organization was "the power of the age," wrote Palmer adding, "without it, nothing great is accomplished" (1895, 55). Davis repeated the theme as second president of the ASSTSN, telling the superintendents convened in Philadelphia that they would need "unity of purpose and united action" to deal with the profession's "difficult and knotty problems" (1896a).

At the NAA's first convention in New York, M. Adelaide Nutting's motion that a committee be created to "arrange about the establishment of our own magazine" was seconded and easily carried (NAA, 1897 [ledger]). Enthusiastic proposals followed but the methods suggested did not seem practical (Riddle, 1920, 6). Nor did Nutting's associate, NAA president, Isabel Hampton Robb, offer a clear vision. The "development of publications and literature" would be of great value to the profession, said Robb, but suggested only more thought and discussion until a consensus of opinions yielded a plan (1898, 310). As a result, the proposal for a journal "hung fire" for almost three years (Roberts, 1959, 41).

Perhaps the ending of the century provided the necessary impetus for action. In 1899 Robb created the Committee of Ways and Means of Producing a Magazine and urged Davis to chair the committee. Then, says Roberts, "Things began to happen" (1959, 42). Committee members were: Harriet Fulmer, a public health nurse from Chicago; M. Adelaide Nutting of Hopkins; Sophia Palmer of Rochester, New York; and, M. W. Stevenson of MGH. Robb was added the next year (Riddle, 1920, 6). As Davis recounted for the 1900 convention, once she accepted the Chair she traveled from Boston to Philadelphia to meet with Robb, to have the work turned "formally over to her, the president [Robb] heretofore having assumed the duties" (Davis, 1900, 81).

Together during Christmas week 1899 Davis and Robb interviewed the publisher for estimates. Davis was "very much impressed" with Lippincott though Robb confessed to Nutting she did not share Davis' "great confidence" (Robb to Nutting, January 1900). In fact Robb, a published author, had no confidence at all in publishers and feared Lippincott would make a profit at nurses' expense. As the new year and the new century began, the Committee met at the Post-Graduate Club with Robb, Davis and Palmer discussing ways that a journal might be financed. The idea of a stock company that had surfaced in the earlier committee was addressed again. At this meeting Palmer agreed to be editor.

It seems that Palmer got under Robb's skin: "Between you and me," Robb confided to Nutting, "I think she (Palmer) has almost too fine an opinion of herself. Perhaps I should not say this but [in] some ways she always makes me feel so" (Robb to Nutting, 1900). It was more than a matter of Palmer's forthrightness contrasting with Robb's gentility. Palmer's co-worker when she edited the *Editorially Speaking* department of the *Trained Nurse and Hospital Review* said that Palmer had a "very intense nature and like all those who are born crusaders had little patience with the slower method of persuasion. [There was] a great restlessness in her manner. She was like a spirited race horse held by the reins of tradition" (Rose, 1940, 112). Palmer's "crusading" differed profoundly from Robb's three-year-long waiting for a "consensus of opinions."

In any event "things began to happen" once the reins were in Palmer and Davis' hands. With "great activity and business sagacity," remembered Mary Riddle (1856-1936) the *Journal's* first historian, on 9 May 1900 only five months after being appointed, Davis presented the Committee's report. The report captures Davis' leadership, intelligence and judgment that her contemporaries so celebrated. From numerous ways, the Committee selected four and then narrowed these to one, and decided to put a journal in the hands of an established publisher (Lippincott). The means were: subscriptions, advertisements, and stocks. The Committee needed assurance that nurses would subscribe, so it distributed 5000 circulars alerting nurses to the proposed journal, received 550 cash subscriptions at $2.00 a piece ($1100) and promises of others, though not the 1500 that Robb sought in January. The publisher assured the Committee that it might count on $1000 in ad revenue each year.

The Committee formed a joint stock company offering stock at $100 per share and sold 24 shares ($2400). Davis personally wrote 300 letters and answered questions. Davis said that no nurse feared she would lose her $100 and that the investors might even gain dividends if the account were properly managed. Robb protested unsuccessfully saying that any dividends should go directly to the NAA (Robb to Nutting, 1900). The fact was, the *Journal* was financed by nurses and not the NAA. Indeed, Palmer would give the

Journal office space in her home at no rental or overhead costs to the NAA for thirteen years. In 1906 Robb and Nutting gifted their first dividend of four dollars to the NAA hoping their example would prompt others to do the same. Robb's expectation that nurses would quickly buy back the stock was optimistic but not realistic. Neither nurses not the NAA were in a financial position in 1906 to do so nor would they be until 1913. Nurses felt they owned the *Journal* by virtue of their support and efforts for it but Robb was correct in saying that the NAA had no control over the *Journal* because it was the property of stockholders, even if those stockholders were fellow nurses. Without the *American Journal of Nursing* Company and Palmer and Davis's unpaid services nurses during the *Journal's* early years, however, it is unlikely that there would have been a journal from 1900 to 1913 (NAA *1897* [ledger], 207-225).

This discord about ownership was still to come when Davis praised the Committee members for their work in distributing circulars, encouraging nurses to buy stock, spurring alumnae associations and schools to "take hold of the movement." She lauded Miss Stevenson, especially, for writing to all the hospitals in Canada. Not least of her praise was that for the members' support that greatly encouraged and cheered her on when she was inclined to be discouraged and the "frail craft" swamped. Continuing her maritime metaphor which called to mind her earlier life in sea port New Brunswick, Davis spoke of Lippincott as the company which would ensure the excellence they wanted and would prevent "shipwreck." The only negative remark Davis passed during her report was aimed at the Committee's receiving $41 for its work. Considering the stationery, postage and printing costs, "not by the most penurious economy," she said, "could the expenditure be kept within that limit" (Davis, 1900, 80-82).

Stating several times that the Committee had exceeded its powers, Davis suggested that it be given the "power to act." The motion: "In view of [the] fact that continued business management will be needed in [the] conduct of the magazine for some time to come, I move that the present committee be reappointed as a standing committee with power to act until such time as their services may be safely dispensed with" was quickly seconded and passed unanimously. Then followed a vote of thanks to Miss Davis and her Committee for their "untiring zeal in this work" (NAA, *1897* [ledger]). During the discussion, Palmer answered superintendents who wondered how to purchase stock. She said the amount had been raised at Rochester in a very few minutes. "The alumnae associations only need to have the matter brought before them," she said, "to have the same enthusiastic belief in the success of the magazine that the committee feels" (Davis, 1900, 82). "Enthusiasm mounted high," remembered Katharine DeWitt fifty years later, "one after another [nurses] rose to pledge money for the purchase of stock in the *Journal* yet to be" (1950, 590).

Nurses exclaimed that "there was every evidence that the *Journal* [would be] a great success" (Davis, 1900, 82). Perhaps Mrs. Cadwalader Jones had softened the nurses in her welcoming address the day before the Committee's report. The New York socialite said the great object of the NAA should be to "draw all members together" and added that every profession or trade had a well-edited journal. She advised, "There should be a journal devoted to the interests of the alumnae throughout the country and it should be taken by every member, and so well supported that it may be really useful" (1900, 73).

Davis became president of the Board of Directors and when the *American Journal of Nursing* Company was incorporated in 1902 she and Palmer were signatories along with Lavinia Dock, Anna Maxwell and Pauline Dolliver. Only Dock had no MGH ties. Palmer set up editorial offices in her rooms at the Rochester General Hospital and with the contributions from associate editors got out the first issue of the *American Journal of Nursing*, October 1900, only five months after the convention. Her first editorial alerted the membership that the aim of the editor and her associate editors was to "present month by month the most useful facts, the most progressive thoughts, and the latest news that the profession has to offer in the most attractive form that can be secured." Palmer called upon the NAA's now almost 4000 members "from every sector of the country-north and south, east and west" to aid the editor so that "every kind of information of value to nurses" would appear on the *Journal's* pages. Not only would the *Journal* then be informative, it would also be educational (Editor, 1900, 64).

The major article of the inaugural issue was Dock's "What We May Expect from the Law." Palmer's agenda was to educate nurses about their rights as citizens and to get laws passed that would identify the trained nurse from "imposters and incompetents" (Palmer, 1900, 98). Ironically, a former pupil of the BTS would provide the telling example. Jane Toppan had been discharged from the BTS in 1891 "for cause." Nonetheless, for the next ten years doctors hired her for cases around Boston and Cambridge. Investigation into the deaths of four members of one family exposed and ended Toppan's nefarious career (Poison, 1901).

The success of the *Journal* was such by 1902 that Palmer was able to report: "Certainly we have a right to say that the *Journal* is the official nursing journal of this country" (NAA, *1897*, ledger], 11). The *Journal* became "a medium of communication between nurses, a history of nursing progress, [and] a guide and leader in nursing thought" (Riddle, 1920, 12). A quarter of a century had passed since Palmer and Davis had met as pupils. Thanks to Davis' "business sagacity" and Palmer's literary editing, the *Journal* survived and prospered.

MISS SOPHIA F. PALMER
Editor-in-Chief of THE AMERICAN JOURNAL OF NURSING

Miss Sophia F. Palmer. Editor in Chief
of the *American Journal of Nursing*
(reprinted with permission of the *AJN*)

Miss Mary. E. P. Davis, Chairman, Committee
on Periodicals of the Associated Alumnae
of Trained Nurses of the United States
(reprinted with permission of the *AJN*)

SOURCES CITED

Boston Training School Papers, Center for the History of Medicine, Countway Library, Boston, MA.

Burgess, May Ayres. 1928. *Nurses, Patients and Pocketbooks*, New York: Grading Committee.

Davis, Mary E. P. 1896a. "The Address of the President," *Third Annual Report of the American Society of Superintendents of Training Schools for Nurses*, 3-7.

---. 1896b. "Post Graduate Course," *Trained Nurse and Hospital Review* (8): 9-10.

---. 1900a. "Report: The Committee on Ways and Means of Publishing a Magazine." Third Annual Convention of the Associated Alumnae of Trained Nurses, *American Journal of Nursing* (1): 80-82.

---. 1900b. Letter. Deaths. Dr. Simeon Palmer, *Boston Evening Transcript*, 12 May 1890.

DeWitt, Katharine. 1950. "The *Journal's* First Fifty Years," *American Journal of Nursing* (50): 590-591.

Editor. [Palmer, Sophia] 1900. "The Editor," *American Journal of Nursing* (1): 64-66.

---. 1901. "Miss Mary E. P. Davis," *American Journal of Nursing* (2): 74.

---. 1918. "Alumnae Subscriptions," *American Journal of Nursing* (18): 215.

Jones, Cadawalder Mrs. 1900. "Address of Welcome to the Associated Alumnae," *American Journal of Nursing* (1): 71-74.

Munson, Helen W. 1934. *The Story of the National League of Nursing Education*. Philadelphia, W. B. Saunders, Publishers.

Nursing Associated Alumnae 1897. American Nurses Association Collection, Box 33, History of Nursing Archives, Boston University.

Palmer, Richard & Eunice (Eds.). 1973. *Palmer Families of Plymouth and Duxbury*, Vol III, Somersworth, New Hampshire: New Hampshire Publishing.

Palmer, Sophia F. 1900. "State Examination for Nurses: Address to the State Federation of Women's Clubs," *Trained Nurse and Hospital Review* (12): 98-99.

---. 1895. *"Training School Alumnae Associations,"* Annual Report of the American Society of Superintendents of Training Schools for Nurses, 55.

Parsons, Sara E. 1922. *History of the Massachusetts General Hospital School of Nursing*. Boston, Whitcomb & Barrows.

"Poison in the stomach," *The Boston Globe*, (20 October 1901): 1-5.

Records of the Women's Board of St. Luke's Hospital of New Bedford, 1884-1887.

Riddle, Mary. 1920. "Twenty Years of the *Journal*," *American Journal of Nursing* (21): 6-12.

Robb, Isabel Hampton. (1898) 1976. "The Spirit of the Associated Alumnae." In Lyndia Flanagan (Ed.) *One Strong Voice*, 301-311. Kansas City: American Nurses Association.

Robb, Isabel Hampton. (1899) 1976. "Early Lesson." In Lyndia Flanagan (Ed.) *One Strong Voice*, 311-331, Kansas City: American Nurses Association.

Robb, Isabel Hampton to M. Adelaide Nutting. January 1900, *M. Adelaide Nutting Collection*.

Roberts, Mary M. 1959. *American Nursing: History and Interpretation*. New York: Macmillan Company.

Rose, Annette Sumner. 1940. "Sophia Palmer." In Pennock, Meta Rutter (Ed.) *Makers of Nursing History: Portraits and Pen Sketches of Prominent Women*. New York: Lakeside Publishing Company.

Teele, A. K. Ed. 1887. *History of Milton Massachusetts*: 1640-1887. Boston: Press of Rockwell & Churchill.

NURSING AT THE 1903 SOLSTICE

(originally published December 2013)

The ancient Celts divided their year into two halves: the bright half and the dark half. On the eve of the dark half, October thirty-first, the boundary between the world of the dead and the world of the living dissolved, allowing the dead to mingle with the living. For the Celts, the turning of the year was a time of great energy. Although very much diluted over the many centuries that have since passed, vestiges of the Celtic New Year Samhain (saween) survive. Trick or treaters wander dark neighborhoods at Halloween, and the next day the Church marks All Saints Day. Each in its own way pays tribute to the continuing presence of people from the past.

As full of energy as these New Year festivities were, they were reminders as well of the life threatening darkness that was spreading over the earth. At mid-December just as the earth was deepest in darkness and the sun the furthest away, the sun "stood" still at the southernmost point of its rising and setting. Then the year turned from darkness towards the light and days would begin to lengthen and nights to shorten. Ancients gathered at Stonehenge in England and at New Grange in Ireland where they marked the moment of solstice. On this December twenty-first, their twenty-first century successors will do the same.

On the sixteenth of December only six days before the 1903 solstice, nurses gathered in Massachusetts to deal with the shadows that had descended on their young profession. To their credit the nursing leaders knew that hospitals provided the best experiences for learning nursing. Annual reports with photographs of pupil nurses dressed in their starched uniforms suggested their value to the hospital. Shadows soon darkened this bright picture. As hospitals continued to change into treatment facilities and their wards into the site of medical education, pupil nurses were pressed into being an ever-renewing supply of cheap labor. Their education and training became secondary to the needs of hospitals.

That dark time energized nurses. By the start of the twentieth century nurses had created alumnae associations, professional organizations (the precursors of the Massachusetts Association of Registered Nurses, the American Nurses Association and the National League for Nursing) and published a professional journal (the *American Journal of Nursing*). All the same, this professional assertiveness failed to loosen the grip hospitals held on nursing Not to be defeated, nurses turned to the law and submitted their bill to the Massachusetts Legislature: *House Bill #564 An Act to Regulate the Practice of Professional Nursing of the Sick*.

Staffing the Executive Committee were: Annie McDowell of the Newton Hospital School of Nursing, Clara D. Noyes of St Luke's Hospital School of Nursing in New Bedford, Rachel A. Metcalf of the Worcester City Hospital School of Nursing, Elizabeth Tisdale of the Massachusetts Homeopathic Hospital School of Nursing (precursor to Massachusetts Memorial Hospital School of Nursing), and Josephine S. Hinkley of the Salem Hospital School of Nursing. Overseeing the entire operation was the determined Mary E. P. Davis, the Chair of the Legislative Committee of the Massachusetts State Nurses Association (MSNA), who also had much to do with the professionalizing strategy mentioned above.

Essentially the *Bill* had a dual focus: protect the public from people who passed themselves off as trained nurses, and protect the education of nurses. The same forces that had undermined nursing's autonomy impeded the success of legislation for seven years. During those years nurses in many other states were already signing Registered Nurse after their names. To give the matter some context, leadership was a male prerogative as the twentieth century began. Whether in the home or in the hospital autonomous women were rare if they existed at all.

Many men in medicine and men in nursing openly supported nursing's legislative strategy. Those opposing the *Bill* met behind the closed doors of Beacon Hill parlors as the medical elite in Boston was also its social elite. Some men in nursing joined these men in medicine in their opposition to the bill. Most were graduates of specialty hospitals that treated a specific population of patients, such as those in psychiatric hospitals and tuberculosis sanitaria. Not having graduated from a general hospital's nursing program, these men failed to meet MSNA's criteria that were serving as a gatekeeper to the profession prior to legislation. Men in nursing who did meet MSNA's criteria were among the first registered nurses when the *Bill* passed into law in 1910.

Nursing's autonomy remained a goal still to be achieved as the new Board of Registration in Nursing comes under the Board of Registration in Medicine. Nursing endured that dark time but day after day and year after year they sought a brighter future for the profession. That nursing students are able to concentrate on their nursing studies as the 2013 solstice nears is due to the action that their predecessors initiated one hundred and ten years ago at another winter solstice. The light of knowledge comes more from computer screens than it does from lamps these days, but insight-by-insight the wish that brought students into nursing solidifies into professional commitment. Even as they are gaining these insights nursing students become a solstice for their patients standing with them at the boundary between health and illness.

And when these nursing students complete their studies, they will find themselves at another boundary, the one that exists between being a graduate and being a registered nurse. That they will be able to take the licensure exam speaks to the success of Davis, McDowell, Noyes, Metcalf, Tisdale and Hinckley in 1903, who confronted the forces that would darken the young profession's bright promise. Thanks to these and other nurses from the past, nursing in 2013 is an autonomous profession. Its brightness emanates from nursing students and registered nurses to the benefit of the people for whom they care.

1910: THE BOARD OF REGISTRATION IN NURSING IS ESTABLISHED

(originally published March 2010)

2010 marks the centennial of nursing registration in Massachusetts. From April 29, 1910 when Governor Eben [eezer] Draper (1858-1914) signed *An Act to Provide for the Registration of Nurses* into law, through the decades to 2010, the Board of Registration in Nursing ensures that each nurse it registers meets the minimal standard of competency. As Mary E. P. Davis (c.1840-1924), who spearheaded the quest for registration told nurses at a public hearing in Dean Hall in Worcester, Massachusetts, the law would protect the public from "counterfeiters, fakers, incompetents and exploiters" (Report).

People had always nursed others. Trained nurses were not opposed to this. They were opposed to those who had not graduated from a training school in a general hospital passing themselves off as trained nurses. Nurses wanted to protect the public, to be sure, but they were not free of self-interest. They also wanted to protect their own earning power.

Economics had also influenced their days as pupils. Hospitals in 1873 pupil nurses also assumed the domestic chores of ward maids, washing bandages, patients' faces, and the dishes. They mopped floors and carried clothes to the laundry. These tasks were "incidental" and had little to do with nursing, said Mary E. P. Davis, but the training interspersed between these tasks was "fundamental." Despite having to do non-nursing tasks, the hospital, the Massachusetts General Hospital in Davis' case, provided the opportunity to "get what we were after" (Parsons, p. 45). Then, as now, nursing was learned at the patient's side.

The cheap labor of pupil nurses became increasingly necessary to the economic vitality of hospitals especially as they transformed into treatment centers. The bright caps and white aprons of young pupil nurses conveyed a message of care to those who were hesitant to turn to hospitals for treatment. As the Training School Movement caught on, more and more Massachusetts hospitals added glossy photographs of pupil nurses in their crisp uniforms to their annual reports.

By 1903, there were 47 training schools in Massachusetts, 28 of which had been established in the 1890s. Even the best of them were not good, for nursing's leaders were caught in a snare. Patient care was alluring as a training milieu but nursing had been grafted onto the hospital's domestic chores which endangered the nascent profession. As necessary as pupil nurses were for patient care (few graduate nurses practiced in the hospital setting), hospital administrators and doctors would not honor nursing as an autonomous discipline. Part of the problem was the patriarch-ism of the day. Men were the heads of hospitals as they were the heads of their families. Women were not expected to be independent. In fact, they were disenfranchised: as they would not get the vote until 1920. Most significant of all, hospitals were not educational institutions and pupil nurses were not tuition-paying scholars.

Medicine's control over the fledgling profession is understandable given the context of the times. What was regrettable then and remains so to this day is how medicine's control stymied the best efforts of nurses to make sure that pupil nurses were educated as well as used. As the nineteenth-century neared its end, nurses focused on professionalizing strategies. They gathered alumnae of training schools into alumnae associations, created what would become the American Nurses Association (1896) and the National League for Nursing (1893) and published the *American Journal of Nursing* (*AJN*) (1900). These feats of organization testified to nursing commitment to its discipline. Still, those achievements were insufficient to establish nursing's autonomy. Their next step was to enlist the aid of the public. What was not accorded by professional courtesy, nurses reasoned, might be obtained by the law. Ultimately, nurses wanted nursing education, and thus its future, to be in nursing's hands.

Fortuitously, a shocking instance had presented itself in Jennie Toppham who after being expelled from the Boston Training School (BTS), was hired by doctors in Boston and Cambridge to care for their patients. When four members of a family Miss Toppham was caring for died suddenly though they had been well along the road to recovery, alarms were set off. Miss Toppham was accused, tried and found guilty of poisoning her patients with morphine, then an unrestricted and easily obtained drug.

Headlines, such as "Poison in Stomach" splashed across the daily papers as the trial progressed (*Boston Globe*, 10/31/01, 1-5). The editor of the *AJN* hurled a shot at the doctors hired

Nurse Toppham while at the same time celebrating the BTS for holding to professional standards and protecting the public. The Toppham case and other far less scandalous cases pointed to the need for nursing control of the profession and public protection.

During the winter of 1902, nurses from the Massachusetts General Hospital, Boston City Hospital, the Newton Hospital training school alumnae associations and Boston's Nurses Club planned their next move. They wasted no time scheduling a mass meeting for February 26, 1903. Almost three hundred nurses and many of their medical allies crowded into Faneuil Hall, that mild winter day. The resolution was read:

> Resolved: We the trained nurses of Massachusetts declare in a mass meeting assembled, that it is expedient and advantageous to have a bill passed to regulate the practice of professional nursing in the State of Massachusetts.

Before the quest for legislation could proceed, they organized and established the Massachusetts State Nurses Association (precursor to the MNA and MARN). Mary E. P. Davis was nominated for president from the floor, but she declined the in order to chair the Legislative Committee. Mary M. Riddle (1856-1936), then of the Boston City Hospital and former superintendent of the Newton Hospital (1904), accepted the position despite her other obligations. She was then in her first term as president of the Alumnae Association (precursor of ANA) and on the Board of the *AJN*.

MSNA submitted its bill: *An Act to Regulate the Practice of Professional Nursing of the Sick* to the Massachusetts Legislature. Missing the point entirely, Governor John Lewis Bates (1859-1946) dismissed the bill as unnecessary. Medical men and women, he stated, could handle the matter. The Legislative Committee withdrew that bill vowing to present another the next year.

This time the loudest complaints came from men in nursing, who favored the registration bill but protested their exclusion because they had trained in specialty hospitals. Their schools, such as those in psychiatric hospitals, had prepared them to care for a specific population and not for nursing. They joined with doctors whose opposition spilled over onto the pages of the *Boston Evening Transcript*, the newspaper of Boston's elite, accusing nurses of being a trust and a trade union. *The Boston Globe*, the paper of ordinary Bostonians, concluded that the men opposed the bill because nurses were the "nominators and examiners" (1903, 3). The level of the opposition was in many ways a measure of the nurses' united power. The medical men, however, were more powerful, as time would show.

From 1903 to 1910, MSNA's Legislative Committee sent eight different bills to the Legislature. Concessions made by nurses led to the 1903 *An Act to Regulate the Practice of*

Professional Nursing of the Sick, which several iterations later became the 1910 *An Act to Provide for the Registration of Nurses.* Nurses wanted a board of five nurses who had graduated from at least a two-year training school and had eight years of nursing experience. The 1910 Act also called for a five-person board but it was of mixed composition. Governor Draper appointed Edwin Harvey, M.D., the Secretary of the Board of Registration in Medicine, to be a member ex-officio; Charles Drew, M.D., the superintendent of City Hospital in Worcester which had a training school (established 1883); and, three nurses, Mary M. Riddle, president of the MSNA and now president of the Superintendents Society (precursor to National League for Nursing), Lucia L. Jaquith, superintendent of the Memorial Hospital in Worcester, and Mary Elizabeth Shields, an 1887 graduate of the MGH Training School for Nurses, representing the Boston's Nurses Club.

The Board of Registration in Nursing was situated in the Board of Registration in Medicine's offices, Room 159 of the State House. Clearly, the narrowed focus of the Act, the two medical men on the Board, and its setting in medicine's territory indicated that though doctors were in the minority, they were still in charge. That the doctor suggested that Riddle should chair the Board supported that nursing's power was derivative, a gift from medicine, and not a professional right.

Piling indignity on indignity, Section 5 of the new law permitted untrained nurses who could provide testimony of having done nursing for the five years before 1910 to apply for licensure until 1911. That particular provision must have galled nurses who had tried so hard to erect a boundary between the trained and untrained. If they had to swallow this bitter pill, they made sure their heartburn would be visible on the record:

> -the untrained nurse with five years of so-called experience, [is] evidently being regarded by the law as an equal in professional ability and fitness for service in the sick room to the trained nurse, [who has had] three years of constant drill and experience in a general hospital. This clarification in the opinion of the Board, is very unjust, both to the trained nurse and to the public; nevertheless, such is the law given to the Board to administer.

Another provision must have provided solace. Section 10 clearly stated that anyone falsely claiming to be a registered nurse or who used "R.N" would be fined no more than one hundred dollars. In addition, anyone being registered under an assumed name would be fined no less than one hundred dollars nor more than five hundred dollars, and/or imprisoned (Registration, 1910, 6).

The law was not the expected panacea but it did give the trained nurse a legal status. On October 1, 1910, on the *AJN*'s tenth anniversary the law went into effect. Three days later, the new Board of Registration in Nursing met in the BORM offices. Of the 630 applicants they reviewed, 592 were approved for registration. Among those listed were: William Bunting, Charles Edward Ludwig (McLean Hospital Training School 1889), Frank Gilmore Magruder, John Harrison Strawser and Fred Lincoln Whitcomb, the Commonwealth's first male registered nurses.

When the certificates were distributed November 15, 1910, the first one went to Mary M. Riddle. In one year's time, November 10, 1911, she would administer the first State Board Examination to one hundred and two nurses. For a century now, the Board of Registration in Nursing has repeated the task each year determining which graduates will be distinguished as R.N.s.

REFERENCES

Davis, M.E.P. Report of the Periodical Committee, *MNA Collection*. History of Nursing Archives, Howard Gotlieb Archival Research Center, Boston University [hereafter MNA Collection].

Garvey, J. M. 1985. Diamond Jubilee of Nursing Registration in Massachusetts. In *Eyes on the Future*. Canton, MA: MNA.

Meeting of the Graduate Nurses, Faneuil Hall Boston, February 26, 1903. MNA Collection.

"Nurses Organize." *The Boston Globe* (27 February 1903).

Parsons, S. E. 1922. *History of the Massachusetts General Hospital School of Nursing*. Boston: Whitcomb & Barrows.

---. 1910. Registration of Nurses, Public Document, No. 91. Commonwealth of Mass.

Report of the Periodical Committee, MNA Collection.

NURSING'S BEGINNINGS AT THE BOSTON PSYCHOPATHIC HOSPITAL

(originally published March 2012)

The finishing touches were being placed on the new building at 74 Fenwood Road as 1912 began. The four-story red brick building was modest compared with the Great Quadrangle of five marble buildings that since 1906 had housed Harvard's Medical School nearby on Longwood Avenue. Millions in private philanthropy financed those buildings as millions more funded the Peter Bent Brigham Hospital with its graceful Grecian columns that would open in 1913.

The Commonwealth of Massachusetts ensured that psychiatry would be part of medicine's scientific revolution in what would become the Longwood Medical Area. Though to a lesser extent than other state hospitals across the country, the Commonwealth's hospitals had become "quasi-prison" establishments, where psychiatrists were unquestioned and un-criticized "far from the healthy conflicts and honest rivalries that keep [doctors] up to the mark" (Mitchell). The Commonwealth's response was the Boston Psychopathic Hospital (BPH) accessible by foot, trolley and car that opened June 1912 at 74 Fenwood Road in partnership with Harvard's Medical School.

Elmer E. Southard personified the unity of that relationship as superintendent of the Hospital and as Harvard's Bullard Professor of Neuropathology. He moved the psychopathic department from the Boston State Hospital to the BPH. With Emil Kraepelin's careful observation and distinct categorization at his Munich clinic as a model, Southard focused the BPH on: first care, observation and short intensive treatment; studying patients on the wards and investigating brain function in the laboratory; providing consultation and out patient services; and, educating doctors, nurses, researchers and other special workers.

If Southard's research was readily transferred from Boston State Hospital, its model of nursing care proved a poor fit. Attendants there were used to the custodial care of patients where domestic duties dominated the real nursing care. Although women attendants were called nurses none had been trained in a nursing school. Southard did not approve of the nursing care provided and saw it primarily as vigilance nursing. He felt that they were not qualified for the nursing care required in BPH's active treatment setting (Southard).

Sara E. Parsons, the nursing superintendent at the Massachusetts General Hospital, knew what was required. After graduating from the training schools at the MGH and the McLean Hospital she practiced at the Butler Hospital in Providence Rhode Island, the Adams Nervine Asylum in Jamaica Plain and the Sheppard and Enoch Pratt Hospital in Baltimore. She wanted nothing less than the best care for the mentally ill but the superintendents of training schools at their 16th annual convention in 1910 rejected the idea of educating nurses to provide high quality psychiatric care. Summarizing the discussion, the president said that as much as superintendents would like to care for the mentally ill, "their urgent necessity of nursing every patient in our hospitals, every hour of the day and night by means of our student body" made it impossible to provide an affiliation in a psychiatric hospital or introduce psychiatric care into the diploma school curriculum (Parsons).

It only stood to reason that the mentally ill should be as well cared for as the physically ill. Though Southard intuitively knew that the mentally ill should be as well cared for as the physically ill, that ideal was still a long way off in the future as Southard tried to tackle the nursing problem at the BPH. He hired Mary L. Gerrin, a graduate of the Boston City Hospital Training School for Nurses as superintendent, nine graduate nurses and 30 attendants. No longer would patients and attendants be separated by gender with women caring for women, men caring for men and men not answerable to the female nursing superintendent as was done in state hospitals. Nurses were assigned to the night shift indicating that patient care was a 24-hour phenomenon and more than a matter of custody. These changes were not without conflict. There were wholesale discharges and un-repented resignations of attendants of moderate skill, reported Southard, some of little or no value and others of real harm. Under Gerrin's leadership hours spent on nursing duties rose and those spent on domestic tasks fell. Significantly, with better nursing care, the number of accidents fell.

Gerrin reported her findings on the differences between watching patients (vigilance nursing) and caring for them (constructive nursing) at the conference, Modern Development in Mental Nursing at the Psychopathic Hospital, held at the BPH February 16, 1914. When her paper was published that fall in the *Boston Medical and Surgical Journal* (precursor to the *New England Journal of Medicine*) an analysis of the changes accompanied the narrative

(Gerrin). M. Adelaide Nutting, representing the national nursing community, presented as well. More than likely Parsons suggested this speaker. The former head of nursing at the Johns Hopkins Hospital and its nurses training school, Nutting was the first professor of nursing at Columbia's Teachers College. Only four years before as President of the Society of Superintendents of Training Schools for Nurses she had rejected Parsons' proposal to educate nurses for psychiatric care. At the BPH conference, however, she stated "such instruction should form a part of the general training of all nurses" (Nutting).

Eventually the profession concurred. The BPH, later renamed the Massachusetts Mental Health Center, became the clinical site for hundreds and hundreds of nursing students, first from the diploma programs and then from universities. At the BPH/MMHC centennial in 2012, they learn to care for patients in MMHC's new building at 75 Fenwood Road across the street from its original site.

REFERENCES

Gerrin, Mary L. "Impressions of a general hospital nurse on beginning work in the Psychopathic Hospital (Boston, MA)," *Boston Medical and Surgical Journal*, (171, September 24, 1914): 483-485.

Mitchell, S. Weir. 1894. "Address before the 50th Annual Meeting of the American Medico Psychological Association, May 16, 1894," *Journal of Nervous and Mental Diseases* (21): 413-437.

Nutting, M. Adelaide. 1926. "The training of the psychopathic nurse," in *A Sound Economic Basis for Schools of Nursing*. New York: G. P. Putnam's Sons, 133-140.

Parsons, Sara E. 1910. "Report of the Committee on the Nursing of the Nervous and the Insane," in *Proceedings of the Sixteenth Annual Convention of the Society of Superintendents of Training Schools for Nurses,* Baltimore: Maryland, 98-104.

Southard, Elmer E. *Third Annual Report of the Psychopathic Department of Boston State Hospital year ending November 30, 1914*, 20-22, 32-34.

GERTRUDE WELD PEABODY (1877-1938):
ALLY OF INSTRUCTIVE DISTRICT NURSES

(originally published September 2011)

As the daughter of a Harvard minister/professor, the sister of a Harvard educated doctor and the niece of a Harvard president, Gertrude Weld Peabody (1877-1938) had a social standing that was further enhanced by her American roots that reached back to 1635. Her father, Professor Peabody was a liberal Unitarian who preached on the moral issues of industrialized society. Her brother, Dr. Francis Peabody, epitomized the emergence of scientific medicine that followed the Flexner Report of 1911. He introduced research at the new Peter Bent Brigham Hospital and later at the Thorndike Laboratories at the Boston City Hospital. Her uncle, Charles Eliot, transformed liberal arts education at Harvard and in 1906 opened the new Harvard Medical School along Longwood Avenue. Its costs were partly defrayed by the Rockefeller Foundation.[1]

A similar level of accomplishment was not required of Gertrude Weld Peabody. As a daughter of a family privileged with the "treasure of God's bounty," however, Peabody was expected to serve those less fortunate than herself. Accordingly, when she was twenty-five years old, she volunteered her services to the Instructive District Nurses Association that Phebe G. Adam and Abbie C. Howes had founded in 1886 in association with the Women's Education Association and the Boston Dispensary.

The IDNA was part of the upsurge of feminine activism in the decades that followed the Civil War (1861-65). Not only was the IDNA founded and led by women, it used the trained nurse—then only thirteen years in existence—to achieve its objective of caring for the poor in their homes. Directed by moral principles and supported by generous Bostonians, the IDNA was an act of beneficence to be sure. It was also a response to the scandalous level of disease in Boston. No longer could Bostonians ignore a death rate that continued to climb, consumption [tuberculosis] that claimed one-fifth of the population each year, and other infections such as scarlet fever and diphtheria that disrupted health and shortened life. And, no longer could the Boston-born population merely separate themselves from the poor immigrants who had from 1845-1900 so flooded the City that by 1875 they had become a 58.4% majority of the population.[2]

Between February and October during the IDNA's first year Amelia Hodgkiss and Colina E. M. Somerville, graduates of the training schools at the New England Hospital for Women and Children and Boston City Hospital respectively, cared for 370 people, in their homes and taught them principles of healthy living during 4305 visits.[3] In 1893 Somerville told nurses gathered at the Chicago's World Fair about the individuals behind these numbers. Among the patients she cared for were: a little girl with bronchial pneumonia, a little boy recovering from pneumonia who was still very weak and stiff, a hundred year old woman with the grippe for whom she made an eggnog, a two year old girl with bronchitis, a woman with a leg ulcer, a young girl with phthisis [tuberculosis], a family of seven children each with a painful skin disease probably contracted from adopting a stray dog covered with sores, a woman with erysipelas [streptococcal infection], a woman with a bruised and crushed ankle of one month's duration who should have been in the hospital but had five little children, a boy with acute rheumatism whose legs she wrapped in cotton and wool bandages, a woman whose face was badly burned when a can of milk exploded while she heated it, a nine year old whose feet were frostbitten, a woman with gastritis and an intoxicated young woman with a severe burn on her neck sustained when she fell against the stove.

Somerville taught the husband of this woman how to make gruel, brought milk for a baby being fed tea and taught its grandmother how to prepare food properly. Pleased with her successes, Somerville concluded, "Almost everyday I find some former patient carrying out many of the simple directions that have been given during some former sickness."[4]

Peabody believed that nurses such as Somerville were the epitome of the Public Health Movement. She became their vocal champion during her thirty years with the IDNA and as an officer in the National Organization of Public Health Nursing (est'd. 1912). Socially, as well, she spread the word on their well-trained intellects and high-minded spirits as they applied principles of sanitation and hygiene principles in their care of the poor.

Peabody stood with district nurses when the Rockefeller Foundation rejected nursing's proposal for a study of nursing education similar to medicine's Flexner Report. She wrote directly to John D. Rockefeller, Jr. with whom the Peabody's often worshipped during summer vacations in Maine. The Foundation responded to his October 1917 inquiry saying that indeed the Foundation was deeply interested in the work of public health nursing. Thanks to Peabody's intercession, the Rockefeller Foundation supported nurses as they asked, "What constitutes a proper training course for the public health nurse?" That question culminated in *Nursing and Nursing Education in the United States* (1923) familiarly known as the Goldmark Report. After Harvard rejected the task of implementing the study's recommendations, Yale accepted and began its nursing school. Meanwhile, Peabody's alliance with district nurses continued ending only at her death in 1938.

[1] Mary Ellen Doona, "Gertrude Weld Peabody: Unsung Patron of Public Health Nursing," *Nursing and Health Care* XV (February, 1994): 88-94.

[2] Mary Ellen Doona, "Wise Thinking about Health," presented at Nursing in the Community: From Our Roots into the Next Millennium," at Bunker Hill Community College, May 24, 2000.

[3] Secretary's Notebook: January 19, 1886-January 25, 1887. [Instructive District Nurses Association] *Boston Visiting Nurses Association Collection* Box 2, Folder 1 History of Nursing Archives, Howard Gotlieb Archival Research Center, Boston University

REMEMBERING THE PAST OF
MASSACHUSETTS NURSING

(originally published September 2004)

The importance of memory in keeping a profession whole cannot be stated too strongly. Essentially, memory is related to function, as nurses who have cared for persons suffering from Alzheimer's disease or amnesia know all-too well. As memory fails, autonomy decreases. Professional autonomy is also dependent on memory. Nurses need to know what happened in the past if they are to function in the present, and make wise decisions for the future,

Once, history was told in songs in the manner of the Iliad, the Odyssey and Beowulf. Inspired by Clio, the muse of history, poets proclaimed the deeds of the past, the rhythms of the poet's song helped people to remember the past, and see themselves in relation to that history. Clio and the eight others daughters of Mnemosyne, the goddess of memory, represent avenues to knowledge, epitomized in Greek mythology by Apollo, the god of light.

Light assumes an encircling darkness. As Greek myth teaches and nurses know, there is a profound price for sitting in the dark. Shadows can be misinterpreted. Some errors have little consequences, for example, the threatening intruder that is shown to be a coat rack once the light is turned on. More serious for nursing are nurses who prefer the darkness of fiction over remembered fact. They not only stay in the dark, they rob the profession of its vitality.

The light shone on Florence Nightingale (1820-1910), a monumental figure in nursing's long story, casts Crimean War (1854-56) nurses into the darkness. Thanks to an uncritical acceptance of her point of view, those nurses were cast as Sairey Gamps and Betsy Prigs, Charles Dickens' brilliant characterizations of negligent nurses who liked to drink and sleep. In truth Crimean War nurses such as Elizabeth Davis, Martha Clough and Isabella Croke cared for sick and wounded soldiers in hospitals on Russia's (now Ukraine's) Crimean Peninsula. Fanny Taylor cared for soldiers at the Koulali Hospitals. And, Kate Doyle nursed soldiers at the Scutari Hospitals at Constantinople. Not knowing about these and other Crimean War nurses robs nursing of its life.

Clio's trumpet was used for a false purpose in Woodham-Smith's panegyric biography of Florence Nightingale. The author was an unabashed fan, and took as her own enemies those who Florence Nightingale saw as her enemies. Woodham-Smith's biography is flawed, but that did not keep unenlightened nurses from repeating the errors of the biography as historical fact, Florence Nightingale abhorred Joanna Bridgeman, and called the Irish num, the "Brickbat" and the "buffalo calf" among other ungracious names. The unskeptical Woodham-Smith repeated the slurs, and did not consider their context or circumstances. The fact was Florence Nightingale was envious of the praise for Bridgemam's leadership at the Koulali Hospitals and her skill in nursing patients. She feared that the growing fame of the nursing nun would eclipse her own reputation. Worse, Florence Nightingale, a woman of her self-righteous Victorian time, could not countenance Bridgeman's daring to deal with her as an equal. Worst of all, Florence Nightingale's bias against the Irish blinded her to Bridgeman's nursing experience,

Captured by the Florence Nightingale mystique, nursing history did not hear Clio's trumpeting the nursing care of Mary Seacole. Once obscured by Florence Nightingale's monumental status, the Jamaican "doctress" as she called herself, had a better chronicler of her nursing care in William H. Russell. The candid war correspondent wrote Seacole into Clio's history book, recording that her healing arts cured many men of diarrhea, dysentery and other camp illnesses that claimed the lives of thousands of soldiers. Many of the officers already knew Mother Seacole, as they called her, from their time in the West Indies,

Seacole was attentive to the officers whose patronage of her canteen was her income, but compassion went beyond the clink of change. She cared for the sick and wounded lying on the rough boards of the Balaclava pier waiting for the "hospital ships" to unload their cargo of horses and munitions before being loaded themselves for a week's journey across the Black Sea to the filthy Scutari Hospitals. Seacole went among these men, most of them dehydrated from infections and wounds, and many of them dying, giving them drinks of hot tea. In this way, Seacole who had paid her own way to the East, cared for soldiers even after the British Government refused her services, and Florence Nightingale ignored her presence, Seacole epitomizes nursing autonomy driven by compassion not by position, and thanks to Russell's first person account, her story is part of nursing's history's available evidence.

Clio was not well-served in the stories of Florence Nightingale's acclaimed nursing care, cleaning up of the environment and reducing the mortality rate. The light that research shone on these nursing "truths" reveals first, that as a lady, Florence Nightingale was not expected to do any direct nursing care, Her task was to superintend other women as they cared for the soldiers, Florence Nightingale was a week's steamship ride away across the Black Sea at her desk in the Scutari Hospital in Constantinople (now Istanbul) supposedly superintending nurses on the Crimean Peninsula. Before she had been in the East very long, Lord Panmure, the Secretary of War, effectively relieved Florence Nightingale of this impossible task of superintending nurses from a distance, and gave her responsibility for dispensing the gifts of clothes, food and articles that the British people had sent the soldiers. As to lowering the mortality rate, this too is in the realm of nursing myth. The record shows that in the spring of 1855, a sanitation commission lined the walls of the hospitals to rid them of fleas and lice; cleaned the drains of carcasses of dead animals; and, purified the water supply. This lessened the occurrence of typhus, typhoid fever and dysentery. The coming of spring with its good weather lessened the incidence of other illnesses. The mortality rate dropped dramatically because of the sanitation commission and the warmth of Mother Nature.

Facts are better than fiction. Florence Nightingale is remarkable for freeing herself from the mindless life of the leisured lady whose only task was to display the family's wealth and status in her dress, manners and travels. She | is remarkable, as well, for throwing the considerable powers of her mind at the glaring inequities of her society that her widely-read contemporary, Charles Dickens, had so graphically detailed. Nursing reform was her chosen field, and the Crimean War (1854–56) provided her with the opportunity to test her ideas. That this well-positioned lady chose to superintend nursing in the East over the social whirl at home, still earns her great praise. Her concern for soldiers raised her Government's view of the soldier from a brute to a person. For this, Florence Nightingale cannot be too highly, nor too often, praised.

Thus Clio's horn has trumpeted much fancy and little fact in the story of Crimean War nursing. The blast was so loud that the same false notes can still be heard one hundred and fifty years later, Nursing institutionalized this } distortion of its past making it more difficult to understand what has happened since and what is happening in the present. As nurses training was established in Boston following the Civil War (1861-1865), at the New England) Hospital for Women and Children (NEHWC), the Massachusetts General Hospital (MGH) and the Boston City Hospital (BCH), the training schools blindly accepted the received stories about Florence Nightingale.

Establishing priority has ever been Clio's task and this she assigned to the training school at the NEHWC when the hospital moved in 1872 from what is now Boston's theater district to a new site in the rural Roxbury. The women doctors may have been responding to the American Medical Association's 1869 recommendations about training nurses. More likely, the nursing done during the Crimean War and America's Civil War (1861-1865) made the idea of nurse's training schools an idea whose time had come. NEHWC's nurses training program began with Linda Richards (1841-1930) as its first pupil. She and her classmates were pupil nurses, while the interns studying medical practice were referred to as students. This was a distinction with a difference as time would tell.

Richards' journey to nursing paralleled much of what was happening following the Civil War as Massachusetts changed from an agricultural to an industrial economy. She left her home in Lyndon, Vermont for work in the straw hat industry in Foxboro, Massachusetts. Unfortunately for Clio's devotees, a fire fed by dry straw, gay ribbons and other flammable materials, such as glue and lacquer, destroyed all the documents which might have shed more light on Richards' tenure at the Union Straw Works. Other fragile sources were in safer repositories, Posterity knows that Richards worked in Foxboro thanks to her application for missionary nursing that is preserved in the American Board of Commissioners of Foreign Missions Collection at the Houghton Library at Harvard.

After one year in the training program, the thirty-two year old Richards accepted the first nursing diploma, which many years later, alumnae of her School gave to the Smithsonian Institution in Washington, D.C. Waltham's Dr. Alfred Worcester would promote Richards as America's Florence Nightingale, and dub her America's first trained nurse. At the same time nurses claimed Richards as their own, making her the icon of the new profession. The struggle between nurses and doctors for Linda Richards was pervaded by the patriarchies of the time, and epitomized the larger and longer struggle of whether nurses or doctors would control nursing.

While Richards was progressing though her year of nursing and lectures at the NEHWC, a group of Boston's elite women were creating the Boston Training School (precursor to the MGHSON). These ladies, many of them doctors' wives, daughters and sisters, had the leisure to devote their energies to such worthy social causes. The task was a personal one for Mary E. Parkman who knew at first hand the need for nurses. During her husband's lengthy illness in 1854, his medical students from the MGH nursed Dr. Samuel Parkman until typhoid fever took his life. Other women in the group were more concerned about the consequences of urbanization as Massachusetts industrialized. Young women were rushing into the city from rural areas in Massachusetts, New Hampshire, Vermont and Maine seeking jobs in the new economy. The socialites feared these young women might be lost to the dark side of society, namely prostitution and crime, if they failed to find work. Their nurses training school offered another option.

Several years later, Sarah Cabot related how the Ladies Committee took Florence Nightingale's Notes on Nursing and chose what they wanted for their Boston Training School. Mrs. Parkman added her experience of having met Florence Nightingale and visited St. Thomas Hospital where she saw the trained nurse in action. The school opened November

1, 1873, the third of the three "Nightingale schools" founded that year. The other two were in New York and Connecticut. The founding mothers wanted America's "first trained 'nurse" to lead their new school. Linda Richards declined this offer, and took a position at Bellevue Hospital in New York. After a year there under the leadership of Sister Helen, Richards returned to Boston in November 1874 and accepted the role of nursing superintendent at the BTS with a salary of $600 per year, raised the next year to $900 per year. Thanks to the Ladies Committee's diligently recording their meetings, Sara Parsons was able to use these primary sources now preserved in the Countway Library in Boston's medical area, in her 1923 history of the MGH's School of Nursing.

Two of Richards' students at the MGH far exceeded their teacher, and would go on to shape American nursing, Sophia Palmer (1853-1920) was a Boston woman whose roots went back to 1621 in Cape Cod, with other relatives serving with Miles Standish, and still others, fighting in America's Revolution. Contemporaries described her as a woman of wide experience, conspicuous ability and great determination. She had a worthy colleague in her sharp-witted and intelligent classmate, Mary E. P. Davis (1840-1924). Davis, the daughter of a Captain in the English army, immigrated to Boston from New Brunswick, Canada.

These classmates, and then, colleagues were part of the phenomenon that increasingly drew women into economic and political life. The prime concern of Palmer and Davis as the nineteenth-century turned into the twentieth was the professionalization of nursing. By 1893 the nursing leaders were organized in the American Society of Superintendent of Training Schools, Both Linda Richards and Mary E. P. Davis served president in its early years. In 1896 Palmer and Davis organized nurses alumnae associations and helped to establish the American Nurses Association (formerly the Associated Alumnae). With Palmer as its editor (1900–1920) and Davis as its financial manager (1900-1910), the American Journal of Nursing published its first issue in October 1900 for an audience of nurses then numbering almost 2500. The Journal began with a circulation of 550 subscribers. Twenty years later 15,000 nurses ware subscribing to the nurse-owned journal, and reading the latest findings on nursing care. Palmer and Davis were influential in making nursing a profession: They had assumed the authority to meet à society's need, established a body of Knowledge 'and organized for self-management.

Then came the business of survival as opponents preferred that nurses be subservient. Dr. Alfred Worcester decided that nursing should become medicine's art as medicine became increasingly a scientific discipline. The presence of the trained nurse was presented as evidence that a hospital was part of this scientific revolution, Hospitalizing the asylum, as psychiatry's return to mainstream medicine was called, required nurses in bright caps and white aprons.

Many hospitals promoted up-to-dateness by enhancing their annual reports with photographs of their pupil nurses.

Davis' memories of her student days at the MGH in 1876 give a glimpse of just how difficult survival was. She recalled:

> We did the sweeping . . . we washed the bedsteads and bedside tables . . . we had to mop [the ward] . . . we did the dusting, we carried the clothes to the laundry and the poultice cloths and used bandages to the rinse house . . . and ironed them. We washed dishes twice a day . . . We realized early in our training that many things we had to do had little relation to nursing. We took the training as a fundamental not as an incidental occupation ... the incidentals were many and grievous, we saw the opportunity to get what we were after. Along with it was developed the mental attitude that has placed nursing in the rank of a profession.

Palmer and Davis knew what they were after, and believed in nursing enough to spend their lives in its elusive pursuit.

Two years after that student experience at the MGH in 1878, Edward Cowles MD, a doctor during the Civil War, was establishing a nurse's training school at the Boston City Hospital. From its beginning, the BCH was designed to care for the poor and indigent. This freed the MGH from having to care for non-paying patients. Overseers of these two charitable institutions distinguished between the virtuous and the vicious poor. The virtuous poor were those whose illness was not a fault of their own, whereas, the vicious poor were those whose illness was brought on by "immoral" behavior. The majority of these poor were Irish immigrants who had flooded into Boston at mid-nineteenth century and dramatically changed Boston's demographics by diluting the hegemony of native Bostonians, before long the poor were politicized and able to pressure the ruling class to lessen and finally eliminate its authoritarian moralism.

Richards headed the new nursing department at the BCH but her tenure was punctuated by frequent illnesses from infections that laid her low, Her associate, Lucy" Lincoln Drown (1847-1934), was often called to step into the breach. Then, when Richards left for Japan in 1885, Drown succeeded to the nursing superintendent position where she continued until she retired in 1910. Described by contemporaries as a gentlewoman, Drown would serve Clio as historian for Massachusetts nurses, knowing from her own family's legacy how the past shaped the present. Drown had roots that reached back to Colonial Boston. Her ancestor, Shem Drown, fashioned the grasshopper weathervane that still graces Faneuil Hall. He rests in a grave in the historic Copp's Cemetery in Boston's North End, on her mother's side, Drown descended from Mordecai Lincoln, an ancestor she shared with Abraham Lincoln. Still another maternal ancestor for this nurse who cared for Boston's newest inhabitants was James Ridway of Dublin, Ireland who entered Colonial Boston as a servant. Closer to her own heart was her forty-one year old father, Captain Leonard Drown, who left his bones in Williamsburg, Virginia to mingle with the bones of other fallen soldiers of America's Civil War.

While Richards and Drown were heading nursing at the BCH, a greater drama was occurring across town at the NEHWC, Ironically, the hospital founded for women doctors who had been denied entry into Boston's hospitals because of their sex refused admission to its intern program to a woman because of her race. This egregious error forced the founding feminists to reconsider their original mission. First, they had to look back over sixteen years to their origins, and then, see how far they had strayed by not keeping their history part of their present. Once an oppressed minority, these women realized they had become the oppressor. After some soul searching, they not only corrected the offense, they welcomed the Negro woman into the internship program (here, as throughout the paper contemporary terms are used). Then they searched for ways to correct a similar bias occurring in their nurses-training program. They invited Mary Eliza Mahoney (1845-1926) who worked in the hospital to enroll in the nurses training program in 1878. Mahoney graduated in 1879 and worked in private homes, as did almost every graduate of the training schools. As a trained nurse, Mahoney had higher earning power, a fact she acknowledged some thirty years later when she praised her school for its openness, and for not being "selfish" as other Massachusetts training schools had been.

Nurses were an economic force within the hospitals. Nursing leaders planted the new profession in the hospital because they wanted preparation for nursing to be clinically-grounded. In many hospitals, however, pupil nurses replaced ward maids whose salaries became the pupil nurse's payment. This exchange of money was not a stipend supporting education. Rather, the pupil nurses' labor (not tuition) paid for their training. In many, if not most cases, they were short-changed. It would take years before pupil nurses would be truly students. But till then, housekeeping and other non-nursing duties took precedent to learning to care for patients.

Because nursing education took a poor second to housekeeping duties, the superintendents realized that pupil nurses were in positions of authority but insufficiently educated to make complex clinical judgments. To guard against error, the training schools created rigid protocols, often calling them ethics that pupil nurses had to follow. Combined with the inadequacy of their education, these stringent measures crippled inquiry and killed autonomy. The successors of Palmer and Davis focused their pupil nurses on the image of Florence Nightingale which kept their eyes diverted from the reality of their circumstances. This, reductionistic contemplation of the past was the ultimate distortion of nursing's history, and made it difficult for pupil nurses to understand their present. Remarkably, nursing kept alive the best of its traditions and defined its boundaries, in theory if not in practice, as it envisioned a future when nursing would be autonomous.

While much is known of nursing's noted, most nurses are nameless and faceless, leaving much of nursing's history in the dark. What was nursing like for these young women at NEHWC, MGH and BCH? Infectious diseases were the leading cause of death in this era. Many pupil nurses contracted infections as they cared for persons suffering from typhoid fever, tuberculosis, pneumonia and meningitis. Some pupil nurses died. Lucy Lincoln Drown sent exhausted pupil nurses from BCH to her widowed mother in Cohasset, Massachusetts where they might rest and recover. What was it like for young men in specialty hospitals such as the McLean Hospital? How did these pupil nurses fare in that pre-medication era as they cared for persons suffering from mental disorders, later labeled schizophrenia, mania and traumatic neuroses? There are statistics galore on these pupil nurses, but the individuals themselves lost the power of agency once they were conglomerated into the numbers of social history. Much more should be done to rescue them from the darkness of statistical anonymity so nursing can throw light on its particulars, contexts and circumstances.

Finally, the idea of Clio serves as a command to Massachusetts nurses to remember the past so they can understand the institutions they have inherited. Massachusetts nurses must shine a light on its past, and keep unbroken the thread to that past. That thread is fragile in some spots and fraying in others spots, yet nursing's present and future are hanging by that thread. Although speaking of the House of Representatives, the late Charles Ruff's directive is one Massachusetts nurses might also heed. He said that we must cast an eye to the past, looking over our shoulders to be sure that we've learned the right lessons from those who have sat in this chamber before us. We also must look to the future to be sure that we leave the right lessons to those who come after us.

Remembering leads to deeper understanding, a necessary preliminary to an enlightened autonomy.

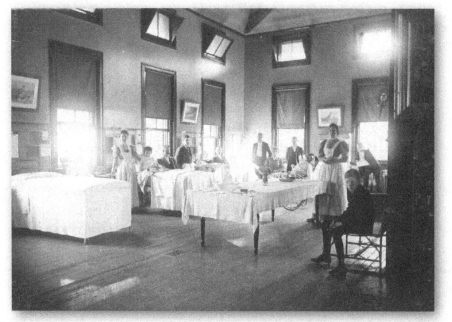

Ward A at the Massachusetts General hospital Christmas 1894 (Sarah E. Parsons Collection)

1908 AND THE ESTABLISHMENT OF THE NATIONAL ASSOCIATION OF COLORED GRADUATE NURSES

(originally published December 2008)

One hundred years ago colored* nurses founded the National Association of Colored Graduate Nurses (NACGN) during a time when racial prejudice was growing in the United States. In 1908 the force of state laws in the South and indifference in the North increasingly separated the races with the Supreme Court countenancing the violation of Constitutional rights. The Court's 1896 decision (*Plessey v. Ferguson*) that children could be educated in racially separated schools gave tacit approval to the Jim Crow "laws" that followed in other public spheres, such as transportation, hotels, restrooms and workplaces.

The lawlessness that was common in the South erupted in Springfield, Illinois in mid August 1908. For two days people rioted against colored people culminating in several being lynched, others killed and still others wounded. That such a riot could occur so near where Abraham Lincoln (1809-1865), the *Emancipator*, once lived, spoke to the rising tide of prejudice against colored people in the North. Progressives, shaped by Theodore Roosevelt's *Square Deal* policies decided the time had come to exchange patience for active protest against the "new slavery" (Kellogg, 1967, 7).

Just one year before they had met in Boston at the Niagara Movement's third annual convention. There, in Faneuil Hall that had cradled America's founding principles and in the city where William Lloyd Garrison's (1805-1879) *Liberator* had spoken out against slavery, the "disturbers of the unjust peace" as Vernon Jordan (2008) would call such heroes one hundred years later, prepared themselves for what lay ahead. In 1908 these Progressives decided they would use the upcoming centennial of Abraham Lincoln's birthday – 12 February 1909 – as the occasion to measure the nation's progress since Lincoln's death. They issued *The Call* to sixty prominent people "to join in a national conference for the discussion of present evils, the voicing of protests, and the renewal of the struggle for civil and political liberty" (1909).

Ever on the side of social justice, nursing's public health nurse Lillian Wald, was among the sixty distinguished invitees. Her Henry Street Settlement House in New York's lower East Side hosted the opening reception on May 30, 1909. Later, she persuaded financer Jacob Schiff, whose philanthropy underwrote the health services provided by Henry Street, to extend his generosity to the new organization that evolved: the National Association for the Advancement of Colored People (NAACP). Ironically, a few months before when Springfield, Illinois celebrated the *Great Emancipator's* Centennial no colored people were invited to attend. America's house was divided then and would remain divided for some time to come.

Lillian Wald and her colleagues proved the exception to the rule. Just as she had provided meeting space at Henry Street for the fledging NAACP, she did the same for New York's colored nurses seeking their rights as Americans and professionals. The record is silent on how she and the nurses became partners in forming the National Association for Colored Graduate Nurses (NACGN) in 1908. It seems likely that the relationship arose from the colored nurses she employed at Henry Street as visiting nurses. Lavinia Dock, nursing's premier historian, who had witnessed their practice testified to their value as good nurses and noted their "intelligent altruism" (1912, 198). Her love for the new profession is evident in her insistence on its being inclusive. She decried the "anti-social feeling" and the barriers that were being erected as nursing grew in size. She vowed that that "injustice" would not be done ..."in the impersonal realm of education and state examination" (1912, 198).

The NACGN with *Service for Humanity* as its motto met the next August in Boston. The NACGN chose the sixty-three year old Mary Eliza Mahoney (1845-1926) to personify the new organization. The petit Mahoney —she was under five feet tall and less than one hundred pounds– praised her training school, the New England Hospital for Women and Children, for its pioneering inclusiveness. Its correction of an injustice in 1878 had made possible for Mahoney to earn her living as a trained nurse for thirty years.

So it was in 1908 that the NACGN disturbed nursing's unjust peace. In 1951 the NACGN was absorbed into the American Nurses Association, signifying that its goals of advancing nursing standards, breaking down discrimination and developing leadership among colored nurses had been achieved.

WORKS CITED

Dock, Lavinia. A History of Nursing, vol Ill., (New York: G. P. Putnam's Sons, 1912).

Jordan, Vernon. "Reflections: The Jordan Gospel." *Newsweek*, 3 November 2008, 52-53.

Kellogg, Charles Flint. NAACP. *A History of the National Association for the Advancement of Colored People.* (Baltimore, Md.: The Johns Hopkins University Press, 1967).

The Call (1909). In Kellogg, 1967.

Please let Clio's Corner know the name of the first African American graduate of your nursing program.

Nurse	School of Nursing	Date
Mary Eliza Mahoney	New England Hospital of Women and Children	1879

*Contemporary term used.

THE EMERGENCE OF THE SCHOOL NURSE

(originally published September 2005)

This fall the school nurses of Massachusetts will celebrate the 100th anniversary of school nursing. They will pay tribute to Annie McKay, a Canadian born and educated nurse that the Boston Instructive District Nurses Association (precursor to the Boston Visiting Nurses Association) chose as the nurse who would introduce nursing into the school system. What did McKay face in 1905 as she stepped into this new field for nurses? This question can be answered only after reviewing what the times were like, and especially how those times impacted on children.

The twentieth century arrived in a blaze with electricity succeeding steam as the nation's energy. If dynamos created this new source of energy, new perspectives created another kind of energy. Avant-garde artists such as Picasso, Renoir and Monet announced in their brilliant art that there were other ways of presenting the human experience. Sigmund Freud pointed out hidden wells of energy in the human psyche in his book. *Interpretation of Dreams*. Enrico Caruso's glorious tenor sang out from the phonograph; Elgar composed the first of his Pomp and Circumstances marches; and, American composers, such as Irving Berlin, picked up the pace with syncopated rhythms and ragtime jazz. Electricity picked up the beat of the human heart on the newly invented electrocardiogram.

The world began to shrink once Marconi beat out the telegraph from Cornwall to Newfoundland. Steamship travel between New York and Ireland took only five days and three quarters of an hour if you were sailing on the speedy *H.M.S. Lusitania*. Within a decade of the new year, the first Model T rolled off the assembly line and the Wright Brothers flew thirty miles in only forty minutes. Those seeking luxury welcomed the new Rolls Royce Company.

And in faraway Persia (now Iran) people started drilling for oil. America was on the move and not yet dependent on foreign oil.

Fashion changed as a consequence of all this new energy. The female silhouette softened as corsets were modified to feature bosoms and hips. Hemlines rose to the ankles and the walking skirt became ordinary. Yet fashion setters were ambivalent. At the same time that bloomers appeared in answer to the bicycle craze and the walking skirt permitted longer strides, the popular hobble skirt limited a woman's steps. Hats loaded down with feathers and frills rested on hairdos whose volumes of curls required hours of attention. The Arrow Collar man, so the ads promised, was the epitome of good grooming, his magnificence was real and his chin was noble. A bowler hat in winter and a Panama hat in summer completed the look over suits that had become less formally tailored.

More than electricity and fashion were changing America. A million plus people entered the United States each year during the peak years of immigration. The population rose from 31 million in 1860 to 92 million by 1910. Boston, for example, had been pretty much a homogenous culture before the influx of immigrants. It would take years and years before old Bostonians made an accommodation to the new arrivals In the meantime in Boston and elsewhere, capitalism saw in these huddled masses a source of cheap labor that would create higher profits. Reformers railed against the abuses of capitalism and its casual use of human beings, especially children, in its quest for profit. One cartoon published in the *Women's Journal* shows a child caught in a spider's web of greed, profit, luxury, poverty, ignorance, and indifference. Another cartoon personifies capitalism as a man with a huge maw of a mouth into which he popped child after child as if they were snacks.

The National Child Labor Committee founded in 1904 to persuade Congress to address this national scandal of child labor marshalled the facts: Two million children under 16 years of age were employed in the United States. Many of them were employed in textile factories where their nimble fingers easily operated the machinery and their cheap labor generated huge profits. The long range cost to the country of unfulfilled potential was ignored. Of those two million children, 580,000 between the ages of one and fourteen could neither read nor write. Children who made money for others had no power to change their own situation. An 1892 law that limited child labor to an eight hour day in Chicago factories, for example, was repealed three years later by dint of manufacturers' persuasion. Government was the servant of business.

Congress attempted to get around capitalism's use of child labor but its Keating-Owens Act was ruled unconstitutional by the United States Supreme Court. Not until 1938 when

President Franklin Delano Roosevelt (1882-1945) signed the Fair Labor Standards Act into law 18 June 1938 was child labor prohibited in all industries providing services in inter-state commerce. The law further stated that the minimum age for employment outside of school hours would be fourteen, employment within school hours would be sixteen, and only those over eighteen years of age might work in hazardous jobs. Those changes were still to come at the turn of the twentieth century when children who should have been in school were working twelve and more hours a day. Most worked in factories, others worked in sweat shops in their homes.

Theodore Roosevelt (1858-1919) who became president in 1901 at the assassination of President William McKinley (1843-1901) brought a reformer's energy to the office. When he was elected in 1904 and later when he ran as a Progressive, Roosevelt tried to bring about social reform. He sought to give both business and labor a "square deal." At the same time, he broke the monopolies, advocated for women's rights, child labor laws and saw the pure food and drugs act become law. His focus on child labor was especially welcomed by reformers who had long decried the practice. In some cases children went back to school. In most cases they remained in capitalism's grip.

Women increased the volume of the cries against child labor. During these same years Jane Lathrop (1858-1932) joined with like-minded women at Jane Addams' Hull House founded in 1889 in Chicago that dealt with social misery. In 1893 Lillian Wald (1867-1940) created the Henry Street Settlement House in New York City that had a similar objective. Andover House founded in Boston in1891 cared for people living crowded together in poor housing. In these and other settings, women gave voice to the voiceless even as they cared for their physical and social needs. Their efforts would be nationalized in 1912 when the Children's Bureau was established to oversee child labor, infant mortality, juvenile delinquency, mother's pensions and illegitimacy. President William Taft (1857-1930) empowered the Bureau to "investigate and report upon all matters pertaining to the welfare of children and child life among all classes of people." Jane Lathrop would be appointed to head the new federal agency.

In 1905, in the midst of a culture undergoing enormous changes that electricity, new perspectives on life, a flood of immigration, expansion of capitalism and women's activism had created, two events significant for the health of children occurred. German biologist, Robert Koch (1843-1910) was awarded the Nobel Peace Prize for his work in isolating the tubercle bacillus in 1882 and in 1883 the cholera bacillus. The full force of Koch's findings would not be felt until mid-century when the antibiotics that could cure infectious diseases were discovered. In 1905 Koch's discovery kicked off medicine's scientific revolution: Doctors would increasingly focus on seeking the causative agent in the disease process.

If infections could not be cured in 1905, nonetheless, Koch's science countered the prevailing view that infectious diseases were inherited or the result of an absence of God's blessing. In Boston, for example, sin and sickness had long been seen as having a common root. The immigrant poor with their alien ways were seen as a breeding ground for sin. By this time Bostonians had given up hope that they could stem the flood of immigrants into their city and channeled their energies into Americanizing the immigrant population. The nurse would be at the center of their plan of helping immigrants to adopt American ways. Bostonians believed that if nurses could keep immigrants healthy, then their moral health would be assured.

The ideal visiting nurse, it was believed, would go into the poor tenement and with her quick eye and ready tact discern the present emergency of children and how the whole family could be improved. She would show the mother by example and suggestion how to organize the household in such a way as to knit the family. Healthy families meant a physically and morally healthy Boston. Thus Bostonians were generous in funding the Instructive District Nurses Association that Phoebe Adam and Abbie Howes had established. In February 1886 Amelia Hodgkiss, a graduate of the New England Hospital for Women and Children, made the first home visit.

In 1893 Celia Somerville, Hodgkiss's successor at the Association, recounted the kinds of cases she cared for in her home visits to Boston's poor. Infectious diseases prevailed. In her visits she cared for a little girl with pneumonia, a little boy with pneumonia, an elderly woman with the grippe, a two year old girl with bronchitis, a woman with erysipelas, a young girl with phthisis, a little boy with rheumatism and an entire family with a painful skin disease that they probably contracted from a stray dog covered with sores that they had adopted. Burns, frostbite and a leg ulcer were still other problems she dealt with. Less quickly amenable to her ministrations were the sounds of quarreling that came from every room and a woman so intoxicated she could not be roused.

If Somerville was not adequately prepared to deal with psychological problems, the Instructive District Nurses Association had no problem naming the causes of such health problems. The Association knew that it was not sin but long hours and low wages that destroyed physical and psychological health. These diseases and conditions resulted from the abuses of capitalism against the commonweal. To her credit Somerville denounced the owners of the poorly ventilated tenements with their filthy and overcrowded living conditions. She called for other nurses to join her in dispelling diseases and purifying the darkness, disease and foul air of the tenements. The kind of nurses who could do this, said Somerville, were refined, cultured and devoted women of high character who had a strong religious feeling for the task (Somerville, 1893).

This was also the kind of woman that Sara Parsons (1864-1949) wanted to attract to the nursing school when she was superintendent of nurses at the Massachusetts General Hospital in 1910. She worried if she could convince the parents of such women to allow them to come to Boston's West End where saloons and their patrons were such a menace. Every time pupil nurses left the hospital they would have to dodge drunken men. Many of the saloons and the land upon which they rested were owned by highly respected Bostonians which made Parsons question their responsibility to society. One wonders if these men were also the husbands and fathers of the society women who did charitable work among Boston's poor.

Gertrude Peabody, the daughter of Harvard's Professor Francis Greenwood Peabody, the sister of Dr. Francis Peabody of the Peter Bent Brigham Hospital and the niece of Harvard President Charles Eliot chose Boston's Instructive District Nurses Association as the philanthropy by which she would meet her moral obligation to serve God by doing good. Peabody would become an articulate advocate of prevention. She admired visiting nurses because they personified prevention as they daily dealt with the social conditions of families and taught them principles of health and hygiene (Doona, 1994). Until the advent of antibiotics, prevention remained the bulwark against disease.

Koch's Nobel Peace Prize in 1905 was an international event. More local but an experiment of great magnitude in the lives of Boston's children was the introduction of the nurse into the Boston School system that same year. The immediate reason for appointing a nurse was the high absenteeism among school children. Some children were excluded from schools when they had a contagious infection. Many of these children failed to return to school once they were well again. Other children absented themselves from school to work. The pro-child advocates sought an unbroken education for Boston's children. New York City had already introduced nurses into its school system. The Henry Street Settlement House chose Lina Rogers (1870-1946) an 1894 graduate of the Hospital for Sick Children in Toronto, Ontario in Canada for the position. Rogers' interest in children especially recommended her for the position. America's First School Nurse lived up to her promise and more. After successfully establishing school nursing in New York City's school system, she pulled her experience together for other school nurses in *The School Nurse* published in 1917 (Hawkins, 1988).

Thanks to the research of Dorothy Kenney RN, BS, MA a school nurse in Brighton, some facts on Massachusetts' first school nurse have been discovered (Kenney, 2005). Three years after New York City, on 14 November 1905, Boston's School Committee decided to establish school nursing and gave the task of finding a nurse to Boston's Instructive District Nurses Association. The association corresponded with Lina Rogers and asked her for advice about introducing a nurse into schools. Then the Association chose Annie McKay (1867-1944) for Boston's first school nurse. McKay, like Rogers, was a Canadian-born and educated nurse. She and Rogers were contemporaries and it is tempting to think they knew one another in Toronto but the evidence for such a relationship is still to be found.

Like Boston City Hospital's Lucy Lincoln Drown and Newton Hospital's Mary Riddle, McKay had been a teacher before she became a nurse. She was twenty-seven years old when she was selected from a pool of 647 applicants to the Toronto General Hospital School of Nursing for the class of 53 pupils. Following graduation in 1894 she attended the Victorian Order Training School in Toronto and did district nursing for two years with the Victorian Order. McKay added a stint at the Women's Hospital in New York to her credentials before coming to Boston's Massachusetts Charitable Eye and Ear Infirmary. By the time she joined Boston's Instructive District Nurses Association, McKay was one of its best educated nurses, and in the words of the Association, "one of our most experienced nurses." In principle and practice McKay was prepared to care for people suffering from infectious diseases such as those that afflicted Bostonians, namely, tuberculosis, pneumonia, scarlet fever, diphtheria, pertussis, chicken pox, mumps and parasitic diseases. These diseases were claiming the lives of forty percent of those who died in Massachusetts in 1905.

With Boston's Mother's and Father's Club paying her salary, McKay began her work in Boston's South End, one of the city's most congested areas. Three schools were in her charge: the Way School, the Quincy School and the Andrews School. Her primary focus was to teach students how to be healthy by teaching them about cleanliness and personal hygiene. The records show that in two months she had cared for 215 children within the school hours of nine o'clock in the morning to three o'clock in the afternoon. Before and after these school hours she made 576 home visits to them and their families. The illnesses were the usual illnesses afflicting children, that is, eye, ear, nose and throat infections, infections of the lungs (perhaps tuberculosis or consumption as it was then called), impetigo, ring worm and other skin infections and pediculosis. McKay fails to specify the medical and surgical cases that she also saw.

Along with teaching her students and their families the basic cleanliness that would prevent many of the infections, especially the skin diseases, McKay also dealt with the major problem of absenteeism. Like school nurses who followed her, she helped to tell parents when students were free of contagion and well enough to return to school after a bout of measles, chick pox and the like. She was also able to discern whether children were missing school because of work. It would seem that having someone paying attention to such matters did help children to stay in school. One wonders if being the fifth of ten children had given McKay a special sensitivity to children. Her commitment to her own education certainly speaks to her valuing school attendance. Perhaps she helped the children and their families to gain a similar regard for education.

Whatever is the case, the numbers show that students being excluded from school because of infectious diseases and other kinds of absenteeism fell significantly. Praise for Miss McKay's results came from teachers, parents and children. Medical inspectors who worked with McKay also praised the effectiveness of the school nurse. Success followed success, so that in 1906 the Boston School Committee added four nurses. McKay had effectively established school nursing and moved on to other work. She had to return in September to steady the program which by the end of October was able to function on its own. In 1907 Boston's School committee added 33 more with another nurse as supervisor. Once again, charitable organizations paid nurses' salaries. The school nurse passed from experiment to law in 1907 when the Boston Code (Title 15, Section 28) mandated that the Boston School Committee shall appoint all supervisory and district nurses in the Boston school system. That year, too, Massachusetts decided that Boston's school nurse program should be extended throughout the state. Boston's school nurse program was no longer a responsibility of the Instructive District Nurses Association (Kenney, 2005).

The data do not show the individual children behind the numbers nor how their lives were bettered because they were healthy and better able to attend to lessons. The happiness of those healthy children of long ago and the advancement of their learning can only be imagined. Left to the imagination as well is the personal and professional satisfaction that McKay must have felt in bringing new light into the lives of those poor children. Perhaps the only way to gain a sense for McKay's experience is to ask present day school nurses about the experience. Although the problems they have to deal with are far different from those that McKay faced, today's school nurses are as close to children and their needs as was Annie McKay in 1905.

According to Beth Thomson's RN BA CSN (Ret.) (2005) research, the health problems that afflict today's students are: asthma, diabetes, epilepsy, viral infections, sports injuries, mental health problems, attention deficit with hyperactivity disorder and obesity [Table 1.]. The problems are different from those in 1905 but the objectives of Miss McKay and her twenty-first century counterparts, are the same. McKay was concerned with health education, hygiene and nutrition. In 2005 school nurses are concerned with disease prevention and health maintenance. conditions For the past one hundred years school nurses have helped children to be healthier and more able to learn. These nurses are Annie McKay's worthy successors. The light they have shone on children's lives is as spectacular as the blaze of electricity was at the beginning of the twentieth century.

REFERENCES

Doona, M. E. (1994). Gertrude Weld Peabody: Unsung Patron of Public Health Nursing. *Nursing & Health Care*: 88-94.

Hawkins, J.W. (1988). Lina Lavanche Rogers Struthers. In M. Kaufman, J. W. Hawkins, L. P. Higgins & A. H. Friedman (Eds.), *Dictionary of American Nursing Biography* (pp. 354-60). New York: Greenwood.

Kenney, D. (2005). Annie McKay. Unpublished material.

Somerville, C. [1893]. "District Nursing. In Robb, I.H. (1949). *Nursing of the Sick* 1893 (pp 119-127). New York: McGraw-Hill Company.

Thomson, B. (2005). Significant Events in the History of School Nursing. Unpublished material.

SEVENTY-ONE YEARS AGO: THE COCOANUT GROVE FIRE (PART 1)

(originally published March 2014)

Gracefully-fronded palm trees; cocoanut shells surrounding light bulbs; rattan, bamboo and leather covering concrete walls; and, billowing satin covering a plaster board ceiling created a tropical ambiance to the Cocoanut Grove, a popular restaurant/supper club in war time Boston. The exotic, but artificial, décor belied the building's origins as a garage and warehouse complex, as well as its subsequent incarnation as a speakeasy during Prohibition (1920-1933). By November 28, 1942, the Cocoanut Grove was second in popularity only to the Latin Quarter. Indeed that wintry Saturday night 1000 people crowded into the club far exceeding its capacity: 460.

Among the merry-makers who stepped into the vibrant Cocoanut Grove that night were soldiers and sailors enjoying a liberty weekend. Some were stationed in Boston while others were soon to ship out for foreign areas. Already at the club were football fans that had come over from Fenway Park after seeing Holy Cross trounce the undefeated Boston College (8-0 for the season) crushing them 52-12. Along with the military and football fans was the usual Saturday night crowd eager to forget for a while that the United States had been attacked almost a year before at Pearl Harbor (December 7, 1941) and was at war with Japan and Germany.

Fear that Boston might also be attacked was evident in the preventive strategies that Boston had put in place. Even Christmas lights were forbidden that year fearing that they might attract the enemy's unwanted attention. Air raid drills were common throughout Boston. Only one week before, Boston had staged a mock blitz attack of a Luftwaffe with Boston's hospitals practicing responses to such a disaster. Supplies of bandages, plasma, saline, IV equipment and oxygen tents had been significantly increased, while special wards had been set up to receive war victims. At the same time, nursing departments were starting to feel the pinch as more and more nurses left hospitals for military duty.

The Cocoanut Grove provided a welcomed respite from these wartime changes and the fears they created. Patrons dined in the restaurant, danced in the ballroom or had drinks downstairs in the Melody Lounge. Some were waiting for the 10 pm show that was already late as the pianist pounded out *Bell Bottom Trousers*. Then, about 10:15 pm, fire broke out. The accepted origin of the fire has focused on a Melody Lounge worker who had lit a match so that he could replace the light bulb that a patron had unscrewed to provide more privacy for him and his date. Investigators also considered faulty electrical wiring and refrigeration gases as culprits but concluded that the origin of the fire was unknown.

What is known for sure is that the fabric that created the tropical sky ignited. A hissing ball of flames and fumes raced up the four foot wide, steep stairway that became a chimney sucking the fire up into the foyer, where it then sped into the dining room. Within five minutes the entire complex was ablaze.

The ball of flame and fumes, seeking oxygen and customers seeking escape, competed for the same exits. Within two to five minutes of its first appearance, the fire poured through the most possible exits making them useless. The main exit, a revolving door that opened onto Piedmont Street, was not only engulfed in flames, it was obstructed by the bodies piling up in front of it as the toxic fumes asphyxiated the fleeing people. Other exits opened into the club rather than out to the street with a similar result. Worse, some exits barred to prevent customers from leaving without paying impeded escape.

Club personnel who knew of other exits in the service areas rescued some customers. Other personnel smashed the few windows that could be smashed and pushed people headfirst out of them. Some of these escaped the flames only to die from the toxic fumes already in their lungs once they breathed in the clear, cold night air. As one fireman observed, "They dropped like stones."

The fire department had been nearby on Stuart Street putting out a car fire and raced to the scene. They and others battled the blaze and by 10:24 pm, "the fifteen minute fire" was extinguished. Rescue became the priority. Soldiers and civilians became stretcher-bearers. One young nurse sped over from the Copley Plaza where she, her brother and friends had been partying since leaving the game at Fenway Park. They joined in transporting the victims to the Boston City Hospital in newspaper trucks, taxis and other vehicles that had been pressed into service.

Several victims presented themselves at the BCH at 10:30 pm to be followed by three hundred arriving by various ambulances. During one seventy-five minute period victims were arriving at the rate of one every eleven seconds. One hundred and eighty had died in transit and ten to fifteen who were still breathing on admission died within a few minutes of arrival. The young nurse remembers the area outside the emergency room as "just bodies" with a doctor and his associate going from corpse to corpse checking for any viability. One hundred and thirty-four victims were admitted into the wards that had been set aside for war casualties.

The BCH was the usual destination for any emergency treatment which explains the numbers of victims that were sent there in comparison to the Massachusetts General Hospital. The Massachusetts General Hospital began receiving victims at 10:30 pm and in two hours had received one hundred and fourteen. Seventy-five of these, many with the cherry-red faces signifying carbon monoxide poisoning, died on arrival. Thirty-nine were admitted.

Immediately on arrival at the hospitals victims received morphine after which their foreheads were marked in lipstick with an M. All, except military personnel who would have already been inoculated, received an anti-tetanus shot. Plasma and blood were started to treat burns as a systemic problem, a lesson that the treatment of burn victims at Pearl Harbor had taught only recently. Victims also received oxygen to treat pulmonary edema. Four days later, December 2, 1942 the antibiotic era began when penicillin, then still in the testing process, was released to treat infections of victims at the MGH. Its government-funded burn research was already in progress, whereas the BCH received its grant only days before the fire.

On the morning after the fire, November 29, 1942, the *Globe* headlined: 400 DEAD IN HUB NIGHT CLUB FIRE: HUNDREDS HURT IN PANIC AS THE COCOANUT GROVE BECOMES A WILD INFERNO. The final count of the disaster was 492 dead and 166 injured but that number excluded the injured who did not seek hospital treatment. The psychological trauma is still to be calculated.

In 1952, Dr. Stanley Levenson remembered the treatment at the BCH fifty years before. "What pulled the patients through…was intensive nursing. You simply kept them going, kept them breathing, getting them to cough, urging them on, physically clearing their airways, lending moral support. We had great attending doctors… residents, medical students, and most of all, we had wonderful nurses."

At the seventy-first anniversary of the fire this past November, thanks to the efforts of Mike Hanlon, Ken Marshall and Paul Miller, the Shawmut Ave Ext at Piedmont Street has been renamed Cocoanut Grove Lane. Mayor-elect Martin Walsh united with survivors, relatives of the victims, Bay Village neighbors and historians in their determination that although the Cocoanut Grove no longer exists, the fire and its lessons will not slip into oblivion.

REFERENCES

"A young nurse." Personal communication December 5, 2013 and January 14, 2014.

Benzaquin, Paul. 1967. *Fire in Boston's Cocoanut Grove*. Boston: Brandon Press, 1967.

Levenson, Stanley. At BCH Reunion. In "Recalling Cocoanut Grove." *The Boston Globe* (May 25, 1992).

Lund, Charles. Report at the December 8, 1942 meeting of the National Research Council's Subcommittee on Burns. http://www.cocoanutgrovefire.org/home/medical/boston-city-hospital.

MacQuarrie, Brian. "New Connection to a Historic Tragedy." *The Boston Globe* (November 28, 2013): A1 and A12.

Marshall, Ken. Personal communication January 7, 2014.

Reilly, William Arthur. Full Report concerning the Cocoanut Grove Fire. http://www.archive.org/stream/reportconcerning00bost/reportconcerning00bost_djvu.txt .

"The Cocoanut Grove Fire." www.bostonfirehistory.org/firestory11281942.html

COCOANUT GROVE FIRE: NURSING CARE (PART 2)

(originally published December 2014)

The one year anniversary of Japan's bombing of Pearl Harbor – Sunday December 7, 1941 – the "Day that would live in infamy" according to President Franklin D. Roosevelt, was only two weeks away as Boston staged a mock assault by German Luftwaffes. On that crisp fall day, November 22, 1942, fire trucks raced to the scene of the "disaster," first aid was given to those who had fallen, laundry trucks had been pressed into service as ambulances, and the injured were rushed to Boston's hospitals where nurses and doctors were at the ready to care for them.

Although not needed by the mock victims who had arrived at the emergency departments at the Boston City Hospital and the Massachusetts General Hospital, their burn services were prepared. MGH had already received its funding to study burns from the United States Office of Scientific and Research Development. BCH got its funding November 18, 1942 only four days before the mock attack. The grants aimed to extend the insights gained from caring for the causalities at Pearl Harbor. Burns, it was thought, were more than a surface trauma. Rather, the local burn set off a physiological response that affected the entire body. Accordingly, both hospitals were ready with saline, plasma, IV units as well as boric acid ointment, bandages oxygen tents and sulfonamides.

War-time jitters and even paranoia about the possibility of sabotage were constant worries as people and hospitals alike remained catastrophe minded. And then, only six days after the mock attack, November 28, 1942, disaster struck, not from a foreign enemy as expected, but from a fire at Boston's popular Cocoanut Grove dinner club. In spite of the drill of the mock attack, emergency vehicles automatically headed to BCH as was customary for Saturday night accidents. As a result BCH was inundated with victims with MGH receiving far fewer. At both sites the immediate task was separating the dead from the living. Corpses, many with cherry red faces from carbon monoxide poisoning and others who were deeply cyanotic from anoxia were lined up in makeshift morgues.

BCH set up its burn unit on wards G and H, while MGH did the same on the sixth floor of the White Building where at both sites prevention of infection became paramount. Burn injuries were draped with sterile towels as victims entered and would be covered with boric acid ointment or Vaseline and wrapped in gauze. All at once, casualties received morphine that an M written in lipstick on their foreheads noted. Anti-tetanus followed except for military men who would have already been inoculated. Fluids were started aimed at preventing physiological shock. Air-ways that had been damaged from flames, fumes and hot air were cleared. So pressing were respiratory problems that within the first twenty-four hours of treatment, BCH had performed thirty-eight tracheotomies.

Care was definitely "low tech" in 1942; medicine's scientific revolution and its resulting technology were post war phenomena. There were no intensive care units, monitors, blood gases, chemistries or equipment that extend eyes, ears and hands that are so commonplace seventy years later. Fifty years later remembering the limited technology, Dr. Stanley Levenson said, what pulled patients through was "intensive nursing care." The care focused on keeping patients going, keeping them breathing, getting them to cough, clearing their airways, lending moral support and urging them on. The attending doctors were great, continued Levenson, as were the medical students and the residents. "And most of all, we had wonderful nurses."[1]

Among them was Margaret Bushe, RN, the Director of Nursing at BCH. That night when she looked into the admitting room, she said to herself, "This is it! It was the kind of catastrophe, if of a different order, we had been preparing all these months to meet."[2] Bushe rounded up nursing students finding them at a dance they had been enjoying in the nurses home. The young women shed their party clothes, donned their uniforms and were with patients in a flash. Hours later, reflecting on how she performed in the emergency, one student said, "We had no time to get jittery. But when we got to our rooms, we began to think about what we had been through." Unable to tamp down the experience enough to get some rest, they could not sleep. Their counterparts at the MGH had a similar reaction. As much as they wanted to rest, they could not stop talking about their unprecedented experience.[3]

---

1 Stanley Levinson, "Recalling Cocoanut Grove," The Boston Globe, May 5, 1991, 34

2 Margaret Bushe, "Hospital Nurses and Aides Toiled Night and day 'Caring for Boston Fire victims", New York Herald Tribune December 6, 1942, p. 3.

3 Ibid. col 1, p.3.

Nursing students were essentially a hospital's nursing service in 1942. They cared for patients under the supervision of graduates in administrative positions. By the night of the fire there were even fewer graduates nurses. RNs had enlisted and gone off to war zones creating a serious nursing shortage. Then a war like condition came to graduates who had remained. Like them Bushe sprung into non-stop action around 10:30 pm when the first casualties arrived. Three and a half hours later at 2:00 am, she looked down at her hands and found them covered with blood. "Not for two days could I cleanse my hands of the smell of burnt flesh. I hope I never have to look on anything like Saturday night again as long as I live."[4]

The number of victims was fewer at the MGH but the horror was no less. Nurses coming off duty from the evening shift and nurses coming on duty for the night shift "swarmed down to the emergency ward," wrote Oliver Cope MD who documented the burn care at MGH.[5] Private duty nurses from the Baker Memorial and the Phillips House joined nurses on the sixth floor of the White Building. Among them was Grace Follett, a nursing instructor, had never before had seen such trauma. Few had. Etched forever in her memory was the experience of caring for fifteen patients three of whom no longer had faces.[6]

Nurses, students and graduates alike kept their focus on keeping people alive calling up strengths they never knew they possessed to care for the casualties. Those on the wards were spared the gruesome scenes of death just outside the doors of the hospitals. Mary Larkin of MGHSN Alumnae Association's Oral History Project interviewed Marion Bates, MGHSN 1934, then the night supervisor at the MGH. As she came on duty that night she saw the bodies of those who had died on arrival lined up in the hall that had been set up as a temporary morgue. The nonagenarian told Larkin it was, "A sight [she] would never forget." Indeed she took the seventy-year-long memory with her to her grave only recently. Nor did Mary Creagh, a BCH graduate of the 1930s ever fully recover from the trauma of that night. Her son, Kenneth Marshall M.D., remembers her screaming herself awake as she "saw," once again the bodies of people still in their evening clothes lined up as corpses in BCH's parking lot.[7]

Nursing students and nurses rushed to the hospitals that night. In subsequent days nurses came from public health services, others from school nursing and still others from Central Directory for Nurses. Many more came from hospitals among which were: the Massachusetts Memorial Hospital, Corey Hill Hospital, the Women's Free Hospital for Women, the Beth

---

4 Ibid.

5 Oliver Cope, Care of victims of the Cocoanut Grove Fire at the Massachusetts General Hospital, New England Journal of Medicine 1943: 229: 138-147.

6 "Caring for Boston Fire Victims," ibid.

7 Personal communication with: Mary Larkin RN September 26, 2014; Barbara Herlihy-Chevalier RN October 6, 2014; and, Kenneth Marshall MD January 7, 1914.

Israel Hospital, New England Deaconess Hospital, the New England Baptist, the New England Hospital for Women and Children, the Adams Nervine Hospital in Jamaica Plain, St Elizabeth's Hospital in Brighton, the Newton Hospital, and from hospitals as far away as Quincy, Haverhill, Medfield, Northampton and Winthrop.

Overseeing these nurses was the nursing consultant Gertrude Landmesser who was stationed at the Hotel Statler until April 1943. Operating in a similar fashion with 300 Red Cross nurses aides was Eleanor Wallace Allen, the wife of Frank Allen, the former governor of Massachusetts (1929-1931). They mopped floors, changed sheets, sterilized equipment, ran errands, stayed with patients, and gruesomely, searched corpses for identification. Mrs. Allen herself swept up litter getting down on her hands and knees to brush the cinders, pieces of flesh, glass and grit into the dustpan so she would not raise any dust.

By June 26 1943 there were still twenty-three patients of the one hundred and seventy-three (134 at BCH and 39 at MGH) needing intensive nursing care. Eventually these, too, went home. Survivors they were, but each carried within him the terror of his narrow escape from an inferno. To this day, the full extent of that trauma has surpassed any attempt to measure it or forget it. Daily reminders of the tragedy are EXIT signs over doors in public places.

PRIVILEGING THE PAST

(originally published September 2013)

Many of nursing's documents are saved in archives, the foremost of which is the History of Nursing Archives at the Howard Gotlieb Archival Research Center at Boston University's Mugar Memorial Library. Nursing's primary source materials are also preserved in other archives across the Commonwealth including: the Dimock Center (successor to the New England Hospital for Women and Children), the Massachusetts General Hospital Institute for the Health Professions, Simmons College Archives, the Mary L. Pekarski Nursing Archives at Boston College's Burns Library, the McLean Hospital in Belmont, Smith College in Northampton, the Schlesinger Library at the Radcliffe Institute, and the Massachusetts State Archives at Dorchester's Columbia Point.

Massachusetts' nurses are especially mindful of their past because history is in the air they breathe and the sights they see. Monuments, statues and photographs of history makers decorate nurses' milieu. Nurses Hall rests under the golden dome of Bulfinch's State House. The grasshopper above Faneuil Hall was fashioned in 1742 by Shem Drowne, the ancestor of Boston City Hospital's Lucy Lincoln Drown. Even street names are loaded with history. The Linda Richards Building at Dimock Center recognizes the nurse who earned nursing's first diploma in 1873 and Susan Dimock, the doctor who created Richards' nursing program at the New England Hospital for Women and Children.

As sensitive to history as Massachusetts' nurses are, the past is not foremost in their minds. Nurses are present-oriented. The urgent now of helping patients in crises is where nurses are found. Even so focused, they still honor their past. The proof is in the care with which they have collected and preserved the paper trail that their predecessors left behind.

These archives and the primary sources preserved in them are valuable. Perhaps more valuable are the memories in the archive that is each nurse's mind. Stored there, nurses' memories are at once strong and exquisitely fragile. Listen to nurses gathered together with classmates at alumnae reunions. Memory after memory made decades before tumble out in laughter and sometimes in tears. So intense was their learning and so present-oriented was their care, their urgent nows endured in memory.

These memories are fragile because they are not part of the profession's narrative. Nursing's history is all the poorer for their absence. All too often this emptiness is filled with myth-which President John F. Kennedy described as "persistent, persuasive and unrealistic." Myths are distractions he told the graduating seniors at Yale in 1962[1]. Many nurses claim that Florence Nightingale single-handedly reduced the mortality rate at Scutari. That myth persists to this day. It even persuades nurses, but it is not true. That myth and others like it are not worthy of nurses and what they do. Such a myth distracts from the real memories of real nurses caring for real patients.

Nurses increasingly privilege their past. The alumnae of the Beth Israel Hospital School of Nursing gathered their memories into a history of their School in spite of the destruction of its primary documents. The late Alice Seale Davis recorded her experience as the second president of the Nursing Archives Associates. Ann Donovan and Marie Knowles taped their memories about joining the United States Navy Nurse Corps as young graduates during World War II. Alumnae of the St Elizabeth's Hospital School of Nursing videotaped graduates from across six decades as they shared their experiences. Although Ida Luniewicz Thomas, a nursing student from 1936-1938 and, Helen Fagan a nursing student from 1947-1950 are no longer alive, their memories, their voices and their styles have been preserved for posterity.

Bernice (Bea) Bennett Kelly, a 1946 graduate of the Massachusetts Memorial Hospital School of Nursing is still another example of privileging the past. She committed her memories to paper with fellow alumna, Emily Fenner, a self-described "story-writing cheerleader" urging her on. As a result, Kelly's article "An Era Gone By: But Never Forgotten" appeared in the Boston Medical Center's *Nursing Narratives* this year.

Kelly was a nursing student at the moment when nursing headed into the era of its greatest change. Nurses joined the Army and Navy to care for the troops during World War II but that left 46% of the nursing positions unfilled. Hospitals wanted more nurses and so too did the armed forces. The federal government responded by financing nursing education, first with the Cadet Nurse Corps and then with tuition support that moved nursing students from hospitals to colleges and universities. During this same time military nursing transformed nurses from those who carried out the orders of others to professionals who made their own decisions about nursing care.

Kelly was a Cadet Nurse. She had completed the accelerated nursing courses at the Massachusetts Memorial Hospital School of Nursing in thirty months. The next six months she practiced at the John C. Haynes Hospital in Brighton/Allston at once reducing the nursing shortage there and receiving a $30 monthly subsidy from the government. Caring for patients was no easy task. Garbed in gown, mask and gloves; riding in ambulances with her patients; or, running a ward on evening and night shifts, Kelly was one of thousands of nursing students across the nation who staffed hospitals during the 1940s. An astonishing 80% of the nursing care in hospitals was given by nursing students. A registered nurse was available to the nursing student by phone.

The diagnoses that Kelly's patients carried suggest the enormity of her task. They suffered from: meningitis, poliomyelitis, diphtheria, tuberculosis, brucellosis, tularemia, typhoid, anthrax, tetanus, gas gangrene, rickettsial diseases…plus the usual measles, mumps, chicken pox, scarlet fever, pertussis…complicated with pneumonia [and] encephalitis.[3]

Robert Koch had identified the tubercle bacillus in 1882 and successors had discovered the causes of other diseases but treatment lagged far behind. As Kelly reports, "Death and disability [were] often the outcome of these infections"[3].

But change was on the horizon. Kelly participated in a study where every other patient with scarlet fever was given a research drug. Once the research drug had proven its effectiveness, the vaccines, and eventually the need for communicable diseases hospitals ceased. Once the leading cause of death, by 1954 infectious diseases had dipped below cancer and heart disease that were on the rise.

As busy as she was, Kelly was accumulating vivid memories that have lasted a lifetime. More than sixty years later those memories have been freed from the archive of her mind and shared with colleagues and family. Etched in print they are no longer fragile. They are available to nurses yet unborn. In privileging her past, Kelly has added essential facts to the profession's narrative.

REFERENCES
[1] Kennedy, John F. Commencement Speech at Yale University (June 11, 1962).
[3] Kelly, Bernice Bennett. "An Era Gone By: But Never Forgotten.
[4] Ibid.

MARCH 2001—THE BIRTH OF MARN;
THE BIRTH OF HEALTH CARE REFORM: MARCH 2010

(originally published March 2011)

On Tuesday March 23, 2010, American Nurses Association President Rebecca Patton sat in the front row in the East Room of the White House. Beside her were health care consumers. Behind them sat Caroline Kennedy, the niece of the late Massachusetts Senator Edward M. Kennedy, for whom health care reform was the cause of his life. Nearly 300 people filled the rest of the room. ANA's prominence as President Barrack Obama signed into law the Patient Protection and Affordable Care Act (PPACA) signified Obama's recognition of nurses' long and valiant efforts for health care reform. Raising the quality of health care had been ANA's mission since its beginning in 1896. Throughout the process from bill to law, Obama referred to nurses as the "beating heart of the health care system."

The signing ceremony had special significance for Massachusetts' nurses. Only ten years before, the Labor Relations Cabinet of the Massachusetts Nurses Association (MNA) started proceedings to end MNA's 98-year affiliation with the ANA. Throughout the spring, summer and fall of 2000, pro-ANA members spoke at Town Hall Meetings throughout the State, on the pages of *The Massachusetts Nurse,* in response to the Hot Line questions on MNA's web site and in mailings to the membership.

Pro-ANA supporters argued that ANA represented nurses in all their diversity including staff positions, advanced practice, management, education, research, the military, health care policy, and as attorneys. ANA's united voice spoke for nurses, patient care, educational preparation, just wages, ethical practice and a safe nurse-patient milieu. Sadly the year 2000 saw the deaths of nurses who believed in ANA: Minnie Cohen who had served MNA as its president from 1967-1969; Mary Anne Garrigan, founder of the History of Nursing Archives at Boston University; Eileen Callahan Hodgman of the Beth Israel Hospital; and, Mary E. Macdonald of academia and the Massachusetts General Hospital. The pro-ANA nurses campaigned valiantly and argued eloquently, but on March 24, 2001 at Mechanics Hall in Worcester, Massachusetts two-thirds of members present voted to end their affiliation with ANA to become a labor organization for staff nurses.

Pro-ANA members were sad and anguished over the vote. Distraught as they were that relationships with colleagues had ended they focused on continuing their relationship with ANA. As Eleanor Vanetzian said, "Unity with the ANA was in the best interest of the public [we] served... and the best potential to represent all nurses and recipients of nursing care." When William Galvin signed the document on March 23, 2001 MARN was incorporated and the Massachusetts Association of Registered Nurses (MARN) became the constituent member of ANA.

Barbara Blakeney recalls, "We wasted no time...to build a new, vibrant organization." David Keepnews emphasizes, "MARN welcomes *all* nurses." MARN's first days were "energizing and exciting," Peggy Blum remembers, knowing at that point, "We were on our way!"

Wisdom galore shaped the new association as its leaders brought to bear their long experience in organizational leadership. Marie Snyder, a nurse and attorney, drew up the Articles of Organization to incorporate the new Association. Its purposes were:

> fostering the continued development of professional nurses and high standards of nursing; [and], providing an environment which encourages exploration of common interests and develops collaborative relationships with other nursing groups within the Commonwealth; initiating and influencing legislation and affecting public policy; providing for quality in nursing practice, nursing education, and the continuing education of nurses; and such other legal purposes as are consistent with a professional nursing organization (March 23, 2001).

MARN's inaugural officers included: Karen Daley, President; Barbara A. Blakeney, Vice-president; Margaret T. Barry, Treasurer; and, Cynthia A. LaSala, Secretary. The Directors were: Peggie Griffin Bretz, Maura K. Fitzgerald, Jackie Hayes, David M. Keepnews, Mary J. McKenzie and Eleanor V. Vanetzian. Others who signed the document on March 19, 2001 were: Linda Moniz, Mary Anne MacKusick, Donna Mae Donahue, Sherry Merrow, Elizabeth Grady, Carmela Townsend, Patricia M. Brigham, Claudia Ellis and Judith Mealey.

MARN marks its tenth anniversary on March 23, 2011 with Anne Manton its president and Karen Daley, MARN's first president, now the president of ANA. MARN members from the edge of the Atlantic Ocean to the hills of the Berkshires are joined with nurses throughout the country. These ANA members are a powerful force as health care reform begins to improve the quality of care for all.

SOURCES CITED

American Nurses Association. (2008). *ANA's Health System Reform Agenda*. Washington, DC: Author. Retrieved from www.NursingWorld.org.

Articles of Organization. [Incorporation]. 2001. Commonwealth of Massachusetts.

Flanagan, Lyndia, compiler. *One Strong Voice: The Story of the American Nurses Association* (Kansas City, MO: ANA, 1976).

Patton, Rebecca (2010). "The Future of Health Care is Now." MARN Conference Randolph, MA, November 10, 2010.

GOVERNOR SARGENT'S REORGANIZATION BILL IMPERILS THE BORN

(originally published June 2010)

The RN after a nurse's name is the stamp of legitimacy. No matter how many degrees graduates of approved nursing programs earn, until they pass the State Board Exam, proving their competency, they cannot be hired as RNs. Since 1910 RN marks the transition from the <u>aspiration</u> to be a nurse to the reality of <u>being</u> a nurse. For the public, RN signifies safe nursing practice.

The Board of Registration in Nursing's daily work of protecting the public, approving schools of nursing and licensing nurses was proceeding as usual as the 1970s began. Nursing's major issue at that time was the American Nurses Association's declaration that preparation for practice must take place in institutions of higher learning. The State was rightly proud of its many hospital nursing schools but the one hundred year era of diploma programs was coming to an end. Twenty had closed during the 1970s while the number of baccalaureate programs increased to ten and associate degree programs to nineteen. As nursing argued about which program best prepared the practitioner, the country was in an uproar.

The public's trust was sorely tested by controversies like Watergate, the Vietnam War and the exposure of the Pentagon Papers. These issues would recede into the background of nursing's consciousness on March 19, 1973 when Governor Francis Sargent submitted his bill H6120 <u>An Act to Reorganize and Modernize State Government by Creating a Department of Human Services</u> with a plan to expedite its passage. Nurses were especially interested in the Health Services Regulation Administration section of H6120 and its implications for nursing. On March 21, 1973, nurses gathered in Framingham for the Massachusetts League for Nursing convention listened as the Governor's Secretary of Human Services, Peter Goldmark, Jr. and his assistant, Charles Stover, could not answer questions about the impending legislation. The Governor, though scheduled, did not appear. In September, 1972, Alan Posner of Consumer Affairs met with the State's twenty-eight Boards without sharing details about the proposed new department, which forced those attending the meeting to conclude that there was a "hidden plan."

Not to be stymied by this pattern of silence, the Board of Registration in Nursing wrote to the Secretary of Consumer Affairs October 18, 1972 stating its concern that there would be no opportunity to review and comment on H6120. The Board's letter was ignored. Human Services, which would succeed Consumer Affairs when the government was reorganized, was equally reticent. BORN Chair, Gellestrina "Tina" DiMaggio said that the Board was tossed like a football between the two Secretariats. In the jargon of the 1970s, the control over the flow of information constituted stonewalling. Worse, the Commonwealth's 100,000 nurses had no voice and were given no hearing. The public, whose lives depended on the quality of nursing care were given less.

The Board was fortunate in its leader. DiMaggio, the Associate Director in Mary Macdonald's nursing department at the Massachusetts General Hospital was used to dealing with complexity and leadership was as natural to her as breathing. She and her fellow nurse appointees on the Board: Phyllis Migliozzi (Worcester City Hospital School of Nursing); Estelle Lombardi (Youville Hospital School of Practical Nursing); Catherine Garrity (License Practical Nurses of Massachusetts); and, Ann Jackson were equally skilled.

Mary Baroli, the BORN's Executive Secretary, who DiMaggio states "was a very smart woman" facilitated the Board's work. Lombardi remembers Baroli as a nurse who was "all business" and who expected everyone serving the Board to behave likewise. Though excellent leaders, DiMaggio and Baroli were unable to convince the Division of Personnel, and later, a legislator, that Board members' salaries must be competitive with the nursing market if the Board was to attract qualified nurses as staff. Alas, salaries remained low in spite of the Board's surplus of $215,000 which exceeded the cost of running the BORN.

On February 15, 1973, DiMaggio alerted Consumer Affairs about the upcoming vacancies of critical personnel and its implications for the State Board Exam in August. The retirements of Eileen Bean, (Registrar), the Executive Secretary and a nursing supervisor between March and June 1973, had a direct impact on the Board's ability to give the national exam. The illness of Board appointee, Marie Andrews, and her death in 1973 further added to the strain. Yet the Board staff carried out their tasks so well that few on the outside knew of the difficulties.

At the direction of Louis Resteghini, the Director of Registration, DiMaggio prepared a fact sheet on the BORN's functions and activities hoping to reach beyond the information impasse to "responsible" officers in Consumer Affairs. At the same time, she sent a memo to nursing schools, practical nursing schools, the Massachusetts Nurses Association, the Massachusetts League for Nursing and the Massachusetts Hospital Association alerting them of the staff openings on the Board.

Besides dealing with the uncertainties surrounding the upcoming change, they conducted the Board's business: granting and renewing licenses, approving new nursing programs, overseeing standards for 101 nursing programs, conducting and reviewing the results of the State Board Exam, investigating schools whose graduates had a high failure rate, reviewing reciprocity requests, evaluating foreign graduates' credentials, conducting competency, exposing imposters and responding to questions from consumers, national organizations and government agencies.

On February 15, 1973, one month before Sargent submitted his bill DiMaggio and the Board received part of report from Verani (Secretary for Consumer Affairs) revealing some details of the Governor's "hidden plan". Meanwhile, rumors about a possible relocation of the Board from its 15th floor offices in the Saltonstall Building on Cambridge Street to an undisclosed location.

At this point DiMaggio called for a meeting with William Bicknell, MD, the Commissioner of Public Health, and Verani and Resteghini of Consumer Affairs on March 6, 1973. Bicknell did not attend but sent Kathy West (Assistant Commissioner of Public Health) and Derek Robinson (Depputy Commissioner). Dan Hillman, Assistant Secretary (legal) of Consumer Affairs was also present. At last, the two secretariats – Human Services and Consumer Affairs - which had been throwing the BORN around like a football were at the same table with the Board.

After DiMaggio presented her report and its comparative data on fiscal 1967 and 1972, West and Robinson disclosed their plan. The functions of the Board, was to be transferred to Health Systems Regulation Council (HSRC) where five consumer positions would outnumber the three professional positions. The Board's two nursing supervisory positions would be transferred to the Health Personnel Board (HPB), which would make recommendations on licensure and investigations. Both HSRC and HPB were advisory, reporting to the Administrator of Health Services Regulation Administration for final decisions. The BORN's positions of Registrar, Executive Secretary and two other supervisory positions would be abolished, effectively eliminating the sixty-three year old BORN.

There would be no professional nurse at the licensure level.
And worst of all, non-nurses would be establishing standards
of nursing education and nursing competency!

To be continued in the next Clio's Corner.

REFERENCES

DiMaggio, Gellestrina. Re: Mary Baroli to Mary Ellen Doona.

H6120 *An Act to Reorganize and Modernize State Government by Creating a Department of Human Services.* Massachusetts State Archives.

Kuba, Anna. To Donald C. Hillman, April 5, 1973. <u>MNA Collection</u>, History of Nursing Archives, BU.

Lombardi, Estelle. Re: Mary Baroli to Mary Ellen Doona.

Minutes of the Board of Registration in Nursing, Massachusetts State Archives.

NURSES PROTEST GOVERNOR'S PROPOSAL TO ABOLISH THE BOARD OF REGISTRATION OF NURSES

(originally published September 2010)

On March 6, 1973, Dr. William Bicknell's office of the Public Health Commissioner, announced that the Board of Registration in Nursing (BORN) would cease to exist on July 1, 1973 with the passing of Governor Francis Sargent's bill to reorganize state government. The BORN's most immediate concern was the State Board Exam scheduled to be given to more than 3000 graduating nursing students in August, 1973. Without a BORN, the exam could not be given.

BORN Chairwoman Gellestrina DiMaggio had no choice but to direct BORN members to "respond to the changes that 'reorganization' will bring about although clearly developed plans or legislation [are] not available to the public or the profession" (BORN Minutes, March 20, 1973). Indeed, the printed copy of the bill would not be available until April 6, 1973. Consequently on Mach 23, 1973, the BORN's Executive Secretary, Mary Baroli alerted the Council of State Boards of Nursing, "Effective immediately, Massachusetts will not proctor candidates for the examination" Reciprocity – interstate licensure – was at an end.

On April 3, 1973 the BORN and leaders of the Massachusetts Nurses Association, the Massachusetts League for Nursing, the Licensed Practical Nurses of Massachusetts, Inc. and the Massachusetts Student Senate, along with Frances Lenehan, Chief Nurse of the Department of Mental Health and Ann Thomson, Chief Nurse of the Department of Public Health, met with Van Lanckton, the Deputy General Counsel for the incoming Office of Human Services. The nursing leaders protested that *Section 311* of H6120 stated that "any person" employed in an approved health care facility (including hospitals and clinics) could provide "nursing service" to patients "under the supervision of a registered nurse or a licensed practical nurse." This provision effectively changed the definition of nursing, repealed mandatory licensure and would pave the way for institutional licensure.

Van Lanckton told the nursing leaders that it was "too late" to delete *Section 311* from H6120. Two days later, April 5, 1973, the presidents of the four nursing organizations: Anne G. Hargreaves (MNA), Mary Conceison (MLN), Catherine Garrity (LPN of Massachusetts, Inc.) and Paul Coss (Massachusetts Student Senate), issued a legislative alert to their respective memberships detailing the potential impact of H6120 and Health Systems Regulation Administration for Massachusetts' 100,000 nurses. The National League for Nursing supported Massachusetts by passing a unanimous resolution urging the Governor not to abolish the BORN. ANA members read the editorial in *American Journal of Nursing* describing the Governor's bill as "regressive" (1973, p. 1167).

Nursing was the first of the professional boards to respond to the Governor's proposed reorganization. The Massachusetts Medical Society, the Massachusetts Hospital Association, the Massachusetts Legislature and the media aligned themselves with nurses. Support also came from 790 nurses and doctors from two of Boston's hospitals who petitioned the Governor stating that his bill eliminated professional expertise, restrained improvement and jeopardized reciprocity between Massachusetts and other states. Many professional supporters saw reorganization as the consumerization of health care with cost, not quality, shaping patient care. Commissioner Bicknell countered saying reorganization was "extraordinarily progressive" and nurses' opposition was "absolute arrogant irresponsibility" (1973).

The blizzard of letters arriving at the State House spoke in nursing's favor. Legislators received so many, they had to create a form letter response. Mindful of nurses' voting power, they penned in notes about a mother, wife, or daughter who was also a nurse. Nursing staff from the MNA and MLN, dropped by legislators' offices to personally explain their opinions about how essential the BORN was to ensuring quality nursing care. Nurses won the support of the public because almost everyone knew a nurse as a family member, a friend, a neighbor or as a recipient of nursing services (April 26, 2010).

Nursing students reacted "vigorously" to reorganization (Conlin, 1973); no strangers to social activism of Civil Rights and Women's Rights Movements of the 1960s and 1970s. Their dream of becoming an RN was dissolving just as it was within reach. They understood that *Section 311* of H6120 allowing <u>anyone</u> to practice nursing invalidated their nursing education. Likewise, nursing's leaders who had been part of nursing's renewal following World War II foresaw how nursing would deteriorate if the BORN's commitment to ensuring safe nursing practice were discarded. The public would also be left unprotected by allowing non-nurses to establish nursing standards and determine competence.

Bicknell's office confidently stated that the exams would be given and then did an end run around the BORN by sending the Commonwealth's lawyers to ANA to work out a process. The exams could not be given, wrote Anna Kuba of the Council of State Boards of Nursing since the Council's contract with Massachusetts specified that a BORN had to administer the national exam. Elimination of BORN on July 1, 1973, meant that there could be no exam in August 1973. Kuba had "no alternatives to offer" (1973).

Trying to quiet the nurses' protest, John Verani the outgoing Office of Consumer Affairs tried another tactic. He asked the BORN to divorce reorganization from the August exam, and endorse his press release stating that the exams would be given while his assistant met with the new Office of Human Services to assure continuity of the positions of Registrar and Executive Secretary under reorganization. The BORN could not join Verani's press release because the exam was not guaranteed "unless and until the provisions of the contract can be met and the contract is approved." Following this the BORN voted unanimously to oppose H 6120 and directed DiMaggio to "communicate this opposition to the Governor, House Speaker David Bartley, Senate President Kevin Harrington, Senator Jack Bachman, Chairman, and Representative Michael Flaherty, House Chairman on Social Welfare" (BORN Minutes, April 17, 1973).

During the next week a number of press releases and remarks were circulated about the testing program as "totally unfounded." The Registrar and the Executive Secretary positions were replaced. The exams would proceed as usual. Specific questions raised by the nursing organizations had not been answered. DiMaggio rebutted these and other statements saying fears had not been "allayed" and the changes were structural and substantial (April 24, 1973).

REFERENCES

Baroli, Mary. To [Council of] State Boards of Nursing (March 23, 1973). *BORN Collection*, Massachusetts State Archives.

"Comm. Bicknell attacks nurses' stand on H6120, accuses nurses of 'arrogant irresponsibility'," *MNA Bulletin* (Spring, 1973): 6.

Conlin, Alice Y. ["Terry"] to State Nurses Associations (April 23, 1973).

Coss, Paul. To Mary Ellen Doona (April 26, 2010).

DiMaggio, Gellestrina. "The Board Members at the March 21, 1973 Meeting…". *BORN Collection*, Massachusetts State Archives.

---. Response to the Fact Sheet Released by Secretary of Human Services-Peter C. Goldmark, Jr. under date of April 24, 1973. *BORN Collection*, Massachusetts State Archives.

H6120 *An Act to Reorganize and Modernize State Government by Creating a Department of Human Services*. Massachusetts State Archives (April 6, 1973). Massachusetts State Archives.

Kuba, Anna. Correspondence to Donald C. Hillman (April 5, 1973). *MNA Collection*, History of Nursing Archives, BU.

Minutes of the Board of Registration in Nursing, BORN Collection Massachusetts State Archives.

Schutt, Thelma M. "Outrage in Massachusetts," *American Journal of Nursing* (July 1973): 1167

RESCUING THE BOARD OF
REGISTRATION IN NURSING

(originally published December 2010)

That the Board of Registration in Nursing (BORN) was able to celebrate its centennial this past October was due in large part to the efforts of nurses in the spring and summer of 1973. They rallied against Governor Francis Sargent's proposal to abolish the BORN. His bill, H6120 would mandate that non-nurses establish standards of nursing education and determine the competence of nurses. Massachusetts nurses were determined that the safety and welfare of the consumer of nursing services would not be so endangered.

Neither their knowledge nor their experience was sought in the development of H6120. Nurses tried another tack. They provided the Governor with an opportunity to address 300 nurse educators when the Massachusetts League for Nursing met on March 21, 1973. He refused, continuing his pattern of withholding vital information from nurses and neglecting to solicit nurses' input.

By this time Mary Macdonald of the Massachusetts General Hospital had analyzed a draft of H6120 confirming what until then had been only rumored; non-nurses would in fact be making nursing decisions. In essence sixty-three years of the BORN's protection of public from the incompetent nurse was being discarded. With the publication of Macdonald's analysis on April 17, 1973 the BORN voted unanimously to oppose H6120. The Massachusetts Nurses Association, the Massachusetts League for Nursing, the Licensed Practical Nurses of Massachusetts and the Senate of Student Nurses fully supported the BORN's decision.

A series of informational sessions with nurses across the Commonwealth followed. Fifteen hundred nurses from Pittsfield, Springfield and Holyoke braved a heavy rainstorm on April 27, 1973 to hear Mary Macdonald, the BORN and Paul Coss, President of the Senate of Student Nurses. There was no question that the audience agreed with the speakers. Thunderous applause greeted Mary Baroli, the Executive Secretary of the BORN, when she told the damp nurses that the forces for H6120 had "only begun to hear from us" (Holyoke Daily Transcript/Telegram, April 28, 1973, 10).

At 3:00 pm on May 1, 1973, just four hours before another informational session was to begin at Faneuil Hall, Peter Goldmark, Secretary for Human Services, told the press that reorganization would not affect nursing standards nor cancel the exams. Nurses knew better. In fact 5000 of them were arriving in Boston. They came by carloads, by busloads, by trolleys and by foot. "The sea of white" rolled in from across the Commonwealth into Government Center. Those who could not get into the standing room only crowd in Faneuil Hall filled the new Boston City Hall, with Mary Macdonald presiding over the former, and MNA President Anne Hargreaves over the latter. Nurses who could not get into either hall filled City Hall Plaza (Boston Herald American, May 2, 1973, p.1).

The next day 250 nurses and nursing students crowded into the State House's Gardner Auditorium and listened as the Governor presented H6120 to the Social Welfare Committee. The audience was not allowed to testify but by their presence and their signs, silent nursing students "voiced" their opposition. Theirs was not a "philosophical disagreement" as the Governor claimed but a realistic reaction to a proposal that would put patient safety in danger. "Let H-6120 die!" said one poster, while another declared, "We care about our patients. Do you?"

The informational sessions continued with 300 nurses attending another one in Holyoke on May 8, 1973. At mid-May another 2000 nurses and supportive legislators filled the Memorial Auditorium in Worcester. On June 12th Hargreaves met with nurses in Dartmouth. "Reorganization was far from dead," said one nurse alluding to Goldmark's position that H6120 in no way threatened licensure. The nurses' protests had gained the Governor's attention. He met in his corner office with Anne Hargreaves (MNA), Mary Conceison (MLN), Catherine Garrity (LPNM), Paul Coss (SSN) and BORN's Gellestrina "Tina" DiMaggio and Mary Baroli. Discussions continued throughout the summer. The BORN was not abolished. Nurses continued to make decisions about nursing education and the competence of nurses as they had since 1910 when the BORN was established. Their successors do the same in 2010.

Nurses and nursing students at Boston City Hall (Massachusetts Nurses Association)

NURSING PRACTICE CHANGES FOCUS

(originally published June 2012)

Years ago nurses were often ordered to give TLC, tender loving care, to patients for whom all other interventions were no longer effective. TLC as its terms are defined is a delicate, sensitive and anxious watching over a patient (Skeats). Medications, irrigations and dressings can be ordered but not TLC, for given its nature TLC originates within the nurse, as art springs from an artist. TLC characterizes nursing's art and a nurse's creativity.

TLC was not an intervention when all else failed as nurses caring for wounded soldiers during World War II discovered. That insight revealed that TLC was nursing practice itself. This was no small matter for prior to that war and for many years to come nursing practice was running a ward, specifically, assigning, directing and supervising the care of others. The nurse was at the apex of a pyramid of personnel and provided only brief and intermittent care while the least educated and experienced ancillary personnel provided the most direct care (Reiter). Thanks to the soldiers they had cared for, military nurses learned that nursing practice was immediate and continuous care.

Following the war, these military nurses used their G.I. Bill benefits (1944 Servicemen's Readjustment Act) to broaden this insight and deepen their knowledge. Some became part of the nation's investment in its mental health that was prompted by the high incidence of psychiatric disabilities among draftees and combat soldiers. The Mental Health Act in 1946 supported these nurses as they earned graduate degrees and then integrated mental health concepts into nursing school curricula.

During this same time, the pendulum of expectation swung towards all nurses being able to care for the mental health of their patients as well as for their physical health. By the end of the next decade, nursing required that all nursing students should have a psychiatric nursing course and that their competency should be tested in the exams for licensure. Nursing itself was re-vitalized as psychiatric nursing became part of all nursing and not merely an after-thought. Thus had wounded soldiers and their nurses influenced the transformation of nursing practice from a focus on nursing a ward to a focus on providing nursing for the patient.

Concurrently, drugs discovered at mid-twentieth century dealt directly with psychotic symptoms rescuing many patients from their illnesses. The long era of therapeutic nihilism that characterized custodial care in large state hospitals was at an end. The recommendations from Congress' Joint Commission on Mental Illness and Health conducted from 1955-1960 were published in 1961 as *Action for Mental Health*. Two years later President John F. Kennedy's Community Mental Health Centers Act of 1963 was signed into law. Subsequently, patients and psychiatric care moved from remote sites to the community.

When June Mellow (12.19.24-10.2.04), moved her study of nursing patients with schizophrenia from the Boston State Hospital to the Boston Psychopathic Hospital as it became the Massachusetts Mental Health Center, nursing therapy saw a further refinement of TLC. Nurses were not expected to step out of their usual role, she often said. Instead they were to explore and realize more fully and intensively their personal care of patients. Dr Elvin Semrad, MMHC's Clinical Director from 1952-1976 whose therapy of patients began with an empathic diagnosis encouraged Mellow's research as did Professor Gene Phillips, who urged nurses to *scientize* their art.

During this same time, the American Nurses Association funded a two-year study of interactions between nurses and patients with Harriet M. Kandler, MMHC's Director of Nursing, as the principal investigator. As nurses studied their care, social scientists studied nurses. To give just one example, a study sought to uncover the changes in the nursing student's empathy as a result of the psychiatric nursing affiliation. Then in 1959 the National Institute of Mental Health chose Mellow's nursing therapy for nursing's first doctoral program at Boston University. The patients at the MMHC served as the site of the studies conducted over the next six years, as patients did for graduate and undergraduate students for many years to come.

Overseeing all this expansion of nursing practice, research and education at MMHC was Marilyn Wright Barron Matte. A graduate of the New England Deaconess Hospital School of Nursing, she knew the days when psychiatric nursing was an elective course and not a requirement. She also knew psychiatric nursing when it was tending patients in prolonged baths, during insulin and electroshock therapy and after lobotomies. From 1962 on, however, Matte oversaw nursing practice committed to the healing power of human contact. This was more than the therapeutic use of self as the utilitarians would have it for neither the nurse nor nursing practice was a technique. Nursing practice was nurses, out of the depths of their knowledge and experience, making an emotional commitment to their patients, and delicately, sensitively and anxiously watching over them as they reached out from illness towards healthy human contact. Such nursing practice cannot be ordered.

On June 24, 2012 the nursing department at the Massachusetts Mental Health Center marks its 100th anniversary.

REFERENCES

Reiter, Frances. 1966. "The Nurse-Clinician," *American Journal of Nursing* (66): 274-278.

Skeats, Walter. 1963. *A Concise Etymological Dictionary of the English Language*. New York: Capricorn Books.

Stein, Jess. 1966. *Random House Dictionary of the English Language*. New York: Random House.

AT THE THRESHOLD OF MASSACHUSETTS
MENTAL HEALTH CENTER'S NEXT CENTURY

(originally published September 2012)

O n June 22 and 23, 2012, the Massachusetts Mental Health Center (MMHC) marked its centennial with a symposium in the Longwood Medical Area only a short walk away from the Fenwood Road site of MMHC 's remarkable history in caring for individuals with serious mental illness. Dignitaries from the National Institute of Mental Health, the Commonwealth's Health and Human Services, the Department of Mental Health (DMH), and Brigham and Women's Hospital (BWH) praised MMHC's unique legacy in care, training and research. Papers featured the neurobiological and genetic factors in serious mental illness along with the cognitive therapies designed for detection, early intervention and recovery. The symposium moved from research reports to reality when a young woman recounted her journey from serious mental illness to recovery.

That the MMHC still exists to celebrate its one-hundredth year is due in large part to what its care, training and research meant to its patients. By 1994 the MMHC building had deteriorated becoming shabby and outdated. Hopes that MMHC would be restored were dashed when Governor William Weld moved MMHC's acute care unit to the New England Deaconess Hospital. Worsening finances prohibited the Commonwealth from rehabilitating MMHC on its 3.1 acres site in the Longwood Medical Area. Despite its recognition by the National Register of Historic Places, the Commonwealth announced that MMHC would close but promised "equal or better" services in its place.

Patients knew at first hand that there was no equal to MMHC. To them, MMHC was more than a building. It was care when they were seriously ill; support that helped them move into the community; and professional commitment that helped them to live more satisfying and productive lives. And so patients created the Committee to Save Mass Mental; designed pins that said "MMHC GIVE AWAY? NO WAY!" spoke on radio shows; wrote op-ed pieces for Boston's newspapers; visited the State House; and, lobbied legislators. Amazingly, they were heard. Legislators blocked the governor's plan by forbidding the closing of MMHC without the expressed consent of the Legislature.

That action provided the necessary pause for other voices to be heard. MaryLou Sudders MSW, the Commissioner of Mental Health, listened to these consumers because their action to save MMHC exemplified DMH's mission. Patients were receiving effective and culturally competent care across a wide spectrum of community-based services. Their rights as patients were honored, and their political action showed that patients were a self-determining population actively participating in decisions made about their care. MMHC worked. The question was how it might be saved.

By 2003, however, the building was no longer safe for patient care. MMHC was moved to the Lemuel Shattuck Hospital in Jamaica Plain with the promise that it would be returned to Fenwood Road. Six years later, the BWH announced a public-private partnership between the DMH, BWH and Roxbury Tenants of Harvard (RTH). BWH would build: a new MMHC at 75 Fenwood Road, a BWH clinical and research building on MMHC's old site at 74 Fenwood Road, and an affordable housing complex and community spaces for RTH.

MMHC returned to Fenwood Road in November 2011; to a shiny six-story tower housing Continuing Care, the Commonwealth Research Center, and administrative offices. Partial Hospitalization and the Fenwood Inn, a transitional residential program, opened at 20 Vining Street. Next spring, BWH will open a medical services clinic, completing MMHC's new status as a public/private institution.

Such easy access to physical care will be a boon to a population that dies from physical illnesses (primarily cardiovascular diseases) 25 years earlier than other populations in the United States. Dr. Jim O'Connell (Boston Health Care for the Homeless) who works closely with MMHC said at the symposium that if other populations had such a statistic, a public health emergency would be declared. In a comment worthy of the satirist, one wag stated "dying from physical illness prevents the recovery from mental illness."

Several nurses including Marilyn Matte, Rena Levesque, Sondra Hellman and Ellen Flowers were mentioned in an historical overview at the start of the symposium. Also attending the symposium was Center Director, Laura Rood with her vast clinical, administrative and teaching experience in caring for those with serious mental illness. Mary Maher, the Nursing Coordinator of Partial Hospitalization, said, "I am so proud of MMHC. I am so proud to be at MMHC. There is nothing more rewarding than seeing the patient out there in the community. When they drop in for a visit, I think of it as alumni week."

Ekaterini Poulakos, APRN exclaimed, "How important it is, this work that we do. We need to do much more to help people." Other nurses at the symposium were: Karen Sherman, the RN on Partial Hospitalization and Liaison between Partial Hospitalization and the Fenwood Inn, Veronica Besancon of Partial Hospitalization, Ann Findeisen of the Prevention and Recovery in Early Psychosis Program (PREP), Joanne Wojcik, Sharon Brown of the Clozapine Clinic, and Ann Cousins of MMHC's Commonwealth Research Center.

Mary Kickham Carney, Northeastern University's Cooperative Education Coordinator confessed she <u>had</u> to attend. Her Boston College student experience on MMHC's Service Two in the 1970s focused her vision of nursing and led her into a career in psychiatric nursing. She exemplifies the concept of "the stickiness of MMHC" described by the Joseph Schilkraudt, MD, "People remain attached to MMHC. "

That attachment created the commitment to people with serious mental illness that is as much action for social justice as care that promotes recovery and resilience. That is what the patients were telling the Commonwealth when they were determined that MMHC would not close. Area Director, Cliff Robinson remarked at the symposium, "Every area [in the Commonwealth] should have a MMHC!" A heavy downpour greeted those leaving the symposium, many of them carrying a brick from the old MMHC, the concrete reminder of 100 years of excellence.

Special thanks to Karen Sherman RN, for her help

THE ANA MASSACHUSETTS: PROTECTING THE PRACTICE OF PROFESSIONAL NURSING FOR 113 YEARS

(originally published March 2016)

Fifteen years have passed since March 23, 2001 when Massachusetts nurses chose to remain members of the American Nurses Association and keep the thread to their origins unbroken. Their predecessors had created the Massachusetts State Nurses Association at Faneuil Hall on February 26, 1903. On that warm winter evening they said, "We the trained nurses of Massachusetts declare in mass meeting assembled, that it is expedient and advantageous to have a bill passed to regulate the practice of professional nursing in the state of Massachusetts."

Mary E. P. Davis, who spearheaded the movement, declined the vote from the floor that she be president of the new association. She acknowledged the recognition of her efforts, but chose to focus her best efforts on the legislation process. In 1905 she would become the second president but in 1903 the officers elected were:

President: Mary Riddle- Boston City Hospital Alumnae Association President
Vice President: Pauline Dolliver – Massachusetts General Hospital
Secretary: Sara E. Parsons – Massachusetts General Hospital
Treasurer: Laura A. C. Hughes - Boston City Hospital.

The Massachusetts State Nurses Association was linked with nurses in other states across the country as members of the Associated Alumnae of the United States and Canada, founded in New York 1896.

The young Association contested with those who trivialized nurses controlling their own profession. It was a patriarchal time when men controlled hospitals as well as homes. Not least of the issues involved was an economic one. Pupil nurses were used as an ever-renewing supply of cheap labor though they were promised a nurses training. The law that was passed in 1910 placed the Board of Registration in Nursing under the Board of Registration of Medicine. The nurses, however, had been victorious in making the public more aware of the unscrupulous individuals who passed themselves off as trained nurses. The Associated Alumnae praised Massachusetts newly Registered Nurses for their endurance when it met in convention in Boston the next year. It was during this Boston convention that the Associated Alumnae of the United States and Canada changed its name to the American Nurses Association.

Four decades later as a result of the changes following World War II (1941-1945) the Massachusetts State Nurses Association revised its Articles of Incorporation. On November 8, 1951 it became the Massachusetts Nurses Association. The constant amid the change was the continuing connection with the American Nurses Association. The majority of the Directors of the new organization had been Directors of the old. Except for Katherine McCabe who was then President of the MNA, Helene Lee who was its Executive Director and Alice Davis who would become President in 1953, only the names of the other officers and directors are known at this time. They were: Margaret Bonner, Annie Rogers, Anne E. Nolan, Hilda Mac Kay, Herbert J. Butler, Martha O. Sayles, Kathleen H. Atto, and Florence C. Britt.

It is reasonable to assume that some of these nurses had served their country during the War in Europe and the Pacific. A nation, grateful to nurses for their care of soldiers, funded nursing education through the G.I. bill and traineeships. This investment essentially moved nursing education out of the hospitals and into colleges where education of other professionals took place.

In the spring of 2001 as the Massachusetts Nurses Association neared its centennial, many of its members voted to make the Association a union. Other members chose to remain true to their origins in Faneuil Hall and their predecessors' long history of advancing professional nursing. Accordingly these nurses created the Massachusetts Association of Registered Nurses and continued their affiliation with the American Nurses Association. Officers of the newly renamed Association were:

President: Karen Daley
Vice-president: Barbara A. Blakeney
Treasurer: Margaret T. Barry
Clerk: Cynthia A. LaSala
Directors: Peggie Griffin Bretz
　　　　　Maura K. Fitzgerald
　　　　　Jackie Hayes

David M. Keepnews
Mary J. MacKenzie
Eleanor V. Vanetzian

As officers they oversaw the continued development of professional nurses and fostered high standards of nursing.

Coming from many areas of the Commonwealth and signing their names in broad strokes "in witnesses whereof and under the pains and penalties of perjury" as incorporators on March 19, 2001 were: Barbara Blakeney, Eleanor V. Vanetzian, Linda R. Moniz, Mary Anne MacKusick, Donna Mae Donahue, Sherry Merrow, Elizabeth M. Grady, David M. Keepnews, Jacqueline M. Hayes, Cynthia A. LaSala, Carmela A. Townsend, Peggie Griffin Bretz, Mary McKenzie, Patricia M. Brigham, Karen A. Daley, Claudia Ellis, and Judith Mealey

Constant in the change was the newly named Association's connection with the American Nurse Association. Then on April 1, 2014, the Massachusetts Association of Registered Nurses changed its name to more fully convey this relationship. American Nurses Association Massachusetts stated in a title what it had been its practice since 1903. In office at the time were:

President: Tara Tehan, MSN, MBA, RN, NE-BC
President-Elect: Myra F. Cacace, MS, GNP/ADM-BC, CDE
Past-President: Gino Chisari, RN, DNP
Secretary: Anthony J. Alley, BSN, RN, NE-BC
Treasurer: Diane Hanley, MS, RN-BC, EJD
Directors: Cathleen Colleran-Santos, DNP, RN
        Sabianca Delva, RN, BSN
        Jessica Florentino, BSN, RN
        Linda Moniz, RN, PhD
        Gayle Peterson, RN
        Patricia Ruggles, BSc, RN, CRNO
        Margaret L. Sipe, MS, RN

For one hundred and thirteen years, from February 26, 1903 to today, whether as the Massachusetts State Nurses Association, the Massachusetts Nurses Association, the Massachusetts Association of Registered Nurses or as the American Nurses Association Massachusetts, the aim of its officers, those listed above and others throughout its long history, has been the same, namely, protecting the "practice of professional nursing in the state of Massachusetts."

LAW VALIDATES NURSES' DECISIONS ABOUT PATIENT CARE

(originally published September 2014)

On the last day of June 2014 Governor Deval Patrick signed into law the safe staffing bill that both houses of the Legislature unanimously passed only days before. This new law mandates a 1:1 or 1:2 nurse to patient staffing ratio, that is, one nurse for one patient in intensive care units. Depending on the stability of that patient as assessed by an acuity tool and in collaboration with other nurses on the unit, the nurse might care for a second patient. A nurse-manager or her designee would resolve any disagreement about the staffing.

The law effectively dismisses fixed staffing formulas mandated from a distance in preference for the clinical judgment of educated and experienced nurses in the immediate presence of the patient. The law effectively keeps nursing decisions about patient care in intensive care units within the nurse-patient relationship. In doing so, the law delineates nursing's professional boundaries in this instance, and in time, may influence staffing patterns in other nursing situations.

The law responds to the high acuity levels of twenty-first century care but has its roots long ago in 1873 when a group of concerned women created the Boston Training School for Nurses (BTS). The School was a free-standing entity headed by a nursing superintendent and answerable for its personal care of patients to the BTS Board of Directors. Linda Richards (1841-1930), the second nursing superintendent, demonstrated in her teaching and her practice the trained nurse's personal care of patients.

From the very beginning, however, the Massachusetts General Hospital expected pupil nurses to also sweep, clean and mop. Pupil nurses endured the intrusion of the domestic needs of the hospital into their nurses training. All the while they kept focused on learning to provide personal care to patients. In doing so Mary E. P. Davis claimed nursing developed the mental attitude necessary in a profession (Parsons). Davis and her classmate Sophia Palmer graduated from the BTS in 1878 and spent the rest of their careers erecting boundaries around nursing's personal care of patients.

By the twentieth anniversary of the Trained Nurse Movement in 1893 pupil nurses had become essential to hospitals as they changed from philanthropic to scientific institutions. Dr. Edward Cowles calmed those who reacted to the change, saying that hospitals were "comparatively easy to run now that there [were] trained nurses for the managing and the nursing" (Cowles 1894). The hospital could be "run like a home," Cowles continued, "with the doctor heading the hospital as the husband headed the home." A physician during the Civil War and founder of nursing programs at the Boston City Hospital and the McLean Hospital, Cowles remarked that nurses became a "most valuable instrument in our hands" (Cowles "Nursing").

Dr. S. Weir Mitchell, a leading spokesman for hospitalizing the asylum, added his support of medicine's intrusion on nursing's boundaries. "Why have not more of you started training schools?" he asked alienists (an earlier term for psychiatrist) as a way to get good nurses. "Can you get these at from twelve to eighteen dollars a month? No. But for nothing you can get them, because if you train nurses during the two years, the second year the nurse is of real value" (Mitchell).

Dr. Alfred Worcester was still another physician who defined nursing as being the physician's hand and being a source of cheap labor for hospitals. He had founded his nurses' training school in Waltham and decided that nursing should become medicine's art. Nursing defended itself against such a scheme declaring itself a distinct profession. Worcester's disdain is obvious in his cavalier dismissal of the "so-called leaders of the nursing profession." Their quest for autonomy was "fictitious," and worse, a "dangerous doctrine." As if Dr. Worcester had the last word on nursing's boundaries he stated, "The nurse, first, last and all the while, is only the doctor's assistant. He is the captain and she is his executive officer" (Worcester 1927).

Palmer and Davis had no time for such a reductionist view of nursing. They believed that organization was the power of the age and fostered nurses' concerted action to protect nurses' personal care of patients. Accordingly, they were foremost among the leaders who established the American Association for the Superintendents of Training Schools for Nurses (precursor of NLN) in 1893 and the National Association of Alumnae (precursor of ANA) in 1896. By October 1900 nurses were reading the *American Journal of Nursing* that Palmer edited and Davis managed.

Given the patriarchal dynamics of the time and the fact that women would not have the vote for two more decades, this professionalizing strategy was a considerable achievement. Driving their efforts was the need to stave off intrusions on the integrity of nurses' personal care of the patient. Then in 1903 nurses rallied in Faneuil Hall and formed the Massachusetts State Nurses Association (precursor of ANA Massachusetts). Its goal was to have the law define the trained nurse as one who had graduated from a course of study and practice in a general hospital. Among their supporters were many medical men and a few men in nursing but the opposition was more numerous, more vehement and more highly placed. In 1906 as Harvard's Medical School moved into its magnificent buildings on Longwood Avenue, doctors blocked nurses' quest for laws that recognized nursing's professional boundaries. The opposition "won" in 1910 when the Legislature created a Board of Registration in Nursing (BORN) and placed it within the Board of Medicine. The doctor appointed to head the BORN graciously gave the leadership of its meetings to Mary Riddle of the Boston City Hospital underscoring that nursing's power derived from medicine.

All the same nurses exercised the power that the law had given nursing. Mary E. P. Davis wrote to Worcester in 1919 while he was president of the Massachusetts Medical Society that his Waltham Training School for Nurses (WTSN) was not eligible for membership in the Massachusetts State Nurses Association because his students were sent out to care for people without being fully trained and the earnings of the pupil nurses were given to the hospital. As Worcester neared the end of his life he looked over his struggle against nurses' autonomy. "All went well with us," he wrote, "until the graduates of hospital schools obtained the political and legislative control of nursing" (Worcester 1949).

Nurses realized that the hospital would remain the site of nursing education for a time but kept their eyes on the horizon for a better day. They sought a study that would standardize nursing education as the Flexner Report (1910) had standardized medical education. Foundations rejected their appeals until Gertrude Peabody, a philanthropist with the Instructive District Nursing Association of Boston, advised a family friend about nursing's request for a study of nursing and nursing education. John D. Rockefeller Jr. responded to Peabody's promptings and authorized the study that is popularly known as the *Goldmark Report*.

The bombing of Pearl Harbor December 7, 1941 would do for nursing what the *Goldmark Report* and other studies that followed were not able to do. World War II freed nurses from hospital control and focused them on the *care* of the wounded men. Nurses made clinical judgments according to the presenting data and not from rigid codes of hospital etiquette and traditions. Following the War, nurses earned degrees as they studied their personal care of patients. Among the most articulate voices was that of Frances Reiter who chaired ANA's first position on nursing education that sounded the death knell to hospital based nursing education (American Nurses Association). The state of nursing at that time was such that the direct care of patients was seen as aides' work with the nurse at the apex of a pyramid of personnel directing their care of patients. In effect, nursing had accepted a situation where professional nursing care and judgment were not available to those who needed it (Reiter).

By 1966 the term *nurse* had been emptied of meaning and agency. For example, Reiter used the term *nurse-clinican* to convey the ideal nurse who gave direct care to patients. No longer the physician's hand or cheap labor for hospitals, nurses began to put meaning and prestige back into the term *nurse* and honored their privileged place in patient care. The safe staffing law of 2014 validates the success of this transformation. It took one hundred and forty years and the concerted effort of many nurses to get to this moment. Although currently limited to nurses in the ICU, it is only reasonable to expect that the law will eventually be extended to all nursing situations to the benefit of all patients.

REFERENCES

American Nurses Association. "American Nurses Association's First Position on Education for Nursing." *American Journal of Nursing* (65, 1965): 106-107.

Cowles, Edward. (1894). "The relation of the medical staff to the governing bodies in hospitals." J.S. Billings and H.M. Hurd, eds., *Hospitals, Dispensaries and Nursing: Papers and Discussions in the International Congress of Charities, Correction and Philanthropy.* Baltimore, MD: Johns Hopkins, 69-76.

---. "Nursing reform for the insane." *American Journal of Insanity* (47): 219-229.

Mitchell, S. Weir. "Address before the 50th annual meeting of the American Medico-Psychological Association, May 16, 1894." *Journal of Nervous and Mental Diseases* (21): 413-37.

Parsons, Sara E. (1923). *History of the Massachusetts General Hospital Training School for Nurses.* Boston: Whitcomb & Barrows, 44-45.

Reiter, Frances. "The Nurse-clinician," *American Journal of Nursing* (66, 1966): 274-280.

Worcester, Alfred. (1927). *Nurses and Nursing.* Cambridge, MA: Harvard University Press, 102-104.

---. "The Shortage of Nurses: Reminiscences of Alfred Worcester," *Harvard Medical Alumni Bulletin.* (1949). Alfred Worcester Box, Waltham Historical Society, Inc.

THE SUNDIAL: TAKING NURSING'S MEASURE

(originally published December 2015)

Many have seen Mrs. Mallard who since 1987 has been leading her eight ducklings: Jack, Kack, Lack, Mack, Nack, Ouack, Pack and Quack across cobblestones at the Beacon and Charles Street entrance to Boston's Public Garden. Runners probably consider *Make Way for the Ducklings* secondary to the bronze tortoise and hare in Copley Square dedicated in 1995 anticipating the one hundredth anniversary of the Boston Marathon. These are probably the most popular of Nancy Schon's many bronze pieces of public art. Not to be overlooked, however, is the magnificent sundial at the Massachusetts General Hospital dedicated in 2004 that gives the lie to Schon being known only as "The Duck Lady."

For nurses Schon is much more than that. She is the artist who created a bronze sculpture depicting nursing's ancient and enduring presence in society. Commissioned by the Alumni Association of the Massachusetts General Hospital School of Nursing, Schon chose the sundial that dates from 1500 BCE in Egypt as the symbol to capture nursing's timelessness. Nursing, as ancient as civilization, is a continuing activity that occurs twenty-four hours a day and seven days a week.

Various aspects of the sundial denote time-the past, present and future-as a measure of existence. The biblical creation of the world in seven days is alluded to in the sundial's measuring seven feet in diameter. Its circularity reflects nurses being present at the beginning and end of life. The granite base that is ten feet in diameter on which the sundial rests further echoes that circularity and points to the cyclical nature of life itself with its seasons following each other.

The figures on the gnomon or the stylus whose shadow points out the time are especially significant. Schon chose Greek goddesses: Athena, noted for wisdom; Aphrodite, noted for love and beauty; and, Artemis, noted for her care of nature and childbirth to epitomize nursing's evolution as a profession. It must be said that these figures represent abstractions. Wisdom, love, beauty and care are beyond persons or gender and thus incorporate all nurses throughout the past, present and future.

The figures on the gnomon-stylus vary in size suggesting nursing's evolution as a profession. Florence Nightingale and her lamp representing nursing's past is the smallest of the three, followed by a larger figure holding a book signifying nursing's present with its intellectual requirements; and the last of the three figures holds a world signifying nursing's expansive universality. Lamp, book and globe also indicate the change in the ways nurses have gathered knowledge: first from the light of a lamp, then from a book, and finally gathered from across the world via the internet.

That "nurses care for people both day and night" is conveyed in the gnomon-stylus telling the time, sun time, says Schon while night is symbolized in the area under the gnomon-stylus. An excerpt of Florence Nightingale's pronouncement in 1871 that "Nursing is an art. The finest of arts" is to the gnomon-stylus' left while that of Ruth Sleeper, the late Director of Nursing at the MGH, is at its right. Reflecting nursing as it began its quest for its science in earnest, Sleeper said in 1966, "Always, always more to see, more to learn, more to do...to improve both care and cure." Fittingly given the Alumni's gift of this elegant and eloquent statement on nursing, the cap of the Massachusetts General Hospital nurse has an honored place at the base of the gnomon-stylus.

The sundial is situated between two birch trees on a grassy patch of lawn leading up to MGH's Wang Ambulatory Care Center. The granite base on which the sundial rests provides a comfortable place to sit and ponder. All the while as the sundial is measuring the moment, nurses are caring for patients as predecessors did throughout nursing's history and as successors will do in nursing's future.

Sources
www.schon.com
schon.com/public/sundial.php

THE RN IN MARN

(originally published June 2011)

The Massachusetts Association of Registered Nurses has much to celebrate as it reaches its tenth anniversary. Foremost among its achievements has been its advancement of nursing standards and promotion of professional development that makes its members leaders in the pursuit of quality nursing care. Fittingly, MARN at ten coincides with the first year of the Affordable Care Act, and MARN member Karen Daley's presidency of the American Nurses Association. Health care reform expects that nurses will be used to their full potential, a position to which MARN is also committed.

With so much on nursing's agenda, MARN's tenth anniversary can only be a brief interlude before moving forward. But there is still time for a glance backward over MARN's roots before stepping into the future. Those roots reach beyond MARN's ten years over one hundred and twenty years to the end of the nineteenth-century. Planting those roots was Mary E. P. Davis, the founding mother of Massachusetts' registered nurses.

Davis and her contemporaries expected other professionals to respect nursing as an autonomous, though young, profession. Instead those professionals used pupil nurses as an ever-renewing source of cheap labor. Disappointed but undefeated Davis turned from doctors and hospital administrators to the law. She helped the Commonwealth enact a law to distinguish nurses who had graduated from an approved training school. Registration protected the rights and privileges of the young profession and alerted the public to the unscrupulous and unlicensed.

Davis rallied her contemporaries at Faneuil Hall February 26, 1903. In order to organize nurses to incorporate their vision before legislation could be pursued, a group that would morph into the Massachusetts State Nurses Association. Declining the nomination to be the new organization's first president, she devoted her considerable energies to the registration movement. By 1910, the registered nurse in Massachusetts was a fact.

An unbroken thread connects the ten-year-old MARN with those pioneering nurses at Faneuil Hall in 1903. MARN's affiliation with the American Nurses Association is a continuation of MSNA's relationship with the Associated Alumnae of the United States, the name of ANA from 1896 through 1911. The history of the quest for licensure, the establishment of the professional association in 1903, registration in 1910 and the long line of registered nurses over the past one hundred years is an everyday presence in the title: Massachusetts Association of Registered Nurses.

In 1910 Davis said the RN gave nurses a legal status, and set a standard of excellence in nursing practice and education. One hundred years later her successors in 2011 offer their concise statements of what the RN means to them. For all gaining the RN was a transformative moment. As Alice Friedman of Amherst said, "My RN meant I was a nurse and that I was special." Military veterans of the World War II era (1941-1945), such as Anne Hargreaves and Ann Donovan, respectively, ANA-affiliated MNA past president and staff, looked back over lengthy careers and appreciated that their RNs gave them many opportunities.

Phyllis Moore, past president of ANA affiliated MNA, and former dean of the nursing program at Simmons College exclaimed, "My RN gave me nursing: A career of a lifetime!" That sense of pride and pleasure was an ever renewing source of pleasure, or as Loretta Higgins says, "For every day of the past fifty years, my dream as a two year old patient has been realized in my RN." Another Higgins, though unrelated to Loretta, Millicent Penny Higgins, provides a variation on that theme: "I felt blessed when that first registration notification arrived years ago and feel the same way each time my new one arrives." Jeanne Gibbs adds, "After 44 years, it still fills me with an unabashed pride to say I am a Registered Nurse."

RNs spoke to the RN's autonomy and accountability and centered these in compassion, empathy and strength. Andrew Harding states that the RN denoted "ability, rights and responsibility." Jeanette Ives Erikson, who leads the nursing department at the Massachusetts General Hospital where Davis trained at the end of the nineteenth-century, states that the RN has a "privileged place in society and in the lives of patients and their families."

These statements about what the RN means to individual nurses speaks to their success in providing safe and competent care. Erin Donahue speaks to the power such competence has. She notes, "My RN means making the world a better place one patient at a time." A future RN, Melissa Baker, already knows what the RN conveys. She believes that "being an RN means having hope, knowledge and <u>always</u> caring."

At its tenth anniversary and rooted in the distant past, MARN continues Mary E. P. Davis' quest for nursing excellence and celebrates Massachusetts' RNs.

NURSES IN SERVICE TO THEIR COUNTRY

NURSES IN SERVICE TO SOLDIERS

(originally published June 2004)

The war raging between the Tigris and Euphrates Rivers where thousands of years ago the Fertile Crescent was the cradle of civilization naturally evokes memories of nurses' compassion for warriors, felled by spears, swords, guns and missiles. That compassion has its roots in the Greek command to be hospitable, and the Hebrew command to love one's neighbor. Nursing techniques have changed over all the centuries since them, but nurses' compassion for the soldier remains constant.

In Western Civilization's first epic, Homer relates how Eurycleia cared for Odysseus when the warrior returned home to Ithaca. The great Celtic hero, Finn MacCool, provided nurses for his warriors, called the Fianna. These women nursed the warriors back to health so that they could fight once more. There were no nurses for other heroes, for example, Beowulf died without nursing care. Sadly, such deaths are too common.

More happily, the Knights of St. John of Jerusalem were there for the wounded. The Knights who were from Europe's noble families established their hospital at Jerusalem just prior to the Crusades (1096-1271) when Islam and Christianity clashed about who should control the Holy Places. The Knights, their black garb emblazoned with a white cross, privileged their patients, seeing Christ in each one. Their patient centered motto was: *the sick asked and the knights obeyed.* Their present-day counterparts of the Knights and Ladies of Malta continue their private charity to the sick.

During America's Revolution (1775-1783) George Washington was concerned that the "sick suffered much for the want of good female nurses." As in all wars, women made up a separate corps as camp followers. Sometimes they were prostitutes, more often they were the wives and mothers who nursed their soldier husbands and sons. Washington pressed these women into a nursing corps, and on 27 July 1775 asked the Second Continental Congress to authorize them as nurses for the sick and wounded. Initially they were paid two dollars a month and received one daily ration. Two years later, these nurses were earning eight dollars a month and one daily ration. Catholic nuns were already organized and opened their hospitals to the wounded soldiers and those who suffered with scarlet fever, dysentery and small pox.

Molly Pitcher served at the 1778 Battle of Monmouth earning her name from the pitchers of water she carried to the troops. Washington recognized her service by warranting her as a noncommissioned officer. As the American Revolution began, a beautiful Georgian home in Jamaica Plain, owned by a British loyalist (former commodore in the British Navy) who fled from Boston as the hostilities broke out, was pressed into service as a hospital for the victims of battles with the British in Boston. In 1811 a Naval surgeon recommended that nurses be included among personnel at Navy hospitals. Before long nurses were serving aboard ships during the War of 1812, the first time alien forces invaded the United States. Nurses also served in the military during the second invasion of the United States at Pearl Harbor in 1941, and during the crisis on September 11, 2001.

The Crimean War (1854-1856) marks a moment in nursing's story when neither the military nor medicine organized a nursing corps. The people demanded nurses for the fallen soldier. The British Government, responded to the public outcry, and sent a corps of nurses to Constantinople in October 1854 under the supervision of Florence Nightingale (1820-1910). She was not expected to nurse the soldiers. Her position, as a lady in the class conscious nineteenth-century, was to oversee the work of others.

The Times kept reporting the lists of dead and wounded and the people kept crying for nurses. Two months later, fifteen Irish Sisters of Mercy, under the leadership of Mother Francis Bridgeman (née Joanna Bridgeman) (1813-1888), and a cadre of ladies and nurses arrived to enlarge the nursing services. The Sisters of Mercy had been nursing the poor and sick in Ireland and London for 27 years. Just prior to the War, they had cared for starving people dying of scurvy, typhus and typhoid fever during the Famine in Ireland, and the Hungry Forties in England. Mother Joseph Croke's (née Isabelle "Issy" Croke) journal reveals how much it pained the nurse to have to see so many fine, young men die, though she and her fellow nuns did their best to keep them from death's grasp. These nuns were the best-prepared nurses in the nineteenth-century. Nightingale, by contrast, knew a lot about nursing, but had little actual nursing experience. Worse, she tried to eliminate the Sisters of Mercy as she tested her ideas about nursing. Meanwhile, soldiers at the filthy Scutari Hospitals were not only dying from their wounds, but mostly from scurvy, typhoid fever and typhus. Since the Sisters of

Mercy were already veterans of caring for people during times of famine it seemed ironic that they be eliminated.

America's Civil War (1861-1865) saw the continuation of women breaking their roles as angels of the hearth to become angels of battlefields and hospitals, Nurses served aboard the U.S.S. Red Rover as their predecessors had served aboard ships during the War of 1812. On land, Clara Barton (1821-1912) left rural Oxford, Massachusetts to care for soldiers. Louisa May Alcott (1832-1888) nursed soldiers in a Washington, D.C. hospital far away from her home in Concord. Barton's efforts are institutionalized in the American Red Cross. Alcott's experience of her caring for men suffering with, wounds, typhoid fever, diphtheria and their dehydration from fevers and wounds, the soldiers must have appreciated Walt Whitman's (1819-1892) unstintingly providing them with drinks.

The mortality rate in both the Crimean and Civil Wars was so high that women, who once expected be cared-for wives, found themselves having to earn their own living as single women. Nursing provided the perfect opportunity for women to excel in the field of caring. Not only did it extend women's work within their own homes into hospitals, women lost none of their prestige as ladies when they became nurses thanks to the fame of Florence Nightingale, Louisa May Alcott and Clara Barton. The first training schools at New York, Connecticut and Massachusetts began within a decade of the Civil War's end.

Five years after the United States and Spain celebrated the 400th anniversary of Columbus' discovery of America, and showcased the impending century's new energy source—electricity—at the 1892 World's Fair in Chicago, the two countries were at war with each other. The headliner event that sparked the conflict was the explosion of the battleship, the *U.S.S. Maine* in Havana harbor. "Internal combustion," the Spaniards claimed, but some Americans said an external mine caused the blast. Spurred on by competing newspapers in a circulation battle, America went to war against Spain with the rallying cry, "Remember the Maine and to Hell with Spain!" The war that began in April 1898 ended that same year in August.

Sara E. Parsons (1864-1949), a recent graduate of the Boston Training School (precursor of the School of Nursing at the Massachusetts General Hospital (MGH) and founder of the nursing department at Providence, Rhode Island, provided nursing care aboard the *S.S. Baystate* that plied the waters between Cuba and Boston. Typhoid fever raged through the camps, due to the decreased sanitation of the filthy camps and their water supply. Twenty-one nurses died, twenty of them from typhoid fever, and one from malaria. Within a decade after the Spanish American War, the Government established the Army Nurse Corps (1901) and the Navy

Nurse Corps (1908), making military nursing a part of the Government. The Air Force Nurses Corps would be established 1 July 1949.

Even before the United States entered the Great War, that a later generation would call World War I (1917-1919), navy nurses were serving aboard transport ships, namely, the *U.S.S. Mayflower* and the *U.S.S. Dolphin*, Sara Parsons and Eva Waldron, her associate at the MGH, oversaw the nursing corps, made up of MGH nurses in *Base Hospital No. 6*. Carrie Hall, for whom Parsons had served as mentor, headed the nursing corps of the base hospital the Peter Bent Brigham Hospital sent to France. Marion Parsons, a 1910 graduate of the Boston City Hospital, joined the Harvard Medical Unit in France in 1915 and then joined the Boston City Hospital unit in France when it was formed in 1916. These three nurses continued as nursing leaders at the state and national levels after the war, having a major impact on the development of the nursing profession over the next decades. Many of the younger nurses who made up the nursing corps became the leaders of the next generation.

Sara Parsons, along with her colleague Dr. Richard Cabot, testified before Congress on the need for rank for nurses in the military. Parsons provided example after graphic example of how nursing care was thwarted and patients jeopardized because men would not follow nurses' orders. To cite just one example, men continued to spit on the floors though they had been provided with sputum cups. Given the prevalence of infectious diseases, especially tuberculosis, this was no small matter.

More urgent, was the influenza pandemic that swept the United States and Europe killing at its peak in the fall of 1918, 200 each day at Fort Devens in Massachusetts. The pandemic would claim 675,000 in the United States and 20-50 million world wide. Sara Parsons wrote from France commiserating on the deaths of nurses at the MGH even as she was caring for other flu victims in Talence, France. She was also grieving the death of Lucy Fletcher, a *Base Hospital 6* nurse who had died of meningitis. In spite of the infection, Sara Parsons was unable to persuade men to follow her nursing orders. Men were not accustomed to obeying women in civilian life, and were not about to follow the orders of women who held no rank in the military.

Ironically, these nurses were spending their lives caring for the soldiers. In fact almost 300 nurses died during the War, many of them died from influenza. Patriarchalism reigned, however, so these nurses had no status, nor for that matter did they have the vote until a year after the War ended. Cabot, ever a foe of conservative forces that impeded progress, and an ardent supporter of nurses and change, argued that nurses had done the same work as the commissioned doctors in *Base Hospital No. 6*, and logically, should also be commissioned officers. Interestingly, Julia Stimson, a Worcester, Massachusetts native and the newly appointed superintendent of the Army Nurse Corps with no wartime experience at this point, sided with the conservative forces at the hearings. Nurses did not get rank and Stimson went on to a 20 year career as Superintendent of the Army Nurse Corps.

In July 1940, a year before World War II (1941-1945) broke out, the various national nursing organizations formed the Nursing Council on National Defense, as their WWI predecessors had formed the Committee on Nursing of the U.S. Council of National Defense. Stella Goostray of Boston's Childrens Hospital headed the Boston section with the aim of increasing the numbers of nurses for the soldiers while at the same time seeing that there were sufficient nurses for hospitals at home. Still, nurses were not ready in December 1941 when Pearl Harbor was attacked, but within six-months 5000 nurses had enlisted. This time, nurses had rank, either second lieutenant with the Navy Nurse Corps or ensign with the Navy Nurse Corps. A year later the military nurses were commissioned officers earning the same pay and prerogatives as other officers. By the War's end, 57,000 Army nurses and 16,000 Navy nurses cared for soldiers in Europe, Africa and the Pacific. Among these were 500 Negro nurses, held to a quota, who served in the Army Nurse Corps in segregated units.

So generous was nurses' response to World War II, their enlistment often left few nurses on the wards of hospitals in Massachusetts and throughout the nation, making the nurses who remained behind often as heroic as those who left for Europe and the Pacific. To deal with the acute nursing shortage the Cadet Nurse Corps was established 15 June 1943. Young women were recruited and put through an accelerated educational program. By 15 October 1945 when it was disbanded, the Cadet Nurse Corps project had created 179,000 nurses. Along with lessening the nurse shortage, the Corps had the salutary effect of desegregating the nurse training schools.

Because nurses were where the soldiers were, nurses came under the same fire. On 21 October 1944 Frances Slanger from Roxbury, Massachusetts; was the first nurse killed during World War II when she was hit by the shell from a German artillery barrage. At 2:00 a.m. of the morning she died, she had written to Stars, and Stripes, the GI's newspaper, of how awe-stricken she was at the wounded soldier's courage and fortitude. On hearing of her death, grateful soldiers, and a more grateful nation, named its largest hospital ship, a former luxury cruiser, the *USS Frances Slanger*. Slanger was resting under a Star of David but her work continued in the hands and hearts of other nurses who cared for thousands of men on that ship.

Slanger's Purple Heart that was given to her family now resides with her papers in the Nursing Archives at the Howard Gotlieb Archival Research Center at Mugar Memorial Library, Boston University. Genevieve Flood who was wounded during WW II and returned home, gave her Purple Heart and her papers to the Mary L. Pekarski Nursing Archives at the

Burns Library, Boston College. Slanger's fellow alumna from Boston City Hospital School of Nursing (BCHSON), Dorothy Morse, Class of 1939 who was with the Harvard Medical Unit just before the United States entered the war, was killed off Iceland when a torpedo hit her ship. The Morse Slanger Library at BCH commemorated their lives. These deaths put in bold relief the reality that being where the soldier was dangerous. Heroic nurses from other parts of the country gave their names to the Blanche F. Sigman, the Ernestine A. Koranda and the Aleda E. Lutz hospital ships. By the end of the War, 200-nurses had died.

Still other nurses were prisoners of: war. Five Navy nurses were captured at Guam when it fell to the Japanese 10 December 1941. They were held in Kobe, Japan until they were expatriated in 1942. Fifty-six Army nurses and 11 Navy nurses were captured when Corregidor fell in 1942, and were held until 23 February 1945. The Army nurses were held at Santos Thomas, Manila, and the Navy nurses were held at Los Banos about 60 miles south of Manila. Helen Cassiani, a nurse from a farming family in Bridgewater, Massachusetts, was among the nurses interned at Santos Thomas. On Memorial Day this year as the World War II Memorial is dedicated, and on 6 June 2004, the sixtieth anniversary of D-Day, the nation will remember these nurses along with the men for whom they cared.

Nursing care close to the front and on troop ships had much, to do with reducing the mortality statistics during WW II. That trend would continue as the United States moved into the, Korean War (1956-1953). Flight nurses and the newly established Air Force Nurse Corps cared for the wounded needing long-term care as they were airlifted to hospitals beyond the battle scene. Mash units (Mobile Army Surgical Hospitals) with their 60 beds stayed as close to the front as possible dealing with the wounded men. Col. Mary Quinn (Ret.), a 1945-graduate of South Boston's Carney Hospital School of Nursing's Cadet Nurse Corps, program, served in the Mash.unit that inspired the book, movie and TV series. Many of the 1500 nurses who served in Korea cared for the "shot-up boys" who came in and out of these Mash units.

Quinn also served during the Vietnam War (1964-1975), as did Carolyn Bartlett, an O.R. clinical nurse specialist. On 20 September 1966 male nurses were allowed to serve in the nurse corps, a ruling that helped expand the nurse corps to its 9500 nurses. Sadly, nine nurses died in Vietnam. Their names are listed on the Wall of the Vietnam Memorial in Washington, D.C. The nurses who served in Operation Desert Storm, and those serving during the war in Iraq are still to be tallied.

The military nurse is enshrined in the hearts and minds of the men they served. A grateful people erected other monuments of stone and marble. Massachusetts nurses are memorialized in the Civil War monument that graces Flagstaff Hill on the Boston Common with its plaque to the U. S. Sanitation Commission, And all that remains of Dorothea Lynde Dix (1802-1887), who oversaw the Civil War nursing corps after a lifetime of crusading for the mentally ill, lies under a monument in the Mount Auburn garden cemetery in Cambridge. In 1914 Massachusetts' daughters of veterans erected the beautiful monument in Nurses Hall at Boston's State House, showing a nurse caring for a fallen soldier with its inscription: To the Army nurses from 1861 to 1865: Angels of Mercy and Life amid Scenes of Conflict and Death.

There are other monuments in the Nation's capital, foremost among them, the Nurses Section of Arlington National Cemetery that was dedicated 22 May 1902. Fifteen years later, 12 May 1917, the American Red Cross building in Washington, D. C. commemorated the women of the North and the South who "braved the discomforts of fever stricken camp or crowded ward to lessen the suffering of the sick and wounded." The Ancient Order of Hibernians erected their monument to the Nuns of the Battlefield 20 September 1924. On 22 May 1922 colleagues of the nurses and volunteer women who died during the Spanish-American War dedicated a monument "To Our Comrades," in the Nurses Section of Arlington National Cemetery. On 19 March 1930, the World War Memorial in Washington, D.C. was dedicated to the "Heroic Women with the World War [I]" who had lost their lives. The Vietnam Women's Memorial shows three nurses, one comforting a soldier, the second praying and the third looking to the sky for the rescue helicopter. Nurses are also enrolled in the WIMSA (Women in Military Service to America) Memorial in the nation's capital.

Unlike other monuments, that honored nurses in specific wars, the Spirit of Nursing that was dedicated 26 April 1934 honors all military nurses. Thanks to Quinn's influence, a similar memorial to all military nurses was built in North Weymouth. At the Weymouth Vietnam Memorial Park where traffic rushes by on 3A at the busy intersection of Neck and Bridge Streets, the memorial pays silent tribute to military nurses. On either side of the Nurses Memorial are markers: one to Vietnam Service: 1964–1975, and the other, to the United States Veteran. The Memorial itself features the insignias of the Army, Navy and Air Force Nurse Corps above NURSES MEMORIAL. Inscribed below is an excerpt from Col. Maude Smith's accolade to the military nurse:

> Where the warrior went ... stalwart and brave
> His nurses arrived on the second wave
> To care for the wounded, the crippled, the blind;
> To help ease the hurts of body and mind.
> Where the soldier was and where he is still
> His nurses stood by . . . And they always will!

The author appreciates clarification on military terms that Col. Mary C Quinn (U.S.A. Ret.), Ann E. Donovan LCDR. (N.C.) U.S. Navy Ret. and Mary McKenzie (rank unknown) provided. Any errors that may occur are the author's responsibility,

Army Nurses Memorial

MASSACHUSETTS NURSES AT THE NEW BIRTH OF FREEDOM

(originally published June 2013)

U sing his war powers, President Abraham Lincoln (1809-1865) signed the Emancipation Proclamation on New Year's Day 1863. All slaves in states still in rebellion against the Union, it was declared, were freed "thenceforth and forever." This deprived the South of the labor of three and a half million men, women and children thereby lessening its military power. To insure that this first step in abolishing slavery would not be seen after the Civil War (1861-1865) as merely a war measure valid only during the war, Lincoln sought to amend the Constitution. The popular Lincoln movie recently in theatres and winning award after award dramatizes the debate about the Thirteenth Amendment. Once the Amendment was ratified on December 18, 1865, slavery was abolished. No person in the United States could be held as property.

That approval of the Thirteenth Amendment was still to come on November 19, 1863 when Lincoln dedicated the military cemetery in Gettysburg. In only 272 words the President stated that the men had fought and died for the Union that had been "conceived in liberty," and was "dedicated to the proposition that all men are created equal." Thousands of men had died during the three days of fighting at Gettysburg (July 1-3 1863). Thousands more had died since the war began two years before in April, 1861; and, thousands more would die before it ended in April, 1865. The total lives lost were at least 750,000 and perhaps 850,000. The number of widows and orphans were even more.

To be sure, the costs were enormous but the soldiers did not die "in vain". The United States did not become half slave and half free. The Union endured. The government "of the people, by the people, for the people [did] not perish from the earth." As Garry Wills states,

"With his words [Lincoln] called up a new nation out of the blood and trauma" and gave the United States "a new birth of freedom" (Willis).

Nurses were present at the birth. Hundred of nurses cared for the wounded and closed the eyes of those who died. Dorothea Lynde Dix (1802-1887), Louisa May Alcott (1832-1888) and Clarissa (Clara) Barton (1821-1912) are a familiar trio. Less well known is Mary E. Gardner Holland who mindful of Dix's criteria for nurses wrote: "I am in possession of one of your circulars, and will comply with all your requirements. I am plain-looking enough to suit you, and old enough....I never had a husband, and am not looking for one. Will you take me?" (Holland). After the war Holland collected nurses' memories as well as left one of her own of a soldier losing the battle with tetanus:

> I asked what that shiver meant that passed over him so frequently. "The lockjaw" [answered the more seasoned nurse who had cared for him all night]. The spasms were frequent and severe all the forenoon. Just before noon he came out of one and asked, "Is my case a critical one...." He went into another, and when he came out of it said, "If anything happens to me send my body home." A moment after he said, "Mother!" loud and clear; then his teeth came together with a crash, and he passed away in that struggle, at just about twelve o'clock. (Holland)

Among the nurses from Massachusetts who shared their memories with Holland were: Elizabeth Wheeler, Helen E. Smith and Adeliza Perry all from Worcester; Martha F. Jennison from Templeton; Rebecca "Aunt Becky" Wiswell from Plymouth; Lauretta C. Balch from Lowell; Jane Worrall and Netty Williams from Boston; Nancy M. Hill from West Cambridge (now Arlington, Belmont); Caroline Burghardt of Great Barrington (the Berkshires) and Helen L. Gilson and Rebecca Pomroy both of whom were from Chelsea.

Gilson (1836-1868) served on one of the Sanitary Commission's hospital boats from June 1862-June 1865 helping to transfer the wounded from battlefields to hospitals. She cared for the soldiers at Antietam, Fredericksburg, Chancellorsville, Manassas, Gettysburg and Wilderness. Her "calm and cheerful courage" provided a presence that seemed to revive men "moaning in pain or restless with fever" noted one observer (Reed). Gilson followed the war to the Battle of Petersburg (June 15-18, 1864) where colored* troops were part of the campaign. The brigade shouted, "Hurrah for the Liberator; Hurrah for the President" as Lincoln and General U.S. Grant passed by (Goodwin). The sick and wounded of the brigade were cared for in the Colored Hospital that Gilson organized. Her management was likened to "the ticking of a clock" because of her "regular discipline, gentle firmness, and sweet temper" (Reed).

Rebecca Pomroy (1817-1884), the other nurse from Chelsea, practiced in Washington. Her first patient at the Georgetown Hospital called out to her, "Oh my dear mother!" as he threw his arms around Pomroy's neck, and then died still clutching the startled nurse. Her experience grew as she cared for men leveled by wounds, amputations and gangrene. The fevers as they were called -typhus, typhoid fever and malaria-claimed many more lives than did battle injuries as did diphtheria, measles, pneumonia, tuberculosis, scurvy, syphilis, and small pox. Sometimes nurses were among the fatalities.

Pomroy briefly cared for the President's little boy at the White House. Pomroy refused monetary payment for her services. Instead, she asked Lincoln to visit her patients. Among the hospital staff she gathered to greet the President were former slaves: Lucy who cooked the nurses' food, and Garner and Brown who served their country, Pomroy told Lincoln, by cooking the special diets for the soldiers. When Lincoln shook Lucy's hand, the astonished woman exclaimed she never expected such a thing (Pomroy). Emancipation became more than a word as Lincoln's hand grasped Lucy's. The former slave and the President were equals in this new birth of freedom.

*1860s term

REFERENCES

Goodwin, Doris Kearns. (2005). *Team of Rivals.* New York: Simon and Schuster, 630.

Holland, Mary E. Gardner. (1895). "To the Reader" in *Our Army Nurses: Interesting Sketches, Addresses and Photographs of Nearly One Hundred of the Noble Women who Served in Hospitals and on Battlefields during Our Civil War* compiled by Mary A Gardner Holland. Boston: Massachusetts: B. Wilkins & Company, 19-22.

Pomroy, Rebecca. (1895). *Our Army Nurses*, 438.

Reed, William Howell Reed. (1895) *Our Army Nurses*, 536-541.

Wills, Garry. (1992). *Lincoln at Gettysburg: The Words that Remade America.* New York: Simon and Schuster, 175.

THE ARMY NURSES MEMORIAL

(originally published March 2015)

Bela Lyon Pratt (1867-1917) was a well-established figure in the American art world. His education at Yale and study with masters in Paris and the United States had long ago polished his talents. He was shaping the next generation of artists as head of the Sculpture Department at the School for the Museum of Fine Arts. At the same time he was completing new commissions that joined works that had flowed from his studio, such as busts of Boston's notables; the personification of the Genius of Navigation for the World's Fair in Chicago; and, the Seasons for the Library of Congress to mention only a few of his 180 creations.

Pratt's Spring exhibit in 1911 had special significance for the press for it had been following the brouhaha that the Municipal Arts Commission had raised when the trustees of the Boston Public Library commissioned Pratt to succeed the late Augustus Saint Gaudens to create sculptures for its new building on Dartmouth Street. By April, compromise had calmed injured sensibilities and Pratt was able to create his own designs as the trustees had wanted. His success was on display in two monumental female figures, one designating Science and the other Art. By June of the next year the monumental sculptures had been cast in bronze and placed on either side of the grand entrance to the Boston Public Library, the "palace for the people". For one hundred years they have graced the façade of the building and busy Copley Square.

Another sculpture in the exhibit that spring had none of the controversy that had surrounded Art and Science, and although it also featured a female, she was less monumental at only eight feet in height. Daughters of veterans of the Civil War (1861-1865) had commissioned Pratt to create this sculpture as a memorial to the nurses who had cared for sick and wounded soldiers. These veterans' daughters were probably part of the Grand Army of the Republic (GAR), a fraternal organization of veterans that had been founded a year after the War had ended to provide for its orphans and widows, as well as be of assistance to disabled veterans. Not least of the GAR's mission was that of ensuring that Americans would remember the services of the soldiers, especially those who had died.

Pratt chose the Pietà as his inspiration for the Army Nurses Memorial. The sculpture is pyramidal in shape with the soldier stretched out on the ground still holding his rifle forming its base. The nurse has raised the man's upper body from the ground and has braced it against her knee while she cradles his head in her left arm in preparation to offering him a drink from the cup she holds in her right hand. If the nurse and soldier have become one in this nurse-patient relationship, the nurse remains the dominant figure in the sculpture befitting the nature of her ministrations and the soldier's need of her care. The nurse is greater in volume and weight than the soldier further conveying her physical and moral strength on which the soldier depends. As the pyramid of nurse and soldier converges up to its single point, it is the nurse's head that is at the top, again focusing on her as the active agent in the relationship.

This goes beyond an ironic reversal of the usual male/strength-female/weakness dichotomies. Rather the focus on the nurse's head suggests that the care originates in the nurse's mind. Like Science, she is absorbed in her contemplation of the soldier. The sculpture captures the moment before the soldier revives enough to present his needs. In that moment the nurse is entirely focused on the soldier and ready to be inspired as Art is, to create care specific to his need. All the while like the Pietà, she embraces his head. The quiet composure suggests her competence as well as her confidence.

The weight of the sculpture is at its base as is fitting for its pyramidal structure. The full significance of the sculpture, however, is conveyed in the small space at the apex between the nurse's head and the soldier's head. More significantly still is how the nurse's gaze connects her with the soldier whose eyes are closed. What the critics had said about Art and Science could be said as well for the nurse and the soldier. There is "something very human and personal about them."[1] The great feat of the sculpture is that Pratt captured nursing's essence and cast it in bronze.

The sculpture had been commissioned in 1909, the one hundredth anniversary of Abraham Lincoln's birth. Five years later on Lincoln's birthday, Thursday February 12, 1914 at noon, Miss Dorothy Standish Lewis, granddaughter of Mrs. Ellen Standish Tolman, one of the nurses in the civil war, unveiled the Army Nurses Memorial. The legend on its marble pedestal states:

TO THE ARMY NURSES
FROM 1861-1865
ANGELS OF MERCY AND LIFE
AMID SCENES OF CONFLICT AND DEATH
A TRIBUTE OF HONOR AND GRATITUDE
FROM THE MASSACHUSETTS DEPARTMENT
DAUGHTERS OF VETERANS
1914

Honored above all others in attendance were Mrs. Fannie T. Hazen with four of the seven Massachusetts nurses who still survived fifty years after the War had ended. The ceremony included prayers, orations and music. Then Governor David I. Walsh (1872-1947) accepted the Army Nurses Memorial eloquently defining what it honored, saying:

> To fight and die for one's country is noble and heroic. [To] live, and work in the wake of the battle's wreck, ministering to the stricken, soothing the dying, fighting disease and death through anxious hours-this is the highest form of sacrifice, the noblest test of patriotism, since to it come none of the emotions and glory of conflict, none of the acclaims of country nor the applause of the public forum, neither the blare of the trumpet nor the roar of the drum, and since it is done amid the silence and pathos of the hospital, where few come but the beaten and the bereaved.[2]

Fittingly, the ceremony concluded with Taps and attendees joining as one to sing *America*. The gift given to the people of the Commonwealth one hundred years ago endures. The Army Nurses Memorial graces Nurses Hall in Boston's State House while the art and science of nursing that Pratt idealized in bronze is made real every day in nurses caring for their patients.

ENDNOTES

1   Boston Evening Transcript April 1911 [np] www.belalyonpratt.com.
2   HONOR NURSES OF CIVIL WAR: Gov. Walsh and Curtis Guild Pay Tribute at Unveiling in State House. March 1914. [Source unknown] www.belalyonpratt.com.

CADET NURSE CORPS

(originally published March 2013)

In 1940 as war raged in Europe with country after country having already fallen under Hitler's fascism and Britain besieged, the unspoken fear was that the United States would be next. America was still at peace but as the *American Journal of Nursing's* editor remarked, "The very air is supercharged with tragedy" (Roberts). "Nursing in Democracy" was the theme of the American Nurses Association's Convention that May in Philadelphia where nurses listened to President Franklin D. Roosevelt's radio speech calling for national preparedness. By July the ANA, the National League for Nursing Education and the National Organization of Public Health Nursing had established the Nursing Council for National Defense. At its first meeting in New York in July 29, 1940, the Council along with the Association of Collegiate Schools of Nursing and the National Association of Colored Graduate Nurses urged nursing organizations at the federal level, such as those with the Veteran's Administration, the American Red Cross, and the armed services, to join in creating nursing's concerted response to the President's request.

With Children's Hospital's Stella Goostray heading the Council, Massachusetts was well represented. She and her colleagues anticipated that once the United States entered the war the demand for nurses might undermine the gains the profession had made in establishing educational standards. The Council feared that nursing programs would be shortened. If education were compromised, nursing care would be as well, for students provided 80% of that care.

After Pearl Harbor in Hawaii was bombed, December 7, 1941, and the United States entered the war, an existing nursing shortage intensified. Graduate nurses left hospitals to care for workers in the rapidly increasing numbers of defense plants. Other graduates left hospitals to enlist in the Army Nurse Corps and the Navy Nurse Corps. The late Ruth Smith who served in the Army Nurse Corps remembered the hospital administrator warning her and others that if they left, they would never get their jobs back. This was no empty threat given the scarcity of jobs in an America that was still climbing up from the Depression. The exodus of nurses from hospitals made nursing students and their care even more important.

Sensitive to the urgent need for nurses to care for soldiers as well as civilians, Congress created the United States Cadet Nurse Corps on June 15, 1943. The Massachusetts section of the Nursing Council for National Defense helped to recruit applicants with the help of alumnae associations, nursing organizations and teachers. "Join the Drive for Victory," one poster urged young women. Another shouted BECOME A NURSE. YOUR COUNTRY NEEDS YOU! The Cadet Nurse Corps' poster stated: "Your Country needs you so urgently that the Government [has] made immediate financial aid available."

The Cadet Nurse Corps appealed to young women who wanted to be part of the war effort. It also spoke to their sense of style. Along with having tuition, books and housing paid for, the poster promised potential applicants that they would love the "attractive uniforms" that "fashion experts" had designed for the Corps. Clinical uniforms, a street uniform, topcoat, hat and purse made up the ensemble. The Maltese Cross served as the insignia for the Cadet Nurse Corps. It distinguished each student as part of the war effort and linked her to the Knights of St. John who cared for Crusaders from nursing's long ago past.

A monthly stipend added another inducement. During the first nine months as Pre-Cadets mastered the sciences, they would receive $15 a month; during the next 15-20 months while mastering the nursing curriculum and clinical practice, Junior Cadets received $20 a month; and, from then until graduation, while they were Senior Cadets, they would received $30 a month (The 1945 minimum wage of forty cents per hour provides a comparison). The usual three-year program was completed in 24 to 30 months, accelerated to be sure, but also enhanced by federally funded faculty and equipment.

For the last 6-8 months Senior Cadets practiced in military settings, such as the Veterans' Administration Hospitals and Fort Devens or in civilian hospitals. Thus they fulfilled their pledge to the Cadet Nurse Corps and satisfied the 36 month Board of Registration in Nursing requirement. Students though they were, Cadet nurses ensured care from a professional perspective in hospitals increasingly staffed with aids and volunteers.

Sixty-four years later many of those Cadets are octogenarians. Shirley A. Harrow gathered twenty-two of them in Quincy this past summer. Among the former Massachusetts

Cadets were: Alfa Zalfa Norman of Boston City Hospital School of Nursing; Kitty Larkin Carbone of Lawrence Memorial Hospital School of Nursing; Dorothy Harrington Hall of Massachusetts General Hospital School of Nursing; Dorothy Griffin Utz, Betty Jeffer Truax, and Elizabeth Damon Beecher of Massachusetts Memorial Hospital School of Nursing; Jennie Kleczek Burns and Jan Greenberg of Newton Wellesley Hospital School of Nursing; Marie Fehlow and Rosemarie Battaglia of Quincy City Hospital School of Nursing; and, Charlotte Savage Bourne of Salem Hospital School of Nursing (Sweeney). They were among the 3341 Massachusetts women who answered their country's call. By the time the Cadet Nurse Corps program ended in 1948 125,000 Cadets had graduated into the profession.

REFERENCES
Roberts, Mary. "Federal Legislation-and the World We Live in," *American Journal of Nursing,* (February 1940): 176.
Sweeney, Emily. "Reunited, 22 nurses recall WW II experiences," *Boston Globe* (August 2012).

MASSACHUSETTS AND THE NAVY
NURSE CORPS: 1908-2008

(originally published June 2008)

Massachusetts' nurses join with their Navy nurse colleagues to congratulate the United States Navy Nurse Corps as it marks its centennial this May. Some attended festivities in Newport, Rhode Island while others traveled to Washington, D.C. for a weekend of events culminating in a gala 3 May 2008. The anniversary has inspired a celebratory mood among nurses who proudly wear the single oak leaf and reverentially remember Navy nurses alive now only in memory.

Before the U.S. Navy Nurse Corps was founded in 1908, there had been talk of using the wives of the fighting men or the widows of men who had died. Tradition won out over innovation. The Navy had been all male since 1798 when President John Adams signed the Department into being. So the Navy would remain. Disease and injuries during the Civil War (1861-1865), however, challenged precedent. The Navy fitted a former Confederate barrack steamer into a hospital ship, renamed her the *U.S.S. Red Rover* and set about introducing women and female military nursing into the United States Navy.

Sister Mary Adela (Catherine Morane), Sister M. Callista (Esther Pointan), Sister M. Veronica (Regina Scholl) and Sister M. John of the Cross (Catherine McLoughlin) are the Navy's first nurses. These Sisters of the Holy Cross from St. Mary's Convent at Notre Dame volunteered their services as had others of their order who were then nursing in military hospitals (Holland, 1895, 571-584). Sisters Adela, Callista and Veronica stepped aboard the *U.S.S. Red Rover* Christmas eve 1862 and served until the War was over. Sister M. John of the Cross joined them 1 February 1853 and served until September when she left to take charge of a new hospital in Memphis. Working with the four sisters were two colored* women, Alice Kennedy and Sarah Kinno (Wall, 1993, 81). Sterner (1997, 6) adds the names of Ellen Campbell, Betsy Young and Dennis Downs to the *U.S.S. Red Rover's* crew of women.

The sisters cared for sick and wounded while the *U.S.S. Red Rover* plied the waters of the Mississippi transporting the men from battle scenes to naval hospitals and dropping off medical supplies to stations along the way. From 1862 to November 1865 the sisters cared for a total of two thousand nine hundred and forty seven men (Sterner, 1997, 6). Once the Civil War (1861-1865) was over the *U.S.S. Red Rover* was decommissioned, the sisters returned to Indiana and the U. S. Navy returned to its all male status. A permanent nurse corps was still in the future awaiting a forward-looking leader. In the meantime, during the brief Spanish American War (1898) the Navy relied on such nursing that contract women, four women students from Johns Hopkins Medical School and others provided. Yet the exclusion of a nurse corps was becoming increasingly more passé. The U. S. Army had established its nurse corps 2 February 1901 and the Trained Nurse Movement was continuing to transform nursing care in civilian hospitals. Perhaps U. S. Navy Surgeon General, Rear Admiral Dr. Presley Marion Rixley (1902-1910) had this revolution in mind as he pressed his case for a permanent U.S. Navy Nurse Corps. He argued that men who enlisted in the U. S. Navy expected that they would be cared for if injured or sick. Accordingly, in 1902 he recommended that Congress be asked to establish a Corps. He asked for a complement of forty-nine nurses between the ages of twenty-six and forty years of age suggesting he favored a blend of experience and fresh ideas.

Claiming that they had given the subject "careful consideration" Rixley's superiors nixed the proposal. But Rixley was not to be dissuaded. In his 1907 Report he argued for the "efficient care of the sick and injured" stating that the "lack of proper nursing mean[t] greater suffering." He concluded that the "skillful nursing" which civilian institutions enjoyed was the obvious remedy. Although his argument was valid, it did not persuade his superiors. Disappointed once again, Rixley reasoned that the "proposed departure from long-established custom" was the obstacle (Sterner, 1997, 13). Just two years before the end of his tour as Surgeon General, May 1908, the bill for a Navy Nurse Corps quietly passed Congress. Thus one hundred years ago during the presidency of Theodore Roosevelt, a former Secretary of the Navy, the U.S. Navy Nurse Corps began.

On 18 August 1908 the Secretary of the Navy appointed Esther Hasson (1867-1942) superintendent citing her experience with the Army as a contract nurse, an Army nurse and as a civilian nurse. During the Spanish American War Hasson had served in the Philippines, on the hospital ship *Relief* and in Panama. The forty-one year old Baltimore, Maryland woman was the daughter of an Army major general who had served during the Civil War. Her brother was a graduate of the Naval Academy at Annapolis. More than likely her familiarity with military lifestyles served her well in responding to the question of how she would organize a military nursing department. She also met the criterion of having attended a two year nurses training program having graduated in 1897 from the Connecticut Training School for Nurses.

Nineteen nurses were selected from thirty-three applicants bringing the new Corps to twenty - "The Sacred Twenty." The average age of the twenty nurses was thirty with the youngest being twenty-six and the oldest forty-nine. Three of the twenty were Canadian-born. The others were from Maryland, Michigan, New Hampshire, New Jersey, New York, Pennsylvania, Tennessee, Washington, D.C., and Wisconsin. Although none was from Massachusetts, two of the twenty trained for nursing in Boston. The forty-five year old Canadian-born Sara M. Cox trained under Lucy Lincoln Drown at the Boston City Hospital Training School and graduated in 1890. Prior to becoming a Navy nurse, Cox had nursed with the Army.

Florence Taney Milburn, a Maryland native, was the other nurse who had trained for nursing in Boston. The thirty-five year old Milburn was a 1907 graduate of the Childrens Hospital Training School. A widow, Milburn joined the Navy Nurse Corps the next year. Like Hasson, Cox and Milburn, each of "The Sacred Twenty" had graduated from a two-year nurses training program and was a member of the American Nurses Association.

The Surgeon General with the approval of the Secretary of the Navy appointed Cox, Milburn, Josephine Beatrice Bowman, Clare L. DeCeu, Mary DuBose, Elizabeth Hewitt, Lenah H. Sutcliffe Higbee, Estelle Hine, Della V. Knight, Elizabeth Leonhardt, Margaret D. Murray, Sara B. Myer, Ethel R. Parsons, Adah M. Pendleton, Martha E. Pringle, Isabelle Rose Roy, Boniface T. Small, Elizabeth J. Wells and Victoria White. Each signed on for a three-year period. Four served the three year tour and then left the Navy Nurse Corps. Six served from four to ten years each, while the other eight served from fifteen to twenty-five years. One was discharged because of a speech impediment that interfered with her ability to lead others.

Hasson resigned after only three years. The available evidence is vague but suggests there was a conflict about leadership between Hasson and her commanding officer. Before she left the Navy for service with the U.S. Army Reserve (1917-1919) Hasson had set the tone for what the Navy Nurse Corps should be. During the first few months while the twenty were quartered in Washington, D.C. Hasson shaped the disparate nurses into a unit. Hasson wanted the Navy Nurse Corps to be "a dignified, respected body of women" held together by an esprit de corps that would keep each nurse and the Corps scandal free (Sterner, 1997, 21). Navy nurses, admonished Hasson, were expected to be cheerful, adaptable, able to get along well with others and uncomplaining in their acceptance of duties. One of the Corps' principle tasks was instructing hospital attendees (precursors to corpsmen) to carry out orders promptly and intelligently. Hasson expected that the nurse's own nursing competence and her quiet dignity would set the example of good nursing care. Because the Navy nurse commanded respect, Hasson reasoned, others would follow her leadership.

Before joining the Navy Nurse Corps Hasson had written on uncinariasis, the parasitic invasion of hookworm into the small intestine, for the *American Journal of Nursing*. (A one million dollar grant from the Rockefeller Sanitary Commission from 1909-1915 did much to stamp out hookworm infestations in the South). Once Hasson was superintendent her writings focused on the Corps. Sophia Palmer, the editor of the *Journal*, would have welcomed such articles because they showed nurses across the United States still another opportunity for the trained nurse. It is reasonable to assume that Hasson's articles might have been recruiting tools. In any event, by the time Hasson left the Corps, "The Sacred Twenty" were no longer alone. Sixty-five other nurses had joined them.

Hasson's successor, Lenah Sutcliffe Higbee (1874-1941), another of "The Sacred Twenty" stepped into the leadership position. Then thirty-five years old, the native of Chatham, New Brunswick Canada was the widow of Lieutenant Colonel John Henley Higbee of the United States Marine Corps. An 1899 graduate of the Training School at New York Post Graduate Hospital, Higbee led the Navy Nurse Corps during World War I. One hundred and sixty strong at the eve of World War I (1917-1918) Higbee oversaw the Corps' expansion to fifteen hundred and fifty nurses by 1918. Nineteen nurses died during the war: seventeen were felled by the influenza pandemic, one died of carcinoma and the other of kidney disease. For her "distinguished service in the line of her profession and unusual and conspicuous devotion to duty as superintendent of the Navy Nurse Corps" the Navy awarded Higbee its precious Navy Cross. .

The Navy expressed its gratitude for Higbee's leadership and for the Navy Nurse Corps again during World War II. On 12 November 1944, three years after Higbee had died, the Navy launched the *U.S.S. Higbee* at the Bath Iron Works in Maine with Higbee's sister, Mrs. A. M. Wheaton of Wolfville, Nova Scotia christening the new destroyer. Two months later, 27 January 1945, the Navy held commissioning ceremonies on the deck of the *U.S.S. Higbee* at the Boston (Charlestown) Navy Yard. The Commandant of the First Naval District and Boston Navy Yard, Rear Admiral Felix Gygax U.S.N. turned the ship over to her prospective commanding officer, Newtonville, Massachusetts native, Commander Lindsey Williamson U.S.N. Surrounded by thirty-nine Navy nurses, six senior Cadet nurses from the Chelsea Naval Hospital, its chief Nurse, Lieutenant Commander Edith N. Lindquist read a message from Captain Sue Dauser, the Director of the Navy Nurse Corps. Dauser alluded to the serious shortage of nurses in her remarks. She hoped that the commissioning of the first ship named after a nurse would inspire young people to enroll in nursing programs.

The year before the *Higbee's* commissioning, 13 May 1944, the Cadet Nurse Program created to address the national nursing shortage inducted seven hundred students in a public ceremony held on Boston Common. Other Cadet Nurses were completing their program with a six-month tour of duty at the Chelsea Naval Hospital. Amy A. Reichert was the first to do so. Like their Navy Nurse Corps co-professionals, Reichert and the other Cadet nurses were expected to exemplify excellent bedside nursing that the corpsmen and Waves would copy. As creative a response to the nursing shortage as the Cadet Nurse program was, it was not without its detractors. Hospital administrators who relied on student nurse labor resented the accelerated program because they lost student nurses in the last six months of their program when they were most experienced and most useful to the hospital's nursing services.

Along with the Cadet nurses at the commissioning ceremony were Massachusetts nursing leaders among whom were: Margaret Dieter, the president of the Massachusetts State Nurses Association; Helen Wood, the president of the Greater Boston Nursing Council for War Services; Mrs. Somers Fraser, the chair of the Greater Boston Nursing Council for War Services; Cadet Nurse Rally; Margaret Busche; Margaret Reilly, Metropolitan Branch of the American Red Cross [Peg Reilly served with MGH's Base Hospital No. 6 during World War I]; Mary Maher, the chair of Massachusetts Nursing Council for War Service [future dean of Boston College School of Nursing and UMASS/Amherst School of Nursing] and Dorothy Haywood, a consultant for Greater Boston Nursing Council for War Services [officer at the United Community Services, precursor to the United Fund].

The ceremony concluded as Stella Goostray, standing beneath the *Higbee's* gun turrets, surrounded by Navy nurses and dignitaries and facing a ship yard full of sailors presented the Battle Flag to Commander Williamson saying:

As chairman of the National Nursing Council for War Service it is my privilege to present this flag to the *U.S.S. Higbee* in memory of Lenah Sutcliffe Higbee and the nine thousand nurses who now serve in the Navy Nurse Corps. The nurses of America will watch with profound interest the exploits of the officers and men of this ship. We shall applaud their victories, we shall pray for their safety in battle, and we shall do our utmost to recruit more nurses for the Navy Nurse Corps so that the wounded may never lack for skilled nursing care (Stella Goostray Collection)

The *Higbee* served in the Pacific downing Japanese planes and then saw action again during the Korean War and the Vietnam War. The *Lenah,* as the crew fondly referred to her, was decommissioned in 1979 and sunk in the Pacific 24 April 1986. Her Battle Flag was returned to the National Nursing Council for War Services. Goostray made sure that the flag was sent to the Navy Nurse Corps when the Council disbanded after the War.

Many of the Massachusetts' nurses who served with the Navy Nurse Corps returned to civilian nursing after the war and transformed the profession with their leadership and experience. Others remained with the Navy Nurse Corps. One of these was Ruth A. Houghton, a Methuen, Massachusetts native and a 1932 graduate of St. John's Hospital School of Nursing in Lowell, Massachusetts. Commissioned as an ensign in 1935, Houghton served in naval hospitals stateside and in Hawaii, New Guinea and Australia. On 16 April 1947 she celebrated with other Navy nurses when the law was passed that stated:

> The Navy Nurse Corps shall consist of officers commissioned in the grade of nurse by the President, by and with the advice and consent of the Senate, and such officers shall have the rank of commander, lieutenant commander, lieutenant, lieutenant junior grade or ensign.

Not until 20 September 1966 were men nurses authorized and commissioned as officers, The Corps was then thirty-nine years old.

Meanwhile Houghton continued her education as so many nurses were doing in the postwar transformation of the profession. She earned a bachelor's degree from Boston College (1951) and a masters degree from Catholic University soon after. She continued to rise through the ranks serving as the Detail Officer in charge of duty orders, Chief Nurse of various hospitals and as instructor. Nuclear nursing was introduced during her time. The medals on her uniform stated her achievements. Among the honors were: the American Defense Service Medal with a star, American Campaign Medal, AsiaticPacific Medal, World War II Victory Medal and the National Defense Service Medal. She brought all her accomplishments to bear on the position that capped her twenty-seven years in the Navy Nurse Corps. Houghton became the Director of the Navy Nurse Corps (1958-1962) stepping into the leadership position that Esther Hasson (1908-1911) and Lenah Sutcliffe Higbee (1908-1922) once held.

Massachusetts' nurses congratulate the Navy Nurse Corps at its centennial and celebrate with the Corps the many contributions of Massachusetts nurses who served and are serving with the Navy Nurse Corps.

Commissioning of the *U.S.S. Higbee* 27 January 1945

From left to right: Ensign Francis Durant, Childrens Hospital School of Nursing; Cadet nurse
Dorothy Harkins; Stella Goostray; Commander Lindsey Williamson U.S.N. and unidentified
Naval officer (From Stella Goostray Collection, Howard Gotlieb Archival Research Center)

WORKS CITED

Goostray, Stella. Commissioning of the *U.S.S.Higbee.* From the Stella Goostray Collection,
Howard Gotlieb Archival Research Center, Boston University.

Holland, Mary A Gardner. (1895). *Our Army Nurses: Interesting Sketches, Addresses and
Photographs of Nearly One Hundred of the Noble Women who, Served in Hospitals and on
Battlefields during Our Civil War: 571-584.* (Boston: B. Wilkins & Co, Publishers).

Sterner, Doris M (1997). *In and Out of Harm's Way: A History of the Navy Nurse Corps.* (Seattle,
Wash.; Peanut Butter Publishing),

Wall. B. M. (1993). Grace under Pressure: The Nursing Sisters of the Holy Cross, 1861-1865,
Nursing History Review, 1:71-87.

*contemporary term is used.

MARY ELLEN DOONA, RN, EdD

D r. Mary Ellen Doona has authored "Clio's Corner" in the *Massachusetts Report on Nursing* since 2004. Educated as a Psychiatric Clinical Nurse Specialist, it was by "historical accident" that she also became a nursing history scholar and author.

During the early 1980s she began research in the Linda Richards Collection held by the History of Nursing Archives at Boston University to learn why the nursing profession valued psychiatric nursing less than other specialties. That research also led to her to discover how Mary E.P. Davis founded the Massachusetts Nurses' Association (MNA). In 1982, Dr. Doona published the historical account of the founding of the MNA in *The Massachusetts Nurse* in an article entitled "The Cause is Just."

In 1983, the MNA established the *"Lucy Lincoln Drown Nursing History Society"* and named Mary Ellen Doona as MNA Historian and Chair of the Society. (Lucy Lincoln Drown was one of the first nurse pupils of Linda Richards at Boston City Hospital School of Nursing.) Starting in 1983, Dr. Doona wrote a column focusing on nursing history, entitled "Nursing Revisited" which ran in *The Massachusetts Nurse* for eight years until MNA voted to leave the ANA. In 2004, the *Massachusetts Report on Nursing*, the official publication of the "new" Massachusetts affiliate of the ANA, Massachusetts Association of Registered Nurses (MARN) began publishing "Clio's Corner," written by Mary Ellen Doona.

Dr. Doona's immersion in nursing history has led both to her publication of numerous scholarly works about nursing history and also the leadership that she has provided in preserving nursing history. She served admirably and productively as a member of the Executive Board of the Nursing Archives Associates at the History of Nursing Archives, Boston University, for thirty years. During that time, she was chair of the Education Committee and she served on the editorial board of the *Journal of Nursing History*, published by the History of Nursing Archives for several years. Dr. Doona literally brought nursing leaders alive in numerous presentations in the 1980s and 1990s when she and other nurses dressed in period costume and impersonated early national nursing leaders at meetings of the Nursing Archives Associates, MNA, and at ANA Conventions.

Dr. Mary Ellen Doona began her nursing education at St. Elizabeth's Hospital School of Nursing. She earned her Baccalaureate Degree in nursing and a Master's Degree in Psychiatric Nursing at Boston College and received an Ed.D. from Boston University. Before her retirement, Dr. Doona was a nursing professor at Boston College. Dr. Doona's outstanding contributions to the nursing profession and to educating nurses about nursing history were recognized and celebrated by MARN in 2009 when she was presented with the Living Legend Award.

CPSIA information can be obtained
at www.ICGtesting.com
Printed in the USA
LVHW051512261222
735889LV00005B/365

9 781530 335190